DISCARD

Character and Circumstance

Character and Circumstance

Essays in Honour of
DONALD GRANT CREIGHTON

Edited by
JOHN S. MOIR

Macmillan of Canada / Toronto / 1970

Library of Congress Catalogue Card No: 77-118938

Printed in Canada by The Hunter Rose Company for
The Macmillan Company of Canada Limited
70 Bond Street, Toronto.

I think that an historian's chief interest is in character and in circumstance. His concern is to discover the hopes, fears, anticipations and intentions of the individuals and nations he is writing about. His task is to reproduce as best he can the circumstances, problems and situations faced by another person in another time. He seeks insight and understanding that cannot be gained through application of sociological rules and general explanations.

DONALD CREIGHTON

Publisher's Foreword

Twenty-five years in a historian's view must be but a moment in time, to a publisher it is most of his working life. But from either view it is a long time for a publisher and writer to remain associated, and to remain friends. My first meeting with Donald Creighton was in 1946, soon after I had returned to Macmillans from the army, and been put in charge. We met at an evening party and I found myself in a corner talking with Professor Creighton and Professor Underhill. Both were working on biographies and the prospect seemed to fill them with gloom; and what, they asked, could a Canadian historian do with a biography when it was finished. In a light-hearted way I assured them that they had only to find a good Canadian publisher and send the manuscript in. Their gloom did not noticeably lift.

A few weeks later Professor Creighton and I met for lunch. I had sought the meeting because I already knew something of what his colleagues looked for in Creighton's *John A. Macdonald*. His *Commercial Empire of the St. Lawrence* had already marked him out as a notable historian and a gifted writer, and I coveted the privilege of being his publisher. It is a pleasure to remember the shared excitement of that first long talk. There were so many books that Canadians waited for, and that day it seemed splendidly possible to do a good deal to supply the need. My role was then, as it has been since, to express the confidence in Donald Creighton's capacity that I felt, and to promise all the support we could provide.

The writing of history, or of anything else, is a long lonely business and a publisher is one of the few people in a position to understand this and occasionally to help a little. By the time *John A. Macdonald: The Young Politician* appeared in 1952 and *The Old Chieftain* in 1955 we knew each other well. The books had some of the reception they deserved: critical acclaim, honours from many directions and, for the small Canadian market, a fine sale.

The accomplishment of this great work had required ten years of exhausting research and writing, and increased those strains that are inevitable in the author-publisher relationship. No serious historian who is also fastidious in the balance of a sentence, in the choice of words, and even punctuation marks can easily bear the shallow punditry of many critics. Everything about Donald Creighton is slightly larger than life: his professionalism, his style – and also his wrath. At one point he wrote characteristically of a manuscript reader: "I gather that the real trouble with my biography is that it doesn't correspond to what he remembers of his public school history. I am prepared to admit this; it doesn't interest me greatly. However, to pacify the gentleman and his kind, I have stuck in the kind of pontifical commonplace which I suppose he likes . . . ."

His former colleagues and students will recognize this style with delight and perhaps wince a little remembering old battlefields. To his publisher looking back across many years the relationship seems often to have been that of a fairly experienced scuba diver and a basking shark. But those years have shown great things. *John A. Macdonald* set new standards for the writing of Canadian history, and has been the model, the inspiration, and the despair of those who have sought to copy its style. The books that followed have confirmed and anchored Donald Creighton's great reputation. Colleagues might not agree with all he said, but nothing that he said was unimportant.

This volume is some recognition of the place Donald Creighton has earned. It is the ultimate honour from the guild of his colleagues. My predecessor, Hugh Eayrs, had the honour of publishing the *Festschrift* to Professor George Wrong, so that I welcome this book the more. It is a high point in an association I have always regarded as a privilege, that has often been entertaining and heart-warming, and always stimulating.

JOHN GRAY
March 1, 1970

Preface

These essays have been written and published as a tribute to Donald Grant Creighton, in recognition of his influence on the discipline of history in Canada, particularly in Canadian universities. When planning this volume it was found impossible to invite contributions from all of Donald Creighton's wide circle of friends, colleagues and students. Therefore it was decided to limit the papers to Canadian topics and to restrict the invitations to those who had filled positions in the historical profession for several years. The result of these decisions is the list of contributors that graces the Table of Contents of this volume.

The contributors have chosen their own topics and have dealt with them in their own way. Since no theme was prescribed for the book other than the field of Canadian history it might reasonably have been expected that the essays would have no unifying factor except to do honour to Donald Creighton. When, however, the authors announced their subjects, a common historiographic thread became apparent. That thread of unity is by happy chance aptly expressed in the phrase of Donald Creighton which we have chosen as a title for the volume.

In an interview with Allan Anderson published in the University of Toronto *Graduate*, June 1968, Donald Creighton explained his philosophy of history:

> I think that history's closest association is with literature. I think a good historian ought to be substantially educated in English and French literature, particularly in novels in which the author views society in a wide scope and tries – sometimes in a series of volumes – to convey an impression of an entire age in the history of a nation.
>
> I think that an historian's chief interest is in character and circumstance. His concern is to discover the hopes, fears, anticipations and intentions of the individuals and nations he is writing about. His task is to reproduce as best he can the circumstances, problems and situations faced by another person in another time. He seeks insight and understanding that cannot be gained through application of sociological rules and general explanations.

We believe that the essays in this volume do reflect both the close association of history and literature and their authors' interest in character and circumstance as forces in the history of Canada and Canadians.

The production of the book has been in every sense a joint effort by all connected with it. The editor wishes to express his personal thanks to his fellow contributors for their ready and willing co-operation, and especially to Professors Maurice Careless, Peter Waite and Paul Cornell for invaluable advice in the planning stages. We as authors are collectively in the debt of Mr. John M. Gray of The Macmillan Company of Canada for his personal support of the undertaking, and Mrs. Diane Mew of the same company, whose editorial direction has helped us around many problems and whose efforts have aided the project at every step from its inception through to its final publication.

Together we offer this volume to Donald Creighton, teacher, historian and artist with words, on behalf of all his friends, colleagues and students, and on behalf of the countless number of Canadians and others who have read, enjoyed and profited from his insight and understanding of history.

JOHN S. MOIR
Scarborough College
University of Toronto

Contents

xi

Character and Circumstance

Donald Grant Creighton

JOHN S. MOIR

Donald Grant Creighton was born at Toronto in 1902, to the Reverend William Black Creighton and his wife, Laura Harvie. Donald was the middle child of three in the Creighton family, the eldest being John Harvie, and the youngest, Mary Isabel (Mrs. H. G. Wilson). After some five years in the pastoral work of the Methodist Church, Donald's father had settled in the city in 1900 as assistant editor of *The Christian Guardian*. His election in 1906 as editor of his church's newspaper, a post he occupied for the next thirty-two years, was but one evidence of the rising influence of advocates of the Social Gospel movement within the Methodist bureaucracy. This new wave of reformers within Canadian Methodism shared a common heritage and ideals – almost all were Canadian-born, well educated and articulate, middle class and "Ontario British"; all were concerned with the social relevance of religion and with Canada's manifest destiny to create an open, just, and Christian society. As editor of *The Christian Guardian* W. B. Creighton was ideally placed to propagate the new gospel of "responsibility" towards the multitude of New Canadians arriving in Canada's second Great Migration. He was determined, too, that the pages of *The Guardian* should offer the greatest freedom of expression for the editor and his correspondents. His own opinions on vital issues were never in doubt but his insistence on judging each issue on its own merits made it impossible to categorize him politically or theologically. Such independence of spirit won public admiration but it also occasioned conflicting charges that the editor was "a most blatant Grit" and "a most pestiferous Tory". In simple fact William Black Creighton was always his own man.

His father's character, connections, and reputation certainly influenced Donald Creighton's own development and interests, but it was his quiet and somewhat self-effacing mother who instilled in Donald a love for literature. While Donald was still quite young Laura began to read English novels to him, particularly the novels of the Brontës and Dickens. Donald's appetite for reading was further whetted by English children's magazines and he successfully entered several contests carried in the pages of those periodicals. "W. B." 's editorial position, however, provided Donald with a more serious introduction to the writer's craft. The Creighton household overflowed with books, for as well as the standard classics that filled the many bookshelves, a profusion of books for review in *The Guardian* was brought home in bundles by the elder Creighton. While still attending high school Donald was allowed to practise the art of book reviewing on some of these volumes from *The Guardian* office, but always under the watchful eye of his father, the editor. From high school and book reviews Donald progressed easily to the next step in his education, the inevitable round of lectures and essays as a student at Victoria College in the University of Toronto.

During those expansive years immediately following the First World War, the Burwash residence and dining hall at "Vic" were still new, and life at the college was made somewhat riotous by the demobilized soldiers who leavened the ranks of the undergraduates. Donald began his studies in the Honours course in English and History, where the required wide reading soon confirmed in his mind that inseparable connection between the two disciplines. Ned Pratt had returned to join Victoria's English faculty in 1920, but a greater influence on Donald than his English professors at Victoria was the inspiration of those he remembers as the "remarkable group of young instructors in the Department of History", a group that included John Bartlet Brebner, Hume Wrong, and George Smith. In Donald's words, "They were young, enthusiastic, and managed to arouse an enormous interest in their students." With each passing term Donald's personal interests leaned increasingly away from

English and more towards the discipline of history. The first die of Donald's future academic career was cast by the influence of that band of youthful historians – he would indeed follow his inclinations towards history, but for Donald Creighton history would always remain a branch of literature.

Graduation in 1925 was crowned for Donald Creighton by the receipt of a scholarship which enabled him to read history at Balliol in Oxford and by his marriage to Luella Bruce, the attractive and lively student from Stouffville whose gay spirit and quick mind so admirably matched Donald's own intellectual drive. Donald returned to Toronto in 1927 with an Oxford B.A. to join the department in which he had been a student. His predilection was towards European history, and especially towards the French Revolution as an area of specialization, although in that day and at least for another full generation, university lecturers were hired to teach history at large, on the assumption that they possessed or could acquire competence in any period of the discipline that the curriculum of the day de-manded. The long vacations at Oxford had been spent mostly in France, and now the attraction of the French Revolution carried Donald and Luella back to Paris for a summer of research. The experi-ence of that summer was to prove another turning point in Donald Creighton's career. Research and travel funds in that day were vir-tually unknown, and the Creightons returned to Toronto in desperate financial circumstances, given the meagre salary of a university in-structor in the 1920s. Research abroad was obviously prohibitively expensive, and so Donald turned to historical sources closer to home. "And that is why I became a Canadian historian", Donald Creighton explained some forty years later.

His first venture into Canadian history was intended to be a study of the governorship of Lord Dalhousie, based on the Dalhousie Papers which had recently been acquired by the Public Archives in Ottawa. After a year's reading on Dalhousie Donald became aware of two facts – that he was not very interested in that stiff Scottish earl, and that his research was leading him into a larger study of the constitu-tional conflicts that preceded the Rebellion of 1837 in Lower Canada. This realization led to the publication of his first academic paper, "The Struggle for Financial Control in Lower Canada, 1818-1831", in 1931. Another aspect of the same theme appeared two years later in his article, "The Commercial Class in Canadian Politics, 1792-1840". A further and related paper, "The Economic Background of the Rebellions of 1837", appeared in 1937, the same year that his extensive researches in the area culminated with the publication of *The Commercial Empire of the St. Lawrence,* a decisive event in Canadian historiography.

During these years of preparing *The Commercial Empire* Donald Creighton had become a close friend of Harold Adams Innis, whose own research and publications on the place of staples in Canadian history had considerably influenced Donald's thinking about the interaction of economics and politics in the development of the St. Lawrence region. Together Innis and Creighton were the leading "Laurentian" historians, emphasizing the determining role of the St. Lawrence River in Canada's destiny.

As a result of his research Donald Creighton's interest in Canadian history had broadened to include wider horizons than the empire of the St. Lawrence. Publication in 1938 of his paper on "The Victorians and the Empire" indicated a shift of emphasis in his work towards examining in a historical perspective the ideology and practice of politics. Before he found his new subject in the career of John A. Macdonald, however, Donald Creighton was retained by the Rowell-Sirois Commission to prepare a study of the economic and financial background of the Confederation movement. His draft of *British North America at Confederation* was completed in 1938 and published in 1939. A new historical avenue was opened for him by this examination of Confederation, an avenue which in future years would lead him far afield from Canada and Canadian history. But, at least during the early years of the Second World War, the theme of his publications was still the problems of Canadian Confederation. His rising reputation as a teacher and a publishing scholar had been indicated by his promotion to assistant professor in 1932, to associate professor in 1939, and by the award of a Guggenheim Memorial fellowship in 1940, one of the first given to a Canadian. Four years later there appeared his classic one-volume history of Canada, *Dominion of the North,* intended in his own words, "to explain the different component parts of Canadian nationality in their historic origin, to show why Canada is and will desire to remain a separate North American nation, and to account for its peculiar relationship with both Great Britain and the United States". *Dominion of the North* was acclaimed immediately both for its historical accuracy and its "high degree of literary charm" – "history in grand style", as the Montreal *Gazette* described it.

The last year of the war found Donald Creighton enjoying a Rockefeller fellowship to pursue his researches. His sights were now firmly set on a biography of John A. Macdonald, whose career seemed to epitomize both the drive towards and the fulfillment of Canadian Confederation. Further recognition in the form of election in 1946 to the Royal Society of Canada, the winning of that Society's Tyrrell Medal for History in 1951, and the publication of a succession of papers on Macdonald followed the war years. With Guggenheim and Rockefeller fellowships already to his credit, he received a Nuffield fellowship in 1951 to work in England on Macdonald's biography. When published in 1952 and 1955 his two volumes, *The Young Politician* and *The Old Chieftain*, gained him unprecedented fame both in Canada and abroad, among academics and laymen alike. Each book was awarded the Governor General's Medal for Academic Non-Fiction, a category title which has since disappeared and which at the time irked Donald Creighton as somehow implying that history was a second-class *genre* of literature.

More honours followed in rapid succession: the British Columbia Medal for Biography in 1955, the University of Alberta's National Award in Letters for 1957, a second LL.D. in 1956 (the first had been conferred by the University of New Brunswick in 1949), two more honorary doctorates in 1957 and another pair in 1959. The Macdonald biography was followed in the next two years by several articles, and in 1957 by the small literary masterpiece entitled *Harold Adams Innis: Portrait of a Scholar*, Donald Creighton's sensitive tribute to his closest friend to whom he had dedicated the first of the Macdonald volumes and whose death in 1952 had been a deep personal loss.

After Donald Creighton finished his popular one-volume *Story of Canada* for British readers in 1958, the flow of publications from his pen ebbed and then halted. He was spending all his available time on the preparation of a book to mark the approaching centenary of Confederation. But the routine of writing and teaching was interrupted in 1960 when the British government appointed him a member of the Monckton Commission to investigate and report on a future constitution for Rhodesia and Nyasaland. The journey into Africa and into the political complexities of Britain's devolving empire on that continent was a sharp change from the relative quiet of a faculty lounge and Philosopher's Walk, yet the appointment to the Commission was in itself a further and international recognition of Donald Creighton's stature as an historian of the difficult processes of federalism. After his vastly rewarding experience on the Monckton Commission he returned to the projected volume on Canada's own approach to the federal experiment. *The Road to Confederation* was issued in 1964, the same year he was awarded the Molson Prize of the Canada Council. The approaching celebration of the Dominion's one hundredth birthday was the occasion for another governmental appointment in 1965, this time to the Ontario Advisory Committee on Confederation. Centennial year itself was marked for Donald Creighton by three more papers on the Confederation theme, two more honorary degrees, and the distinction of being made Companion of the Order of Canada, a fitting tribute to the scholar who had done so much to awaken Canadian interest in the story of Confederation.

While Donald Creighton's long list of books and papers had brought him deserved acclaim, publication was only one side of his academic activities. Research and writing had always to be done in such time as remained after teaching and administrative duties were finished. In 1945 Donald had been promoted to full professor in the Department of History, and from 1954 to 1959 he filled the arduous post of departmental chairman. Some relief from the evergrowing burden of lectures, tutorials and marking came in 1967 when he was made a University Professor with responsibility for graduate teaching only. By now his former students were to be found on the faculties of many Canadian and American universities, and the adjective "Creightonian" was applied more commonly to those scholars who shared his view of Canadian history than to his own inimitable literary style.

At home Donald had a fellow author in Luella who had written several successful books. These included school texts, a juvenile biography of Tecumseh, books for younger readers, a social history of the Confederation period, and two novels. Donald had on occasion described himself as a "novelist *manqué*" but he left the family's preoccupation with fiction writing in Luella's hands. By the early 1960s their family – one son and one daughter – had graduated from university, were married and raising families. Donald and Luella now moved some thirty miles east of Toronto to Brooklin, the quiet Ontario village that was once, ironically, a hotbed of Clear Grittism. The tranquillity of Brooklin's treelined streets and comfortable Victorian houses proved to be an ideal retreat for the two authors from the distressing confusion and noise of the distending city, and there

Donald completed his writing of *The Road to Confederation* and its sequel, *Canada's First Century*, which was published in 1970.

Commenting on the quantity, quality, and impact of Donald Creighton's career as author and teacher of Canadian history, his former student William Kilbourn has written, "If anyone has reshaped the tradition of Canadian historical writing it has been Donald Creighton."

Donald Creighton and Canadian History: Some Reflections

J. M. S. CARELESS

To make a full evaluation of Donald Creighton's massive contribution to Canadian history requires more insight and presumption than I have readily at hand. But I would like to offer here some reflections that arise from contemplating aspects of his work that seem to me of particular relevance and significance. These comments are admittedly an incomplete judgment of his writings – but I hope they may indicate something of the stimulus to be drawn from there. And in that, perhaps, lies Donald Creighton's greatest contribution to history in Canada: his capacity to stimulate readers, students, or colleagues to fresh appreciations of a subject so long condemned for ditchwater dullness and pedestrianism.

Donald Creighton creates this stimulus especially, of course, by one of the oldest of tricks, by telling an eminently good story: a dirty trick those might say who seem to hold that to present a carefully constructed narrative, marked by evocative description, immediacy and feeling, is highly suspect, if not actually to be deplored, as smacking too much of the popularist and subjective. Nevertheless,

Creighton's undaunted efforts in our own gloomy science of Canadian history have continued to rouse warm responses to their skill, vigour, and commitment. It may be that his presentation of historical scholarship essentially in the form of literary art does not accord well with newer quantifying social sciences techniques that enable us to prove conclusively what formerly was only perceived by common sense. It may be that his approach invites unfortunate emulation by those who lack his long immersion in English literature. And it may be that he can sweep one along by the impelling force of his narrative and descriptive powers: Canadian history would yet have been immeasurably poorer had he somehow damped down his artistry and withheld his engagement in order to produce more primly withdrawn, soberly pedestrian volumes.

But for all the pervading importance of Creighton's skill as a story-teller (that is, as an historian), the reflections of this paper concern other aspects of his writings. What category of history indeed, would best describe his work – political, economic, social, cultural or what? It is an easy judgment, typical of half-baked opinions by quarter-learned critics, to deem it merely political narrative, as if there were something inherently second-rate in studying the course of past political events and personages in Canada. Obviously, Creighton has written largely on such themes; on the political struggles in the two Canadas in the *Empire of the St. Lawrence*; on the making of federal union in *The Road to Confederation* and the first volume of his meticulously detailed biography of John A. Macdonald; on the politics of the young Dominion in the second. One could add more illustrations; but the obvious point to note is that his treatment of political subjects has in no way been limited to a concern for politics only.

In fact, his scholarship has notably been shaped by an underlying economic conception, based in turn on physical facts of Canadian geography. This is, of course, the idea of the commanding role of the great St. Lawrence transport system in Canadian development; the Laurentian concept, which has linked Creighton with his friend Harold Innis' staples approach to Canadian economic history, but which he has profoundly made his own. The long river trade route, its transatlantic access to Britain, its thrust into the American interior and the British North West beyond, provides a central, unifying theme. Hence the promise and potential of a St. Lawrence-based commercial system runs through Creighton's classic one-volume synthesis of Canadian history, *Dominion of the North*, no less than through *The Empire of the St. Lawrence*. The same conception echoes in his succinct *Story of Canada*; and though the masterwork *Macdonald* reaches out to continental boundaries, it ends as it began, with the great river of Canada.

This stress upon the Laurentian concept assuredly did not make Donald Creighton an economic or environmental determinist. Indeed, his view of the environment has comprehended broad human and cultural forces beyond the purely material – just as the river itself carried immigrants, ideas, and governance inward from Great Britain, as well as staple products outward. Studies like his *Empire of the St. Lawrence* or *British North America at Confederation* might closely consider trade conditions or the state of colonial economic growth; but Creighton is no more "largely" economic than "merely" political in his scholarship.

Can his work then be classed within that convenient catch-all, social history? Certainly he has dealt effectively with social groups and social differences, as between mercantile and agrarian communities of both Upper and Lower Canada in *The Empire of the St. Lawrence*. Certainly he has viewed French-English conflict in social terms, as a struggle between a society that had never known the French Revolution and one produced by the Industrial Revolution, as aptly expressed in his article, "The Struggle for Financial Control in Lower Canada, 1818-1831".[1] Nevertheless, his writing has rather been infused with an awareness of socio-economic forces than primarily concerned with social topics in themselves, such as questions of class structure, social institutions and customs, social mobility and so on. Similarly, he has seldom directed himself wholly to matters of cultural or intellectual history (unless in his admirably incisive sketch of an imperial outlook, "The Victorians and the Empire"[2],) so that one might better note his socio-cultural insights than seek to identify him as a cultural historian *per se*.

What does this leave? Above all, Donald Creighton's deep interest and fully demonstrated talent in biography. His *Macdonald* or his *Harold Adams Innis* come to mind at once; but one should remember that he has dealt with personalities, graphically wording them into

1. *The Canadian Historical Review*, XII, 2 (June 1931), 120-44. (A complete reference to this and other articles and works by Donald Creighton will be found in the Bibliography on p. 235.)
2. C.H.R., XIX, 2 (June 1938), 138-53.

life, in other works as well. In fact, this is the main source of the present reflections: Creighton's power to evoke individuals or groups of individuals in a living world of their own times – and what that may imply for Canadian history. In one sense this ability to delineate and vivify past personality, singly or collectively, is the special art of biography. In another sense it ministers particularly to more effective social history. And that, indeed, deserves reflection in itself.

It is not hard to play the superior critical game and observe that "everyone knows" the literary devices Creighton uses to produce his characteristic effects. The truth is, everyone does not know, as attempted imitations usually demonstrate; because the devices include personal imponderables like sensitivity and perceptive imagination, distinctive vocabulary and a strong sense of style, as well as special regard for details in research and an intuitive grasp of the whole picture to be conveyed. However, one can select certain aspects of Creighton's biographical skill which have specific relevance for the theme in hand. I will choose three for comment: his care to vitalize and humanize historic circumstances through descriptions built up from small but convincing details; his inferential reconstruction of personal conduct, to fill out and enrich the limited records of primary evidence; and his close concern to enter into the hearts and minds of his leading figures, so that one can comprehend and appreciate their behaviour – indeed, by witnessing in them the juncture of "character and circumstance". Together, these three elements particularly mark Creighton's inquiry into the workings of human personality in history. But before considering that in general, let us look at each of the three aspects in turn.

Probably the most notable example of his imparting reality and humanity to past circumstance lies in the well-known description of July 1, 1867, in the Epilogue of *John A. Macdonald, The Young Politician*. There is no need to recount his warmly appealing treatment of the doings of the people of new-made Canada on that day, still less to subject it to some weighty literary analysis. (I am too mindful of the critic who pontificated that Stephen Leacock's humour was "an ingenious mixture of meiosis and hyperbole", which led Leacock to reflect that all he needed to do was to go down to the cellar and mix up a can of each.[3]) But note the judicious use of the

3. Ralph L. Curry, *Stephen Leacock, Humorist and Humanist* (New York, 1959), p. 235.

minutiae of historical evidence through which the picture of Canada on July 1 was built up: not Canada the country, that political and economic abstract; but the living community, the human reality of which Macdonald was but a part, albeit an important one. Creighton's work here almost becomes an essay in collective biography, generalized, interpreted and imaginatively recreated as much of it has to be.

It would not be very difficult to draw other examples from his writings wherein newspaper (and weather) reports, extracts from diaries, memoirs and letters, are selectively interwoven to bring past circumstances expressively and persuasively into the present. I will cite only one instance, which actually does not reveal a wide range of sources nor do much more than present a mood and setting. But the vignette in *Dominion of the North* of the Royal Canadian Regiment sailing from Quebec for the Boer War in the autumn of 1899 seems to convey the immediacy of the event so clearly that it is worth once more repeating here, as a classic illustration of Creightonian technique.

> The deck of the Allan liner *Sardinian* was thick with dark tunics and white helmets; the men had climbed high into the rigging, and one soldier swung his cap from the top of the first mast. Then the big steamer cast off, the first gun of the citadel roared out, and the crowd crashed into the strains of "God Save the Queen". In the clear late-afternoon sunlight of autumn, the *Sardinian* stood out down the St. Lawrence, escorted by a little fleet of gaily decorated tugs and pleasure boats, heralded by the booming guns of the citadel and the screaming whistles of the river craft. Then in a little while the sun went down over Quebec, and from the decks of the *Sardinian* they could watch the spires and ramparts against a gaudy sky. . . . As it grew darker, the ship settled into the long journey down the river towards the open sea. She passed Grosse Isle at seven o'clock and l'Islet at eight-twenty. It was a fine night, with a clear starry sky.[4]

Here is a depiction straightforward and almost simple in content, detailed rather than adorned in style; but dramatic in impact, as the

4. *Dominion of the North*, (Toronto, 1957), p. 401.

departure of a troopship anywhere must be. It shows, indeed, a
perceptive interest in how people saw and shared a significant social
incident: it expresses "human interest". Even though that term by
now has been badly degraded, it appropriately describes a characteristic element in Donald Creighton's writings – one which other
authors at times try to insert in chunks to vary the diet of their dis-
course, but which forms an integrated part of his own. And it might
be said that a sense of human interest also pervades his reconstruc-
tions of an individual's specific actions or style of conduct – the second
aspect of his biographical approach for our reflection.

The primary evidence of official dispatches or private letters, government records or parliamentary debates will usually offer the
historian only a bald outline of individual responses and behaviour.
Newspaper accounts, where available, may provide more observation,
external or biased as it may be; so will the comments of contemporaries (perhaps well grounded, perhaps not) in current missives or
later memoirs. One could go on; but it is not necessary to produce
a handbook on the problem of sources for biographical studies. The
point is, simply, that the course of a person's conduct, like the flow
of his motivation, is registered only incompletely or incoherently in
documents – quite aside from the question of how trustworthy the
documents are themselves. Hence particular actions and behaviour
must often be inferred and reconstructed from the accessible evidence:
weighing its validity is only the initial step. Assuredly, this is a
problem for historians in general, and for other biographers beside
Donald Creighton. What is significant, however, is his skill in
meeting it, most fully exhibited in *John A. Macdonald.*

Research, deliberation, and that vital quality called historical
imagination, here combine to produce a lucid and cohesive account
of the actions and responses of one important individual through a
life of seventy-six years. And in the process much is adduced as
well about the conduct of other individuals with whom that life was
intimately involved. At times we may be informed, just as effectively, of Macdonald's feelings or behaviour when in private. But if
these instances are not to be found explicit in the documentary
record, they still form satisfyingly logical inferences from that record.
Like Shakespearean soliloquies, they have no less validity as illumi-
nations of action because no one but the author could elicit them.

Take, for example, Macdonald's sudden illness after the Red River
troubles, as described in Volume II, *The Old Chieftain.* While waiting

alone in his office before the House opens, he feels the onset of agonizing pain, stands up writhing ("trying to bear the pain, knowing he could not bear it"), clutches the table, sways, and falls "blindly across the carpet"[5]. A graphically detailed picture is conveyed; but there is no sense that it is not in accord with its foundation in factual evidence – rather that it must have happened so. Or consider later in the volume George Stephen, deep in the battle to build the C.P.R., musing in his library on the foes in the way and calling up clan memories from Scotland, which stir him to send the rallying cry of Clan Grant by cable to his kinsman, Donald Smith – "Stand fast, Craigellachie!"[6] Again, it must have happened so.

There are so many deft touches to enliven the presentation of the record: old William Lyon Mackenzie, "chattering with rage", rising to refute a charge in parliament, in volume I, *The Young Politician*[7]; in the same work, George Brown's strong and awkward style in debate – "the stiff arm jerking monotonously up and down like a dull saw on an obstinate log of hardwood".[8] Or, in *The Road to Confederation*, there is Langevin, newly arrived for the London Conference in the fall of 1866, lighting the little gas fire in his frigid bedroom, and gazing out "the streaming window on a typical English November day of wind and heavy rain".[9] A letter cited indicates Langevin's awareness of the miserably wet and windy English weather. The rest is a reasonable inference of what he must have done; a small but typical enrichment of the account, in no way extraneous, fitting naturally into the flow of events. Nor does it really signify that some highly unlikely proof might yet turn up that Langevin had resolutely refused to look out the window or had kept the curtains drawn that day. These are not matters that affect the direction of action or events, but simply fill them in and intensify their reality. They have, indeed, a ring of "higher truth" about them. They are what people would do – or what particular people particularly do – and as such have a due place in the creative art of history.

Of course, they involve the possibility of error; but then, so do the presumed facts of documents themselves. There is always the chance of error (and so of more histories). What is required in any

---

5. John A. Macdonald: The Old Chieftain (Toronto, 1955), p. 69.
6. Ibid., pp. 397-98.
7. John A. Macdonald: The Young Politician (Toronto, 1952), p. 190.
8. Ibid., p. 191.
9. The Road to Confederation (Toronto, 1964), p. 406.

case is strict, judicious care in weighing and inferring. This is not to say that there are not serious pitfalls in efforts to enrich the record. There is the popular ploy, "surely he must have known. . . ." Much may be hung on that flimsy sky-hook – anything the author wants his subject to have known. And there is the meanwhile-back-at-the-ranch device, to give a spurious colour and import to any happening: "As the town drains bill was before the House, a bearded German Jew was labouring tirelessly in the British Museum, while Cossacks rode down serfs on Russian plains." But these are obvious dangers for any historian, exaggerations that need not be discussed here. We may pass instead to the third aspect of Creighton's biographical approach to be considered: his basic effort to identify the thoughts and emotions of the individuals he deals with – to "characterize" them; an old term that has not yet lost all its value.

Once more, this is reconstruction, involving inference and creative imagination as well as analytical description and judgment. Some will argue that the historian cannot accurately categorize the attributes and motives bound up in any personality of the past; that even if we had a full written estimate left by the individual himself, the problem of its accuracy would remain; and further, that we might not still feel satisfied, if, so to speak, a psychoanalyst could yet put Julius Caesar on the couch. All this may be granted. But what more are we saying than that writing any history involves selection and reconstruction from an imperfect, even doubtful, body of recorded data? An historian's value judgments may vary in the weight they carry according to the nature of the evidence in his particular field of investigation; but they are always there. Even the "hard data" of quantified kinds of historical inquiry have remarkably soft spots, and repeatedly involve choice and interpretation.

The fact is, that as history seeks to be a science as far as possible, but like medicine remains an art, so it must accept that the best thing that can be done in the treatment of past human personality is to do its best with the materials at hand. The alternative is to do it not at all. Or rather, if biography is not done by trained historians with techniques of critical analysis, it may be done less validly by popularists more concerned with surface impression than deliberate judgment. I am not herewith disdaining popularity. Most historians hope their books will be widely read – not to mention sold. Besides, a popular writer can still produce sound history; a professional historian can still have decided popular appeal. And here we easily

return to Donald Creighton, in that his incisive handling of personality is surely an important factor in the wide readership and
popularity his books have earned.

It would take too long to discuss his most outstanding work of
reconstructing and presenting past personality, obviously that of
Sir John Macdonald himself. One must pick shorter, simpler instances
of his mode of characterizing individuals. For example, there is his
rendering of the essential attributes of Sir Francis Bond Head in
The Empire of the St. Lawrence:

> His lack of political experience was uncompensated by
> any native capacity for statemanship. It was as a
> soldier, as a traveller, as a gentleman adventurer, that
> he had spent his life. He journeyed on a romantic pil-
> grimage around the Mediterranean; he galloped across
> the plains of South America; and in between these pic-
> turesque excursions he produced graphic and popular
> travel books. This faintly Byronic combination of liter-
> ature and adventure must have gratified Sir Francis;
> and there ran, through his entire career, a strain of
> imitative romanticism and second-rate theatricality. He
> judged life, or liked to think he judged it, upon the
> simple principles of the gentleman soldier of fortune.
> He tried to settle hard situations with big words, full
> of cloudy and grandiose associations; and he governed
> Upper Canada by mouthing rhetoric, striking heroic
> attitudes and making melodramatic gestures. For him
> the governorship of the little frontier province became
> a kind of romantic lead.[10]

Perhaps the sharp powers of Creightonian characterization are best
exhibited in portrayals of colonial governors. At any rate, there is
almost a companion piece in the notable description of Arthur
Gordon in *The Road to Confederation:* the lieutenant-governor of
New Brunswick in the 1860s who considered himself too fine a frog
for so petty a puddle, especially muddied as it was by the local
politicians in office:

10. *The Commercial Empire of the St. Lawrence* (Toronto, 1937), p. 362.
    Republished as *The Empire of the St. Lawrence,* (Toronto, 1950); but
    quotations here are from the original edition.

Yet these were the creatures who actually governed the
province. And he, the Lieutenant-Governor, who was
obliged by the inventions of responsible government to
act on their advice, wielded only an empty and formal
authority. Gordon had a very lofty view of the dignity
of his vice-regal office, as well as a high opinion of his
own abilities. He instructed the Anglican clergy of the
province that after praying for the Queen, they should
petition the deity for "Thy Servant Arthur". He would
have been decidedly annoyed if he had suspected that
it was as "Thy Servant Arthur" that he was soon to
become familiarly and jocosely known in New Brunswick. . . . At the time, the clergy no doubt prayed duti-
fully as requested; but the politicians, far from showing
him a similar respect or treating his advice with becoming deference, seemed hardly to bother to pay any attention to him at all. It was absurd, grotesque, mon-
strous! It was a total inversion of the natural order of
things – an enormity to which Gordon never became
hardened, which he never ceased to regard with aston-
ishment and indignation.[11]

This is clearly a rendition of personality in history, the conveying
of the attitudes and spirit of individuals in the past. Again examples
could be multiplied from Creighton's writing: from Jean Talon yield-
ing to "that instinct for grandeur, that vertigo of ambition, that was
a part of the enchantment of the St. Lawrence"[12] to a brisk delineation
of Sir Allan MacNab – "a hearty simple-minded soul who enjoyed
every minute of his robust existence, and who alternated with genial
ease between a rather ostentatious wealth and an unabashed im-
pecuniosity", and took to railway speculation "like a cheerful child
to jam".[13]

Creighton expressed his own approach to the writing of biography
most succinctly in his article of 1948, "Sir John Macdonald and
Canadian Historians".

Biography is a distinct and special branch of historical
writing. Of all branches it is perhaps most closely related to the art of the novel, and this in both a legitimate and illegitimate sense. In a biography, as in a

11. *The Road to Confederation*, pp. 5-6.
12. *Dominion of the North*, p. 69.
13. *The Young Politician*, p. 176.

novel, the phases of historical development, the conflict
of historical forces, are seen, not in generalities and abstractions, but concretely, in terms of a central main
character, a set of subordinate characters, and a series of
particular situations. A biography may achieve the
vividness and actuality of a novel; but, with even
greater ease and frequency it may degenerate into the
trivial, or dull, improbability of fiction and propaganda.
The complex facts may be cheerfully disregarded for
the sake of dramatic simplicity, or they may be
deliberately perverted for the sake of political justification. . . . On the one hand there is the light-
hearted fictional biography with its gaudy jacket which
has been written with a keen eye, not so much
for facts, as for sales; and on the other there is the
solemn work of commemoration, usually in two fat,
funereal volumes which looks, as Lytton Strachey observed, as if it had been composed by the undertaker,
as the final item of his job.[14]

The fictional biography, he continued, at least displayed "a lively
interest in character and personality". But Canadian biographies had
been of the other kind. They had "a formal official air, as if they
had been written out of the materials of a newspaper morgue or from
the resources of a library largely composed of Blue Books and Ses-
sional Papers". Consequently, the individual subject too often had
remained "an important Public Personage – in capitals – dwarfed
by the circumstances of his 'Times' ". And the result could be seen,
of course, in an arid line of lives of "Robert Responsible-Government,
and Francis Responsible-Government, and Wilfrid Responsible-Government". This bleak picture, one might add, has been notably improved by Donald Creighton's work in history. But what matters at
the moment are less his strictures on bad biographies in this article
than what it serves to underline about his own approach.

Creighton explicitly links biography with the art of the novel,
while recognizing the dangers of melodramatic fiction or political
propagandizing. He stresses the play of specific characters "in particular situations", but notes that the Man must not be swamped
by the Times, or become a mere stereotype for some historical force
in "an abstract and inhuman method of presentation". He wants,

14. C.H.R., XXIX, 1 (March 1948), 3.

indeed, the whole man, a living personality centre-stage, portrayed from whatever sources that will establish his reality; not "an unsubstantial *papier maché* figure made up of old dispatches and newspaper files".[15] In short, Donald Creighton here is preaching what he practises; namely, the very procedures we have been discussing in terms of recreating past circumstances, displaying individual conduct (as in a novel) and emphasing the role of character and personality. All this has naturally a great deal of interest for the writing of biography in Canada, by a Creighton "school" or any other. But what seems to me still more interesting is its significance for application in the field of Canadian social history – which is the final reflection to be offered here.

In this regard, I am certainly not being boldly visionary. Alan Wilson, notably, has already stressed the value of a biographical and individualized approach to much of Canadian history, in a pathfinding article in 1965 that mapped out the rich possibilities of biographies, single or collective, beyond the field of politics alone.[16] In fact, I am merely following up his course, though striving to link it particularly to Donald Creighton's work at one end, to social history at the other. Moreover, what Wilson has urged (and carried through in his own biography of a business man, *John Northway, A Blue Serge Canadian*) Peter Waite has to considerable degree incorporated in his *Life and Times of Confederation*, whose very title expresses its treatment of the union movement as a form of collective biography. It is surely not simply a coincidence that both once were Creighton's students. Nor is it likely that others of his former students, who share similar interest in biography or in the history of human beings as well as impersonal forces, did not learn more from Creighton than just an eager desire to write so-called "romantic" political narratives. In varying ways, they have indeed evinced a broad concern for aspects of Canadian social history.

The study of the social history of Canada has long been urged, assuredly; and valuable work has already been done, some of it by scholars in other disciplines. Still, it is only now becoming in its own right a major field of historical research. The concepts and the data of sociology, anthropology, or geography, behavioural studies in politics

15. *Ibid.*, p. 4.
16. "Forgotten Men of Canadian History", *Canadian Historical Association Annual Report for 1965*, pp. 71-86. See also "Biography as History", by J. M. Gray, in the same issue, pp. 144-53.

or economics, research in education and psychology, the potentialities
of computer programs – all suggest ideas, references, and techniques
for promising development in Canadian social history. From this
background, however, such a development would be naturally
oriented to the methods of social science and directed toward a
quantitative approach. It would probably deal in numbers, statistics,
and encoded categories, lean to theoretical models or abstractions
in handling social groups and functions. While socio-cultural study
of institutions like churches and educational systems, or of ethnic
societies, labour unions, and local communities could offset such a
trend, it is altogether possible that social history in Canada might
develop as relatively faceless and generalized; that it would not deal
with particular people in particular situations. And that, in Creighton's words, would seem "an abstract and inhuman method of presentation".

This is not to deplore, much less condemn, the application of social
science techniques and quantifying methods, which suggest a wide
range of fruitful possibilities for Canadian social history. I seek
rather to promote the other application, no less fruitful, which we
have seen so strongly evinced in Creighton's own approach: the study
of individual personality and of collective biography as integral parts
of social history. They provide the humanizing, particularizing
factor, to link the "hard" data of quantity effectively with the "soft"
data of quality, and make social history neither a set of formalized
abstractions nor a mass of meaningless parochial chronicles. Indeed,
this makes it history; a study of the concrete and the particular,
shaped by art and imagination – but not thereby lacking in con-
ceptual framework or the widest possible foundations of precise and
validated fact.

One may envisage the idea of collective biography applied in a
variety of instances: as the approach for studying a political, business,
or social élite, for analysing the functioning of an entrepreneurial
element, a religious, ethnic, or union leadership, or tracing the
pattern of a regional or occupational grouping. Numbers and categories, figures on income and property, say much; but so do the lives
of as many individuals in the social body as can be practically dis-
cerned and depicted. And here, moreover, inference and creative
imagination will reasonably be applied to the evidence available.
Class relations, family structure, the impact of social policy, can all
be illuminated through a biographical approach, which may even

answer the broad questions more meaningfully. Clearly this is a huge and difficult task. We will never know much about the great anonymous majority; and the larger the social grouping under study, the bigger and vaguer the problem. But the fact is, we have scarcely tried. Diaries and family papers, even newspaper obituaries may deal with all sorts of individual merchants, farmers, or professional men; yet where these do become the subject of historical publication, it is usually still for reasons of ancestor worship or antiquarian interest – rarely as part of some intended scheme for collective social biography.

Nevertheless, an emphasis on individual human personality can be highly valuable for Canadian social history. One may talk of social types, of social conditioning, of stance and role-playing, even of "psycho-history". May not these concepts, too, be illumined by examining the conduct and character of many separate individuals through Canadian history? Computerized data banks may tell us where and how people lived, and by what economic standards, but we also need to judge (we cannot know) what they thought and how they felt. Here again the power of historical imagination is particularly in demand. Through creative art we must work, as Creighton has, to join character with circumstance, to enter into minds and feelings. The approach is as valid and constructive for social history as it is for political. Thus we may seek to handle social motivations also – which one should be able to elicit and infer from the record in the same way as Creighton reconstructs political intentions.

In all these enterprises the modes exemplified in Donald Creighton's writings can teach us a good deal. Setting the stage with detailed human circumstances, conveying the sense of the surrounding *living* community, is vital for the understanding of social processes in history. Describing personal conduct and individual responses are equally essential to the full comprehension of social behaviour, while the penetration of character is basic in giving concrete historical meaning to abstract social categories. Whether these aspects we have observed in Creighton's biographical approach to Canadian history would make him most significantly a social historian is of little consequence here. What is of consequence is the skill of that approach and the force of its example – which may render his influence on history in Canada even greater than now is realized.

Charisma
and Canadian Politics

ROGER GRAHAM

"Not too much pancake. I want my charisma to show through."
So ran the caption of a cartoon in *Saturday Review* depicting a
politician being made up for a television appearance, a pointed
allusion to a kind of Gresham's Law of English usage. For reasons and
in ways that are obscure, certain words are catapulted into fashion
and used so much, with so little discrimination, that they displace
more correct ones, in the process losing their own true, or at any
rate traditional, meaning. In the verbal coinage of politics one of the
agents and victims of this debasement in recent years has been the
noun "charisma". It is, one must admit, an alluring word, resonant
and with a slightly exotic ring, tempting for commentators to toss
off knowingly in their explanations of political events. But what does
it really mean in its political application? One of the curious things
about charisma is that hardly anyone claims to know exactly what
it is but almost everyone thinks he can recognize it. Lately it has
become something of a habit to credit successful political leaders
with a charismatic quality, and indeed to ascribe their success in
great measure to its possession, while writing off their unfortunate
rivals as failures largely because of the lack of that magical gift. As

one scholar has expressed it, ". . . what often happens is that, being aware of the success of particular leaders, and finding their success in some ways extraordinary, writers take the easy way out by attributing it to 'charisma' without giving due consideration to the fact that their explanations follow no recognized criteria. . . ."[1]

However, one should not exaggerate; such emphasis on "charisma" is by no means the invariable practice. There have been too many cases where it was on the side of the loser, or where it could be found in none of the contenders. No one, for instance, seriously suggested that either of the major candidates in the 1968 American presidential election was notably charismatic, while George Wallace, who was more so, fared much worse than many people thought or feared he would. Winston Churchill certainly looked more charismatic than Clement Attlee in 1945 – almost anyone would have – but that was not enough to save the Tories from defeat. If they win the next British general election under Edward Heath some other reason than their leader's charisma will have to be found. However, the British are rather old-fashioned in such matters; they do not seem to put much stock in this as a political factor. Neither, apparently, do the French at the moment, whether despite or because of the Gaullist charisma of *la politique de la grandeur*. As for the Germans, having experienced the real thing in the nineteen-thirties, they may not want another messiah just now, especially when the pleasures of prosperity are so available.

And yet, whatever caveats one may enter, the notion of charisma in politics, or what commonly passes for it, is an "in" thing right now, especially in North America. It is worth remarking that we have been more or less conditioned for a long time to believe that in reality impersonal forces are the main shapers of events and that individuals are pretty much at the mercy of those forces. Nonetheless we are increasingly inclined to treat politics in personal terms, to emphasize style, not content, personalities rather than issues, when attempting to assess the meaning and outcome of political contests. The "cult of personality" is no less prevalent in some democracies of the western type than in certain more authoritarian states, and in fact appears to have become one of the chief instruments of those who plan and direct party campaigns. No doubt there are some obvious reasons for this. Policy questions are so numerous, compli-

1. K. J. Ratnam, "Charisma and Political Leadership", *Political Studies*, vol. XII (1964), 341.

cated, and hard to talk about in any but the most simplified way that it is tempting to think they are in truth beyond the comprehension, and even the caring, of the yokels and numbskulls who are thought by some people to comprise the bulk of the electorate. The "hidden persuaders" employed by political parties presumably find it easier to package and market the "image" of a man with whom the customers can "identify" than a reasoned argument about issues or a set of considered policies. Radio and television, the latter especially, probably encourage an emphasis on the men rather than the matter of politics, even though they might be, and to some extent have been, employed to the opposite purpose. The same may be said of much of the press. Perhaps, too, in a mass society bureaucratically organized, where authentic individuality has to be cultivated with devotion like an orchid in the desert, where depersonalization is a chronic complaint, the leader who stands out from the crowd in his uniqueness, or can be stage-managed to give that impression, is both more noticeable and more commanding, a more exclusive and attractive focus of political interest than used to be the case. For he may embody that sense of personal identity and worth, that dignity, that freedom to decide and to act (however illusory the power and freedom may be in actual practice) that most of us in our hearts would like to have but feel are unattainable. The more most people are assimilated into the mass, the more adulation is bestowed on those who successfully resist the process, as long as they refrain from challenging the fundamental assumptions and conventions of society; that is, bestowed on the superstars of sport, entertainment, the arts, science, technology, business, and politics. And in politics these days nothing is so appealing as the "charismatic" leader who brightens up the scene, relieves the monotony and offers a type of entertainment of his own.

Awareness of "charisma" as a significant fact of political life came to Canada in the 1960s. Like most new things that turn up here, it wafted in from the United States. The concept of charismatic political leadership in its modern form is not, to be sure, an American invention; like a number of other influential ideas it emerged from the seminal mind of Max Weber. But, although there is a body of debunking opinion in the United States, it seems to have caught on particularly well there, both among academics and in the realm of more casual, everyday political comment. It may be that preoccupation with the leader, with his character, personality and style, is natural and appropriate to those who live under a presidential form of government, where a head of state and chief executive with great power is elected to office for a prescribed period. By contrast it seems to be less important to those who enjoy our parliamentary system, where a man becomes the Queen's first minister because the party of which he happens to be the leader happens to have won most of the seats in the legislature. In any case, all manner of notable American public men have been placed in the charismatic category by various observers, including such diverse presidential personages of recent vintage as Franklin D. Roosevelt, Dwight D. Eisenhower, and John F. Kennedy. Not that serious students of the phenomenon down there have confined their attention to figures in the life of their own nation. On the contrary, it seems to be agreed generally by the scholars that, as Weber himself pointed out, a charismatic leader is most apt to appear at the head of some revolutionary movement, whether in pursuit of national independence from imperial rule, a socio-economic transformation, or both. This has led them far afield and certainly helps to explain why they have ignored Canada.

Not to be outdone, though, Canadians discovered "charisma" for themselves in the person of Pierre Elliott Trudeau. True, John Diefenbaker was thought by some to have had it during his glorious campaigns of 1957 and 1958, but one of the hazards of heroism is that it cannot survive a decline and fall. Doubt set in along with disillusionment. Had he been genuinely charismatic after all, for charisma is often thought of as something not only wondrous but beautiful and built into its lucky possessor? Or had Diefenbaker been just a master of colourful bombast with a remarkably mobile face, a highly developed talent for expressing righteous indignation, and an instinct for finding the many weak points in his opponents' armour?

But it was a decade later, according to a widespread belief, that true charisma walked onto the stage of Canadian politics. As luck would have it, the country, in this view, was treated in the 1968 election to a contest between a man who epitomized charismatic leadership and one who epitomized anything but. Both were newcomers to politics; for both, therefore, the slate was relatively clean. How, then, account for Mr. Trudeau's success in winning a majority of seats, which his predecessor had been unable to do, and for Robert Stanfield's inability even to hold the ground his party had occupied, let alone add to it? The answer, clearly, must lie in the marked contrast of personality between the two new leaders, or so some onlookers were inclined to think. Mr. Stanfield bore the cross of guilt by association with the underwear of the same name, the solid, colourless dependability of which he seemed to personify. In 1968 dependability was not enough. Canadians were ripe for excitement and among the exciting things about Mr. Trudeau was that one could dare to wonder privately whether he wore any underwear at all. Politicians in Canada had been kissing for generations but only, in public, those who had not reached the age of puberty. Mr. Trudeau cast such restraint to the winds. Although of middle age he was young in spirit, a far cry from the stuffy, wordy, predictable, ultra-respectable model of the proper Canadian public man. Arriving on the stage at a moment when to be young and in revolt was very heaven, he magically "turned on" a great many of those who *were* young or who, no longer in that happy condition, were caught up in the modern cult of youthfulness. He did not project the familiar image of the father-figure or of the comfortably avuncular custodian of the public weal. He was much too "with it" for that, as witness his unconventionality, his faintly irreverent wit, his apparent readiness to question orthodox opinion and received wisdom. A "swinger" with a flair for fast cars, moderately "mod" styles and outward informality, he enjoyed a reputation as an expert skier, an adventurous skin diver and an accomplished performer of judo. He was a widely travelled cosmopolitan, wise to the ways of the world, a man for whom life was real but a lot more than merely earnest. Had there ever been in Canada a national party leader quite like this? Sir Wilfrid Laurier, let us say, sliding down a banister? Sir Robert Borden in goggles and flippers? Arthur Meighen in a Mercedes? Mackenzie King at judo? R. B. Bennett on skis? Yet no matter how much became known about him, how lovingly the media chronicled his every move, he remained something of an enigma, a slightly distant, reserved intellectual, "a very private person", in the current cant phrase. In sum, here was a public figure fresh and different, a leader most intriguing and – well, charismatic.

II

Or was he? That depends, of course, on how one defines the term but defined it must be, and with some care, or there is no point in using it. One may begin by mentioning some of the things which charisma is not, at least according to those who have devoted serious thought to the subject.[2] It is not enough to be charming, graceful, stylish, magnetic, eloquent, witty, or brilliant. If it were, any or all of these adjectives would suffice to describe a man fortunate enough to deserve them. Panache is not charisma, nor is sex appeal. Great personal popularity with one's followers does not necessarily spell charisma. Neither does an admiring multitude, although this may be symptomatic of the condition. A leader may be wonderfully well attuned to the sentiments and interests of his people without being at all charismatic and, as any student of Canadian history can testify, longevity in office has no relationship to charisma, which indeed is more likely to be a fleeting phenomenon.

If these do not indicate a charismatic presence what does? The function of ruling, "with diligence", was one of the "gifts [*charismata*] differing according to the grace that is given to us" mentioned by St. Paul in his Epistle to the Romans. The possession of power was legitimized by its divine source. "For there is no power but of God; the powers that be are ordained of God" and those subject were enjoined to obey on pain of damnation. This belief that temporal authority enjoyed the majesty of divine grace, that it was charismatic, was a casualty of the secularization of thought in the

2. The basic theory of charismatic authority is set forth in two works by Max Weber. See *The Theory of Social and Economic Organization*, translated from the German by A. R. Henderson and Talcott Parsons (London: William Hodge & Co. Ltd., 1947), chap. III; and *Essays in Sociology*, translated, edited and with an Introduction by H. H. Gerth and C. Wright Mills (New York: Oxford University Press, 1958), chap. IX. The quotations from Weber in the following pages are from these sources. The most elaborate recent discussion of the subject is Ann Ruth Willner, *Charismatic Political Leadership: A Theory* (Princeton: Center of International Studies, 1968). Among useful and interesting shorter treatments are : Carl J. Friedrich, "Political Leadership and the Problem of Charismatic Power", *Journal of Politics*, vol. 23 (1961); Karl Loewenstein, *Max Weber's Political Ideas in the Perspective of Our Time* (Amherst: University of Massachusetts Press, 1966); K. J. Ratnam, *op. cit.*; Robert C. Tucker, "The Theory of Charismatic Leadership", *Daedalus*, vol. 97, no. 3 (Summer 1968); Ann Ruth Willner and Dorothy Willner, "The Rise and Role of Charismatic Leaders", *Annals of the American Academy of Political and Social Science*, vol. 358 (March 1965).

modern age. Although it survived among defenders of the divine
right of kings, the main tendencies of political thought were inimical
to it. However, "genuine charisma originally meant . . . leadership
based upon a transcendent call by a divine being, believed in by both
the person called and those with whom he had to deal in exercising
his calling. In the Christian tradition charisma is a gift of grace."[3] A
very different meaning was given to the term when it was redis-
covered by Max Weber and used by him with reference to secular
rule in some of his writings about the time of the Great War.
Charisma, as he saw it, was only one source of power, and quite the
most exceptional.

Without suggesting that they were mutually exclusive, Weber
distinguished between "three pure types of legitimate authority". The
first, legal authority, rests on a rational foundation, "on a belief in
the 'legality' of patterns of normative rules", and "obedience is owed
to the legally established impersonal order. It extends to the persons
exercising the authority of office under it only by virtue of the
formal legality of their commands and only within the scope of
authority of their office." The second type, traditional authority, is
founded "on an established belief in the sanctity of immemorial
traditions", demanding obedience "to the *person* of the chief who
occupies the traditionally sanctioned position of authority and who
is (within its sphere) bound by tradition". Thirdly there is charismatic authority and here the inhibitions of law or tradition are
removed; ". . . it is the charismatically qualified leader as such who is
obeyed by virture of personal trust in him and his revelation, his
heroism or his exemplary qualities . . .". The normative patterns are
"revealed or ordained by him . . .".

Historians, unlike many of their brethren in sociology and political
science, are inclined to question the validity and usefulness of
typologies of this sort. Neat categorizations somehow flatten the land-
scape, making things seem more orderly, less complicated and more
explicable than they actually were or are. But assuming for the sake
of the inquiry that there are in fact these three "pure" types of
authority, what did Weber see as the characteristics of the third?

He defined charisma as "a certain quality of an individual personality by virtue of which he is set apart from ordinary men and treated
as endowed with supernatural, superhuman or at least specifically

3. Carl J. Friedrich, *op. cit.*, p. 14.

exceptional powers or qualities." It is not simply a matter of a person so gifted believing in his own endowment and in the mission he is appointed to fulfill. If it were, a discussion of charisma in Canadian politics need only conclude that Mackenzie King was the most charismatic of our leaders and let it go at that. Charisma is partly in the eye of the beholder. The charismatic man, wrote Weber, "demands obedience and a following by virtue of his mission. His success determines whether he finds them. His charismatic claim breaks down if his mission is not recognized by those to whom he feels he has been sent. If they recognize him, he is their master – so long as he knows how to maintain recognition through 'proving' himself. But he does not derive his right from their will, in the manner of an election. Rather, the reverse holds: it is the *duty* of those to whom he addresses his mission to recognize him as their charismatically qualified leader." How the apparent freedom not to embrace the leader and his calling can be reconciled with the duty referred to is not made clear. It is clear, though, that the obligation to follow and obey disappears when the leader can no longer "prove" himself. Failure on his part presumably means that the gift of grace has lapsed.

One writer has recently taken Weber's stress on the importance of recognition from below a lot further, suggesting that certain circumstances may bring on a "charismatic response" to a non-charismatic leader. This "situational charisma" is found in "instances where a leader-personality of non-messianic tendency evokes a charismatic response simply because he offers, in a time of acute distress, leadership that is perceived as a source and means of salvation from distress."[4] Franklin Roosevelt in 1933 and Winston Churchill in 1940 are given as examples. But this proposition, by removing in some cases an essential ingredient from the theory advanced by Weber, unneccessarily complicates an already elusive concept. Is it not simply intelligent to welcome, even with a marked display of feeling, a leader who, while neither underestimating the complexities and dangers of the problem nor promising quick and easy solutions, gives evidence of knowing how to come to grips with a desperate situation?

Weber emphasized that in all respects "charismatic domination is the very opposite of bureaucratic domination". It "knows nothing of a form or of an ordered procedure of appointment or dismissal. It

4. Robert C. Tucker, *op. cit.*, p. 744.

knows no regulated 'career,' 'salary,' or regulated and expert training
of the holder of charisma or of his aides. It knows no agency of
control or appeal, no local bailiwick or exclusive functional jurisdic-
tions; nor does it embrace permanent institutions like our bureau-
cratic 'departments,' which are independent of persons and of purely
personal charisma." Elaborating on this contrast, he wrote:

> There are no established administrative organs. In their
> place are agents who have been provided with charis-
> matic authority by their chief or who possess charisma
> of their own. There is no system of formal rules, of
> abstract legal principles, and hence no process of
> judicial decision oriented to them. But equally there
> is no legal wisdom oriented to judicial precedent.
> Formally concrete judgments are newly created from
> case to case and are originally regarded as divine judg-
> ments and revelations. . . . In the pure type of char-
> isma, these are imposed on the authority of revelation
> by oracles, or of the leader's own will. . . . Charismatic
> authority is specifically irrational in the sense of being
> foreign to all rules.

In short, charismatic power is the antithesis of the rule of law; it is
government not by laws but by men free from legal restraints.

As Weber defined it, charisma is in essence "revolutionary and
transvalues everything" because it "repudiates the past" and "makes
a sovereign break with all traditional or rational norms . . .". The
charismatic leader will emerge naturally "in times of psychic, physical, economic, ethical, religious, political distress" to challenge the
existing system of authority and offer deliverance. If he is heard and
accepted his dominion may produce "a radical alteration of the
central system of attitudes and directions of action with a completely
new orientation of all attitudes toward the different problems and
structures of the 'world' ". At the same time, since it is revolutionary,
pure charismatic authority is by its very nature transitory. It "has
a character specifically foreign to every-day routine structures" and
"may be said to exist only in the process of originating. It cannot
remain stable, but becomes either traditionalized or rationalized, or a
combination of both."

Basic to Weber's conception of charisma, then, is a sense of redemp-
tive mission. While he was more concerned with the general nature
of charismatic rule than with the specific characteristics of leaders

and followers, certain inferences may be drawn from what he wrote and from historical experience. The true charismatic leader exhibits messianic pretensions and brings a millennial message, diagnosing the ills of the society to which he appeals in simplistic formulas and, more probably than not, promising salvation through a panacea better designed to elicit an enthusiastic response than to withstand rational scrutiny. In offering a way out from whatever trouble or despair prevails, he may well display impressive powers of demagogic eloquence, thus enhancing his claim to be inspired. As long as he can "prove" the authenticity of his inspiration he will be venerated, and the truth he reveals will be embraced by the believers with a faith and passion equal to his own. Being revolutionary, the leader's attitude and the movement he builds are impatient and tend to be totalitarian. While the quest for power is still in progress, requiring freedom to preach, protest and proselytize, the right of dissent, the virtue of non-conformity to the norms of the external community will undoubtedly be stressed. But the thrust of the movement is towards uniformity; absolute truth demands absolute acceptance and no room will be made for sinners who refuse to see the light.

From this very summary description of "pure" charisma at least two difficulties arise, apart from the primary one of whether or not the theory contributes to an understanding of political power. Weber admitted that none of his three types of authority is usually found in its pure or ideal form, but what degree of "impurity" is compatible with the designation "charismatic"? What compromises may be made with things as they are, with laws and institutions, prevailing modes of thought and the entrenched customs of society? The problem will arise almost anywhere an attempt is made to apply the theory, but especially in a country like Canada where there has never been a genuine revolutionary movement or a root-and-branch rejection of the past. Secondly, how substantial a proportion of the citizenry must a leader attract if he is to be considered charismatic? There is no absolute answer, of course. A man may certainly qualify though never achieving power in the state, or perhaps, for that matter, without even seeking public office; but it is begging the question to say simply that a leader who can "elicit from a following deference, devotion, and awe toward himself as the source of authority . . . is charismatic for *that* group".[5] Doubtless he is, but something more is

5. Ann Ruth Willner and Dorothy Willner, *op. cit.*, p. 79.

needed if he is to be considered historically significant. His supporters must be sufficiently numerous and aroused by issues of sufficient urgency to the community as a whole to permit his mission to be taken seriously and to have a measurable impact on the world.

III

Have there been any such leaders in Canada since Confederation, figures with even "impure" charisma? Very few. One would not expect to find many and none remotely comparable to such quint-essential titans of the charismatic fellowship as Lenin, Hitler or Mao Tse-tung. A society with a well rooted liberal-conservative democratic tradition is the least susceptible to a charismatic faith-healing psychology. This brand of democracy in its actual operation may often seem to be an exercise in calculating cynicism, the practice of institutionalized deception. But, while rejecting notions of revela-tion and salvation in mundane affairs, it rests at bottom on a faith of its own: belief in the inherent rationality of imperfectible men, and therefore in discussion, compromise, gradualism, and the accep-tance of defeat in the knowledge that one will be free to fight again. That freedom allows the rise of charismatic men and movements but they are less likely to appear as the head and shoulders of a national party, performing within the framework of the constitution its celebrated duty of conciliating differences, than as the active agents of a fearful or alienated group. Charisma will blossom more naturally among the ultra-Protestants or Roman Catholics of Ulster, for ex-ample, than among the power-brokers of Westminster; it is more apt to be found in spokesmen for the black people of America than in a man travelling the road to the White House. The same is true of Canada, where the last place to look for it is in one who inhabits, or seriously strives to inhabit, 24 Sussex Drive. Unless, that is, some crisis of overwhelming proportions overtakes the political society as a whole, creating common anxieties and demands. One man's version of salvation may seem damnable to another unless they are united by their suffering and believe in the same explanation of their plight.

It has been notoriously difficult for Canadians to find common ground, even in the midst of some emergency affecting them all, and therefore the prospects for the appearance of charismatic *national* leaders have been more remote than in a country beset by fewer internal divisions. The two world wars did not bring us even such imperfectly charismatic leaders as a Lloyd George or a Churchill – they left R. L. Borden and Mackenzie King in office. The great depression gave us R. B. Bennett who, for all the extravagant promises of the 1930 election campaign or the dramatic pronounce-ments prepared for his delivery in the "New Deal" broadcasts of 1935, could hardly be said to have fitted even the loosest definition of charisma. To be sure, it also produced the C.C.F., with a manifesto nearly millenarian in flavour; but J. S. Woodsworth, however pro-phetic he may have been, was far too patient, prudent, rational, and conventional in method to be counted charismatic. For that matter, our protest movements have not, by and large, been charismatic; the movement, not the man, has predominated, although one need only mention Réal Caouette to indicate that this has not been invariably true.

Canada's perpetual "identity crisis" usually excites only the pro-fessional nationalists, identified by their agonized search for identity. The chronic problem of her survival in North America has not, thus far, brought into prominence an effective charismatic figure. John A. Macdonald, preaching the gospel of the National Policy or sum-moning his countrymen against the "veiled treason" of 1891, might qualify in a marginal way, but all thought of revelations, revolutions and drastic solutions was really foreign to a mind that specialized in shrewd assessments of reality. John Diefenbaker came closer to being charismatic on this issue with his vision, his evangelical affir-mation of faith not only in the continued existence but in the greatness of Canada, his objections to unwarranted intrusions from the south and his penchant for disturbing the peace of the bureau-cratic establishment. In the event, however, he was unable to "prove" himself satisfactorily to many of those who had answered his call. The likelihood that even increasingly acute threats to Canada's sovereignty will throw up a charismatic saviour is, if anything, diminishing, simply because such a large proportion of Canadians cannot be roused to deeply-felt concern so long as the integration of the continent proceeds with the gentle slowness of seduction and not the brutal suddenness of rape.

Above all one might expect charisma to appear in response to the threatened destruction of the country by the separation of Quebec. And this brings us back to Mr. Trudeau. No doubt there were some,

perhaps many, who were won over in the spring of 1968 by the
promise expressed in the slogan "Trudeau and One Canada", and
also by his previous televised encounter with Premier Daniel Johnson.
The slogan was not very clearly explained, and may have been
misunderstood in some places, but it looked to be contrary to the
"two nations" approach to the problem adopted with some equivocal
disclaimers by the other chief parties. Perhaps this was a minor case
of "situational charisma", if one cares to accept that formulation,
but the 46 per cent of the popular vote that went to the Liberals
did not represent a stampede to the one man thought to be capable
of saving the nation. Assuredly it would be a mistake to read too
much charismatic significance into the well-engineered spontaneity,
the ubiquitous mass-produced placards and the swarms of ecstatic
teenagers assembling to pay homage to their latest pop idol as he
swooped from the heavens in his DC 9. Kisses and dialogues do not
charisma make and Mr. Trudeau, for all his off-beat fascination, is
not charismatic, not in the Weberian sense anyway. A charismatic
leader-personality would hardly propose seriously that there should
be more reason and logic in politics, although the suggestion was
so unusual as to verge on the revolutionary. One would expect him
to be not so much concerned with abiding by the existing constitution as convinced of its irremediable defectiveness. And is it
not less typical of such a leader to insist on keeping his options open
as long as possible, while marshalling his task forces and engaging
in protracted re-examinations of policy, than to push forward con-
fidently with all speed along the revealed road to salvation?

Some slightly closer approximations to "pure" charisma have
occasionally appeared, and may turn up in the future, in specialized
movements appealing to the powerless, the dispossessed, the angry,
the impatient, those disillusioned with "the system" or alarmed by
some danger, real or apprehended. And now and then a provincial
leader, operating in a comparatively homogeneous community with a
more readily identifiable common interest than that of Canada as
a whole, has resembled to some extent the charismatic model. Anyone can choose his nominees, past or present. How about Joseph
Howe, for instance, assuming, somewhat belatedly, the moral leadership of anti-Confederation sentiment in Nova Scotia until he "dis-
proved" himself by capitulating to Macdonald? Or Louis Riel,
embarking on his mission to save the Métis "nation"? D'Alton
McCarthy, carrying the crusade for Equal Rights into Manitoba, is

a possibility and so is Sam Hughes, raising troops and hackles in the Great War. Mitchell Hepburn, working up the farmers on the back concessions against the corrupt Tories and their cynical big business friends, might have some charismatic validity. So might Maurice Duplessis, making himself the protector of Quebec against the sinister centralizing ambitions of Ottawa. And René Lévesque, separatist, comes to mind. So many objections, however, could be raised to admitting any of these to the select circle, possibly excepting Riel, that one might just as well continue to regard them as interesting and influential but non-charismatic figures. None of them, at any rate, can rank with the most certifiable Canadian exemplar of charisma in the past century, William Aberhart.

Not that Aberhart's affair with the people of Alberta was a case of "pure" charismatic authority at work; by no means. Quite a few of the elements were there, though: a people in dire distress; the revelation received by the leader in an experience akin to conversion; the false clarity and the winning simplicity of the diagnosis and the cure, expressed in such formulas as the A plus B theorem, in the charts and graphs, in homely analogies irresistibly convincing; the booming confidence and ringing sincerity; the overpowering revivalist oratory, which made a message he was not the first to preach more persuasive than it had been before; the scapegoats, the struggle between "us" and "them"; the call for loyalty, for trust in him and in the experts who understood all; the authoritarian and anti-intellectual tendency, shown in disdain for such established institutions as the courts and the legislature and in the attempt to curb criticism in the press. Social Credit, of course, was far from revolutionary in its economic doctrine and purpose, promising only to revivify the capitalist system. Indeed, the conservatism that underlay the favourable response to Aberhart by so many Albertans was evident; he gave them hope that stability could be restored to a social order they were accustomed to and did not want fundamentally changed. On the other hand, the political theory of Social Credit cut closer to the bone. Here was a reflection of disillusionment with many of the traditional assumptions and much of the institutional framework of representative democracy, along with encouragement of the delusion that the people need only express their general will and it would be done. Taking up this secular gospel, which he seems not to have fully understood – if anyone did – and altering it to suit his needs, devoting his enormous energy and organizing talent to the cause, Aberhart achieved a measure of charismatic communion between leader and led unequalled in Canadian experience. Had television been available to him, no mere make-up man could have obscured his charisma.

Still, if Aberhart, charismatic though he was by Canadian standards, is the best one can offer, the conclusion seems unavoidable that the theory has little relevance to the political life of this country. Perhaps it will in a future that seems bound to be full of seething discontents, when things as they are may come under ever fiercer attack on a widening front by those who see things as they would like them to be. Perhaps some day, somewhere in Canada, from some disaffected group a true charismatic hero will spring. But if experience is any guide the odds are against it.

Lord Monck, His Friends, and the Nationalizing of the British Empire

W. L. MORTON

Charles Stanley, fourth Viscount Monck, governor-in-chief of the Province of Canada, 1861-1867, and governor general of the Dominion, 1867-1868, is a well-respected figure in Canadian history. Those historians who have written intensively on the period of Confederation have reflected the esteem in which Monck was held by his ministers, and have grasped the essentials of his personal character – his amiability, his steadiness, his industry. Nevertheless, his background remains comparatively unknown and what particular contribution, if any, he made to Confederation is still somewhat obscure.[1]

1. The author undertook this essay partly because the role of Lord Monck in Confederation seems to be treated in a fragmentary and inconclusive manner in Canadian historiography, partly because of the discovery of a small, but significant addition to the documents of Lord Monck's career. This consists of letters to Monck in the years 1864-1866 (in the main) from such people as Edward Cardwell, John A. Macdonald, J. R. Godley, C. B. Adderley. These were salvaged at the sale of Charleville in 1931, and are now in the possession of the Honourable Mrs. Batt, Gresham Hall, Norfolk, who has kindly given copies to the Public Archives of Canada.

This essay offers some tentative findings and opinions that may serve to give the background of Monck's thought and bring some sharper definition to his term as governor general and his influence on the shaping of Confederation.

II

Monck was born on October 10, 1819, at Templemore in county Tipperary. His mother, Bridget Willington, was a Tipperary woman, but his father, Charles Joseph Kelly Monck, was the second son of a county Wicklow family. Its seat, Charleville, was near Enniskerry, some miles south of Dublin. The Moncks were a Devon family which had been in Ireland since the 1620s, and the family owned lands in five of the counties of Leinster besides Wicklow.[2]

Monck, then, belonged to the Anglo-Irish landowning aristocracy and was christened into the Protestant ascendancy. Although he was his father's eldest son, he was not likely to succeed to wealth or the family title. Charles Joseph Kelly was a soldier and not well-to-do, and Monck's uncle, second Viscount Monck and Earl of Rathdowne, was still young and vigorous. His heir, when born, would inherit the title and estates.[3] Monck, then, was a soldier's son, well born and well connected, but faced with the relatively modest destiny of a career in army, church, or state.

Nothing has yet been published on his childhood and little is known of his early life. From what can be learned of the upbringing of his own immediate family, it is possible to suppose that he was raised in the active and healthy life of Irish country houses, that he was given a firm religious training in the Church of Ireland, and that he was privately and carefully educated. As a boy, he was the pupil of a Mr. Doyle, whose school and personality may have had important influences on Monck.[4] In 1836, while still only sixteen, Monck was matriculated at Trinity College, Dublin, where he was to study for five years. In 1841 he graduated with the degree of B.A., and was called to the Bar as a member of King's Inn in June of the same

2. Monck was just forty-two when he became governor general. The biographical details are from *Burke's Peerage and Baronetage*, p. 1576; and B.M., Add. Mss. 43, 629, Ripon Papers, Monck to Ripon, June 13, 1881.
3. The second Viscount had, in fact, nine daughters and no son.
4. G. D. Burtchaell and T. V. Sadleir, *Alumni Dubliensis, 1593-1860* (new ed., Dublin, 1935), p. 585. Monck is described as "socium comitatus" of Mr. Doyle. I owe the suggestion of his influence on Monck to Hon. Mrs. Batt.

year. Thus at twenty-two he was in a position to practise law in Dublin, although there is no family tradition that he actually did so; but Dublin was his home for the next eight years.

In 1844 Monck married his cousin, Elizabeth Louise Mary, third daughter of Viscount Monck. From the marriage came the family of two sons and two daughters which was the central pre-occupation of Monck's life; that is, he was never to be wholly the politician absorbed in public life. On the unexpected death of Viscount Monck in 1845 Monck's father succeeded to the title. Monck himself became heir to the title and estate, and in 1849 succeeded on the death of his father.

These few details are all that is known at present of Monck's early life. As such they have little value except to place him as an Anglo-Irish landlord and member of the Church of Ireland, and an aristocrat devoted to the service of his family. They do seem, however, to have value as a contrast to his career. Monck was to earn his way into the English peerage and give his elder son Henry an education and opportunities he had not had himself. But he was to be active in disestablishing the Church of Ireland, in reforming the land law of Ireland, and, probably, instrumental in embodying the principle of nationality in Canada and in imperial policy. None of these latter things was to be expected from his early life.

As a member of the Anglo-Irish aristocracy, however, Monck was to be to the end of his life at once a resident and an enlightened landlord. During the famine of 1846 and the years immediately succeeding, he was concerned and active in local affairs. He was a member of the (Resident) Landlord's Committee, formed in 1846 by the landlords who took their social responsibilities seriously to concert plans for famine relief.[5]

In the work of the Committee he became friends with John Robert Godley of Killegar, like Monck, the son of an Anglo-Irish landowning family. It was the beginning of a friendship that was to last as long as Godley's life, and was, it is suggested, a major influence on Monck, and particularly on his work as governor general. As a friendship it was to be continued in Monck's connection with C. B. Adderley (later Lord Norton), the closest of Godley's associates, and also in the person of Godley's younger brother Denis.[6]

---

5. C. E. Carrington, *John Robert Godley of Canterbury* (London, 1950), p. 33.
6. Lord Kilbracken (Arthur Godley, son of J. R., refers in his *Reminiscences*

The occasion of this friendship, the Landlord's Committee, was one element in the feeling of many Irishmen in those years of distress that Ireland ought to be free and able to look after itself. The Committee therefore might be an element in an Irish nationalist party of all elements, but when Smith O'Brien, then emerging as the leader of the Young Ireland movement, attempted to convert a conference called by the Committee in January 1847, into a political demonstration, "two young friends, Charles Monck and William Monsell", persuaded a majority to vote to exclude the press.[7] It is the first glimpse of Monck in politics, with another life-long friend who was to achieve political eminence.

That friendship with Monsell belongs to Irish politics, however. For Monck's Canadian career it was the development of the friendship with Godley that mattered. The maturing of that connection may be detected, although not traced, by scattered correspondence and reference to visits.[8] From friendship with Godley, it is suggested, may have come the ideas that were Monck's own in his role of governor general. Godley's views on colonial policy were founded on the full acceptance of responsible government. He thought it the just and proper way to develop the colonies into mature communities. To him this meant self-government and self-defence, to be carried even as far as *de facto* independence, but to the point of formal separation only if a colony wished it.[9]

(London, 1931) to Monck as "one of a few of [his] most intimate friends", p. 12, and as "my father's friend", p. 17.

Denis Godley travelled with John Robert to British North America in 1842, when the latter became a strong advocate of responsible government. Denis was an officer in the Highland Regiment, went with his brother to New Zealand, became Monck's civil secretary in Canada, secretary of the Irish Temporalities Commission, of which Monck was chairman, 1870-1881 (B.M. Add. Mss. 44, 468, Monck to Gladstone, Aug. 5, 1881), and secretary of the Irish Land Commission, 1881, (United Kingdom *Debates, House of Lords*, vol. 266, p. 220, Feb. 9, 1882). His nephew described him as being "a strong Liberal", in later life at least (Kilbracken, *Reminiscences*, p. 83).

7. Carrington, *Godley*, p. 33.
8. C. B. Adderley (ed.) *Extracts from the Letters of John Robert Godley* (London, 1863), Godley to Adderley, Nov. 2, 1853, p. 194. ". . . We are all staying at the Monck's for a visit." The Monck Letters, of which copies are in P.A.C. contain one letter from Godley at Killegar to Monck, Sept. 4, [1847] and two from Godley in New Zealand to Monck in 1850 and 1859.
9. J. R. Godley, *Letters from America*, I, (London, 1844), 226-31. Godley here expressed his approval of responsible government in Canada. In 1849 he was to state his final concept of the metropolitan-colonial tie, in a letter to

The working out of this idea seemed to Godley important at once for the United Kingdom and the colonies. In 1850 he, Edward Gibbon Wakefield, C. B. Adderley and others formed a Society for the Reform of Colonial Government. Their purpose was to urge the carrying out of the full implications of responsible government, to the point of full self-government, the assumption of local defence, and the growth of independent nationality. The range of their thinking is shown by Godley's letters. In 1853 he spoke to Adderley of their belief that colonies should fully govern themselves as Greek colonies had done; in 1854 he told Adderley he had written to Joseph Howe of "a British American nationality based either on an equality with, or independence of, this country"; and in 1859 he was to write of "our grand object – the nationalization of British colonies".[10]

Self-government might properly, these enthusiasts thought with Godley, lead to independence, but independence need not necessarily mean separation in form or sentiment. What they hoped for, particularly in defence, was co-operation and reciprocity. The Colonial Defence (Naval) Act of 1865, as Adderley pointed out, was founded on Godley's work for Cardwell as Secretary of War, 1859-1862, and invited colonial participation in Imperial naval defence.[11] What these colonial reformers sought, indeed, was what came to be practised in the Commonwealth from 1921 to 1945. But their ideas confused their contemporaries, and were over-shadowed by the rise of the imperial federation movement. When Monck, with his customary frankness and bluntness, later uttered such ideas to his ministers in Canada (and when Denis Godley perhaps did so less circumspectly) it would seem that misunderstanding and over-simplifications followed.

In British North America Arthur Gordon, when he was lieutenant-governor of New Brunswick, wondered aloud to Monck if Monck had really said he would be the last governor general. "[J. R.] Godley, I remember," Gordon continued, "thought it would be a good thing to get rid of the colonies & made no secret of his opinions." And Edward Watkin, after having been in Canada in 1862, wrote that "Lord Monck told me that he thought in two years Great

Gladstone as "1, an acknowledged allegiance; 2, a common citizenship; 3, an offensive and defensive alliance." Quoted in Carrington, *Godley*, pp. 215-23. It was the third he was working to realize as Assistant Under-Secretary for War, 1854-1862.
10. Adderley, *Extracts*. Godley to Adderley, Nov. 27, 1853, p. 194; Godley to Adderley, Aug. 28, 1854, p. 217; Godley to Adderley, Oct. 25, 1859, p. 286.
11. Lord Norton, *Imperial Fellowship*, p. 35.

Britain would 'cut the painter.' He told J. A. M. [?] through a 3rd
party that he would be 'the last Governor General'." Monck replied
to Gordon that neither he nor Godley held any such opinion, but in
fact he would have agreed both with Adderley who felt the "connection" with Canada must be maintained, and with Cardwell who
declared himself an advocate of colonial independence.[12] Monck himself wished not to destroy the colonial connection but to transform
it into an alliance of convenience and sentiment.

Monck, however, appears never to have been a member of the
Society for the Reform of Colonial Government, although the reason
may have been that he lived in Ireland and in 1850 had no regular
business to take him to England. It may or may not mean anything
that he was not a member of Godley's Canterbury Association
formed for colonization in New Zealand, although he was in full
agreement with Godley on the need for assisted and directed emigration.[13] But of his knowledge and general acceptance of the ideas of
Godley and Adderley on matters of colonial policy and development
there can be little doubt. Godley, for example, was delighted with
Monck's appointment as governor general of Canada, and wrote
Adderley that Monck was "thoroughly 'sound' on colonial politics".[14]

But at that time Monck had no special interest in colonial policy,
as did Godley and Adderley. The famine had left him convinced that
major land reforms were needed to create tolerable conditions of life
in Ireland for all Irishmen. Thus it was that in 1848 Monck made
his first bid to enter politics at a by-election for Wicklow. Defeated
by only ten votes, he had based his campaign as a Conservative on
opposition to the Liberal nominee as an absentee landlord. This
identification with local interests was further reflected in his open
espousal of the principle of compensating tenants for improvements
to the land. In 1852 he was successful in his candidacy for the seat
of Portsmouth, and his reputation as an active member in the Commons was built on his support for liberal legislative measures.

12. P.A.C. Monck Letters, Gordon to Monck, Oct. 7, 1863; *ibid.*, Adderley to
    Monck, Dec. 1, 1862; *ibid.*, Cardwell to Monck, Sept. 1, 1863; P.A.C.
    Newcastle Papers, Watkin to J. Ogden Wright, June 3 [1863 ?]; U.N.B.
    Library, Stanmore Papers, Monck to Gordon, Oct. 15, 1863.
13. United Kingdom, *Debates, House of Lords*, 3rd Series vol. 255, pp. 608-10,
    Aug. 8, 1880: Adderley, *Extracts*, Godley to Adderley, Dec. 16, 1860, p. 298.
14. Adderley, *Extracts*, Godley to Adderley, Aug. 26, 1861, p. 305, and Sept.
    12, 1861, p. 306, adding however, "but he can do nothing, and if he is
    wise will attempt nothing".

Monck's adhesion to the Aberdeen and Palmerston governments in the Crimean War earned him entry into the administration as a Lord of the Treasury and the more responsible post of whip for the Irish supporters of the government. But his enforced withdrawal from Parliament began in 1857 when he failed to be re-elected and was completed by the loss of his Treasury position when Palmerston's government fell the following March. Another attempt at re-election failed in 1859, and for the time being at least Monck's political career was at an end.

He was, however, too useful a man to be forgotten. After two years in private life, he suddenly received, in August 1861, an invitation from the Duke of Newcastle, Colonial Secretary, to become governor-in-chief of the Province of Canada.[15] Suddenly he was back in public life, charged with an important and, in view of the American Civil War which had begun in April 1861, very difficult office.

It must be said that at first sight Newcastle's appointment of Monck is surprising, as many contemporaries, some by no means unfriendly, found it.[16] Monck had shown some promise in British politics, but he had not concerned himself with colonial affairs. Whatever influence Godley and Adderley may have had on his opinions of colonial affairs, he had not spoken on any colonial issue before the Commons from 1852 to 1857. Nor was he Newcastle's first choice for Canada, far from it. As the Duke explained to the retiring governor general, Sir Edmund Head, in informing him of the choice of his successor, he had tried to get the most substantial man he could; and had received refusals from four before he turned to Monck.

Yet the Duke and Palmerston did not consider this a choice of desperation, nor was Monck to be dismissed as a mere Irish peer and "whipper-in". He was well thought of in powerful circles, for on this

---

15. P.A.C., Newcastle Papers, Newcastle to Head, Aug. 27, 1861. Edward Watkin, *Canada and the United States: Recollections 1851 to 1886* (London, 1887) says Newcastle told him five candidates had been approached before Monck.
16. P.A.C. Ellice Papers, R. Lowe to Ellice, Sept. 4, 1861, A. Parker to Ellice, Nov. 19, 1861. Lowe called Monck "an innocent lamb"; National Library of Wales, Lewis Papers, Lewis to Head on Monck's appointments; "He is a man of good sense and judgment, and fair abilities and application. He has never been tried in anything difficult, but I should not be surprised if he acquitted himself with propriety . . ." *Saturday Review*, Nov. 2 and Nov. 8, 1861, with editorials criticizing Monck's appointment as irresponsible patronage.

occasion he was suggested to Newcastle by Delane, the great editor of The Times.[17] Certainly Newcastle and Palmerston were fully aware that the office of governor general of Canada, as long as the American war lasted, would call for exceptional steadiness and good sense.[18] They would not, and they could not, have chosen a man in whose ability and prudence they had not sufficient reason to trust. Certainly the consequences were to approve their choice, for perhaps Monck's chief accomplishment as governor of Canada was that he won the confidence of the Lincoln administration that he would preserve the neutrality of British North America.

Even when his term as governor general was over he from time to time expressed the ideas on colonial policy which he had held while in Canada. These amounted to a liberal colonial policy, leading at once to independence and interdependence. He so expressed himself on three major occasions in the House of Lords. There in February, 1869, in seconding the Address, he urged the complete separation of church and state in Ireland to end the Protestant ascendancy, given up, he asserted, with the Penal Code, and to make the Church of Ireland free as the church was in Canada.[19] In April he spoke out boldly for army reform by coming out for the whole of the Cardwell scheme, and indeed going further in his admiration of the Prussian system. On the matter of redevelopment of the imperial forces, he summed up what his military policy may be supposed to have been in Canada:

> In justice to the colonies, and in order that they may
> place themselves in a condition of self-defence, they
> should be explicitly informed that the withdrawal of
> the troops now going on resulted from no spasmodic
> effort of economy, but from deliberate policy; and that
> in time of peace they must under no circumstance,
> expect to see an Imperial soldier within their limits;
> while in time of war Imperial troops will be handled
> and distributed solely with reference to Imperial stra-

17. A. I. Dasent, John Thaddeus Delane, Editor of the Times, II (London, 1908), 30. Delane is said to have been an old friend of Monck.
18. See for example the correspondence of Palmerston and Newcastle on the further re-inforcement of British North America, Historical Manuscript Commission, Palmerston Papers, G.C./N.E./88/3; Palmerston to Newcastle, Sept. 1, 1861; Newcastle to Palmerston, Sept. 3, 1861.
19. United Kingdom: Debates, House of Lords, 3rd Series vol. 194, Feb. 16, 1869, pp. 33-39.

tegical considerations and will be sent to a colony only
in the event of its becoming the theatre of the decisive
contest of the war.[20]

The Canadian Militia Act of 1863, so hardly teased from the government of John Sandfield Macdonald, had been a stone in the foundation of that policy.

In 1870 Monck took up, in general principle this time, the subject of colonial policy. Carnarvon on February 14, 1870, raised in the Lords the question of relations with the colonies in view of the withdrawal of troops. Monck agreed it was timely to raise the question, but differed from Carnarvon "*toto caelo*" as to the policy he had implied in his question. It was in vain, Monck declared, to protest the dismemberment of the Empire; that dismemberment had already occurred with responsible government. He himself had respected the Canadian Parliament and had found able men among the Canadian ministers. With them he had discussed colonial relations "fully and frankly".[21] The colonies, he asserted, were quite free now, and there was no reason to think that the connection with them would endure forever. Any tie must rest on advantage, at least to the mother country.[22] Carnarvon himself had admitted separation might occur. "But if the event may occur," Monck asked, "is it not our bounden duty to so shape our policy that when the separation actually does come about the colonies shall be enabled to maintain themselves in a position of independency, and that it should be unaccompanied by any ill-feeling on either side?" He then quoted Cornewall Lewis on *The Government of Dependencies* to the effect that the imperial government should prepare the colonies for independence.

He did not, he concluded, seeking to modify the harsh impression the speech had created, ignore sentiment, even if his argument seemed to rest on material considerations. He was, in fact, wholly for union, a union "of common origins, community of sentiment, and identity of interests". But such relations must be prepared for by clearing up all obligations of protection or control. The government, he said

20. *Ibid.*, Apr. 23, 1869, pp. 1420-1436. The speech was published as a pamphlet, *Speech of the Rt. Hon. Lord Monck on the Military Force of the Kingdom* (London, 1869).
21. *Ibid.*, 3rd Series, vol. 199, Feb. 14, 1870, pp. 223-228.
22. *Ibid.*, p. 227. It was this implication that cooled his audience and Monck sought to repair the impression later in his speech.

finally, had disavowed such a policy, but it was in fact pursuing it, and he approved and supported it in doing so.

The speech was Monck at his plainest and bluntest, even to the point of asserting duplicity in the policy of the government. (It is not impossible that this insistence on speaking "fully and frankly" was his greatest political handicap). His plainness shocked John Rose, as he reported to Sir John Macdonald, adding that the speech had won little support.[23] Monck was in fact expressing in the 1870s ideas formed in the 1850s, when already the reaction against mid-Victorian liberal policies was beginning to gather. The speech explains why Monck's views sometimes distressed his friend John A. Macdonald, who sought to preserve the forms of the imperial connection as a diplomatic makeweight against American pressure. Both the thought expressed and the bluntness of expression help explain the rumour of 1862 and 1863 that Monck expected to be the last governor general. Monck probably had expected no such outcome in the 1860s, but he was quite prepared to contemplate a time when there would be no imperial governor: in his opinion, as he now said, "it was for the colonies to decide whether to come or go".[24]

On his return to the United Kingdom Monck had also become involved in Anglo-Irish politics, and so remained until he broke with Gladstone over the first Home Rule Bill in 1886. He sometimes referred to Canadian examples, but his only considerable statements on colonial matters were his emphatic approval in 1869 of the withdrawal of imperial troops from Canada, as a policy, not just an economy, and his blunt assertion that colonial policy should prepare the colonies for independence, with separation as they might choose. It was the pure word of Godley.

III

Is there, then, in this sketch of his ideas and actions before and after he was governor general of Canada, anything to suggest – such evidence as there is admits of no more than tentative suggestion – what opinions on colonial policy Monck held while governor general? To that a second question must be asked, what kind of man was he?

23. P.A.C., Macdonald Papers, Rose to Macdonald, Feb. 17, 1870.
24. United Kingdom: *Debates, House of Lords*. 3rd Series, vol. 199, Feb. 14, 1870, p. 223.

Character is of more than usual importance to a man who, by the nature of his office, must persuade rather than command.

It seems likely that, in so far as Monck had any preparation for the post of colonial governor, it derived in large part from his friendship with J. R. Godley and C. B. Adderley.[25] Both were active and influential advocates of complete responsible government as a preparation for colonial independence in connection with the United Kingdom. Monck, "thoroughly sound" on colonial policy in Godley's opinion, may be taken to have had the same general outlook on the relations of the self-governing colonies with the mother country. Self-government might, indeed would, mean independence, sooner or later, but when it was to come was for the colonies to decide. If they should wish, because of ties of interest and sentiment, to co-operate with the Empire in diplomacy, defence, or other matters, that too was for them to decide. But full political self-government they must assume, perhaps have thrust upon them. Monck, that is, seems to have been neither a Little Englander concerned to cast off the colonies even against their will, nor a Liberal Imperialist granting responsible government with limited powers, much less an Imperial Federationist seeking to create forms of imperial co-operation. He was, before that time, a Commonwealth man.

Monck, however, was severely pragmatic. He would never have advanced such ideas unless he thought the time ripe. The circumstances of his governorship were to afford abundant grounds for thinking that relations between Canada and the United Kingdom, confused since the granting of responsible government in 1849, had to be clarified. Not only had the Crimean War, the first Maori War in New Zealand, the Indian Mutiny and the sometimes menacing guise of the Second Empire of France raised questions of defence latent since Waterloo; there was also the American Civil War.[26] Like Durham he found internal politics in Canada gravely influenced by relations with the United States. He was therefore from his first day of office occupied with most serious questions of diplomacy and defence.

Immediately after his landing at Quebec on October 23, 1861,

25. Their general influence would be increased by Monck's friendship with such radicals and colonial reformers as Robert Lowe, Henry Labouchere and Cornewall Lewis.
26. See W. L. Morton, "British North America and a Continent in Dissolution, 1861-1867", *History*, June 1962.

Monck conferred with his predecessor, Sir Edmund Head. On Head's recommendation, he wrote on the same day to Lord Lyons, British Minister to Washington, to request him to continue the same private and confidential correspondence he had had with Head.[27] Lyons responded cordially,[28] and the two corresponded with increasing confidence until ill health forced Lyons to resign at the end of 1864. The exchange was supplemented by visits of Lyons to Quebec in the fall of 1863 and 1864.[29]

Monck and Lyons saw eye to eye on the matter of Anglo-American relations. The "North" was the undoubted government of the United States, south as well as north, and no offence was to be given it in its efforts to reassert its authority over the rebel states. Certainly no aid or comfort should be given its enemies in or from the British North American provinces. The preservation of the neutrality of Canada therefore became one of Monck's leading purposes.

This diplomatic role was a responsibility he had considerable freedom to discharge, as the Canadian government had no external powers. Aided by Lyons and E. H. Archibald, the British Consul at New York, and by his Attorneys General West, J. S. Macdonald and John A. Macdonald, he was very successful until the release of the St. Alban's raiders by Magistrate Coursol in December 1864. This was the tensest moment of Monck's career in Canada, because it threatened to destroy at a blow the careful diplomacy he and Lyons had pursued for three years.[30] Monck was deeply concerned that he should have sufficient power, as he did not have under existing legislation, to deal with violations of Canadian neutrality. The passage of the Alien Act by the Canadian Parliament in 1865[31] was therefore a relief to him. In some measure the Act may be seen as a personal accomplishment, as was the preservation of Canadian

27. West Sussex County Library, Lyons Papers, Monck to Lyons, Oct. 21, 1861. (I owe thanks to the Duke of Norfolk for permission to quote.)
28. P.A.C., Monck Letters, Lyons to Monck, Nov. 2, 1861.
29. The social description of the latter visit in Frances Monck's *My Canadian Leaves*, conceals the fact that Lyons did not go entirely on holiday, but was instructed by Lord John Russell, the Foreign Secretary, to discuss Reciprocity and Canadian defence with Monck; Lord Newton, *Life of Lord Lyons*, I (London, 1913), 131-33.
30. The St. Alban's raid has received much attention but its consequences in Canada require further study.
31. Province of Canada: *Statutes*, 28 Victoria, Chap 1. The Act, valid for one year unless renewed, gave the governor general power to deport aliens and seize armed vessels.

neutrality throughout the war, despite widespread Canadian sympathy for the South and the presence of great numbers of Southerners in Canada.[32]

Monck had also to turn to matters of defence almost as quickly as to those of diplomacy. British North America had already received imperial reinforcements since the outbreak of the Civil War. But a month after Monck became governor general the *Trent* affair led to the instant dispatch of a far greater imperial contingent. The crisis passed off, but the troops remained in undiminished numbers until well after the end of the Civil War. The affair revealed how grave a liability the obligation to defend British North America was, and how little the provinces were prepared to assist the imperial troops. As a result the imperial government and its chief representative in British North America, Monck, strongly resolved that the imperial obligation to defend Canada should be matched by a Canadian readiness to assist.[33] It was this determination, shared by British public opinion, that made British reaction to the defeat of the Militia Bill in May 1862 so strong.[34] Canada had shown itself unwilling to take its part in its own defence. Monck, with his knowledge of the ways of politicians and of the condition of the Cartier-Macdonald government, knew that the reasons for the defeat of the bill were more various,[35] but he was none the less determined to obtain a satisfactory militia bill.

As titular commander-in-chief he had more freedom of action than he had in civil matters. Moreover, the troops available for the defence of Canada were largely imperial and Monck was an imperial officer. From these circumstances came his bold rebuke to the mayor of Montreal in July 1862, for his boast in Monck's presence at a public banquet that Canada was a free country, free even of the cost of its

32. The term "personal accomplishment" is warranted by the amount of work and correspondence Monck gave to this, although of course the framing and carrying the bill was the responsibility of John A. Macdonald as Attorney-General West: See Historical Manuscripts Commission, Palmerston Papers, Monck to Cardwell, Dec. 15, 1864; Cardwell to Palmerston, Jan. 6 and 15, 1865. P.A.C. Monck Letters, Cardwell to Monck, Dec. 31, 1865.
33. All the provinces were of course involved, but Canada, because of its size and long frontier with the United States, was the decisive one.
34. P.A.C., Monck Papers, de Grey, Secretary of State for War, to Monck, Aug. 28, 1863.
35. P.A.C., Newcastle Papers, Monck to Newcastle, May 23, 1862; Newcastle to Monck, June 6, 1862.

own defence. Britain would defend Canada at no cost to Canadians. It would do no such thing, said Monck in reply; Canadians must play, and pay, their part of their own defence.[36] Hence his steady pressure on his new prime minister, John Sandfield Macdonald, to repair something of the damage done by the defeat of the Militia Bill, and then to get through in 1863 a fairly satisfactory Militia Act.[37]

In terms of Monck's career, the Militia Act prepared the way for his memorandum on the defence of Canada for his ministers in 1865, and the agreement on defence between the Canadian and British government of that year, in which Canada undertook to pay three-fifths of the cost of the necessary fortifications.[38] The Militia Act is therefore an indicator of Monck's work in Canada; defence, indeed, was probably Monck's chief interest in Canada and the Act his principal achievement. It produced in the next two years a fairly competent force in the Militia and the Volunteers, which proved of use in the Fenian raids from 1866 to 1869. More important, the existence of the force showed that Canada was prepared to defend itself. To Monck, readiness for self-defence was a necessary part of self-government and of an independent nationality.[39] The creation of an effective militia was preliminary to the creation of a nation.[40]

36. *Globe*, July 7, 1862, for the report of Monck's speech of July 3. Mayor Beaudry, perhaps carried away, described Canada as "the land of freedom, the land free from taxes, protected at the expense of the Mother Country". Monck replied that Canada enjoyed "practical independence" and yet was protected at others' expense. If Canadians wished "to preserve their independence", they must be ready to defend themselves. It was not unusually plain spoken for Monck, but it was for a governor general even in that day.

37. P.A.C., Monck Letters, Fortescue to Monck, Nov. 5, 1863; "The Act was a great advance in the right direction and will redound to your credit at home, as all your treatment of the defence question has."

38. For the memorandum, see C.O. 42/648, Mar. 21, 1865; for the Defence Agreement, C. P. Stacey, *Canada and the British Army, 1846-1871*, (Toronto, 1963), p. 187; Province of Canada: *Parliamentary Papers*: "Papers relating to the Conferences . . . between Her Majesty's Government and a deputation from the Executive Council of Canada", p. 9.

39. This at least was the thought of Godley and Adderley: Norton, *Imperial Fellowship*, p. 35, by the Society for the Reform of Colonial Government. "Self-defence was soon recognized as a necessary condition of self-government."

40. The standard works for a military aspect of the matter are, C. P. Stacey, *Canada and the British Army 1846-1871*, (Toronto, 1963), and G. F. Stanley, *Canada's Soldiers*, rev. ed. (Macmillan Co. of Canada, 1960).

Monck was, however, primarily a civilian head of state; only the Civil War forced him to be so active in diplomacy and defence. In this role it is probable that Monck followed a significantly different role from that of his predecessors since 1849, Elgin and Head. He made himself more the "constitutional monarch" in internal Canadian matters than either had done. In doing so he was following both the private advice of Newcastle and the main premise of the thought of Godley and Adderley.[41] Responsible government meant self-government, at least in internal affairs, wholly and without qualification in the hands and on the responsibility of colonial ministers.

Monck was quite aware of the nature of his position. "I am," he wrote to Lyons, " – bless the mark – a constitutional monarch, administering a system of responsible government."[42] The test of his role came in 1863, when J. S. Macdonald found he could no longer carry on and advised a dissolution of the Parliament elected in 1861. The Opposition claimed, and might have been granted, the opportunity to form a ministry. But Monck accepted Macdonald's advice and granted dissolution. Macdonald survived the election – one can hardly say won – and formed the Macdonald-Dorion ministry. There was some criticism of Monck in Canada, but his action was warmly upheld by his English friends, Adderley and Lowe, and his unexpected admirer, old Edward Ellice.[43] That is, liberal opinion supported him. Constitutional monarchy was a necessary stage on the road to colonial independence.

But it was not yet constitutional monarchy as Walter Bagehot was defining it. Monck was by force of circumstances an active governor in diplomacy and defence. Beyond that necessity, the equal balance of parties, reflecting support of and resistance to the cry of "representation by population", made him active also in domestic politics, as the balance, or fragmentation, of parties tends to make the constitutional monarch. Monck, therefore, took up the idea of coalition

---

41. P.A.C., Newcastle Papers, Newcastle to Monck, Nov. 29, 1862. C. B. Adderley, *Russell's Colonial Administration*, (London, 1869), p. 46, in which he claims Monck "was the first Governor General to hold a perfectly neutral constitutional-monarchical attitude towards contending parties".

42. West Sussex County Library, Lyons Papers, Monck to Lyons, Mar. 10, 1864, written when Monck was anticipating the crisis which led to the coalition.

43. P.A.C., Monck Letters, Adderley to Monck, June 12, 1863, Lowe to Monck, Jan. 11, 1863.

as the necessary release from the "deadlock". He saw it as the means of dealing with the Canadian crisis and of saving, or remaking, the Canadian union. By his own account he picked up the idea for Canadian coalition from J. S. Macdonald in March 1864; he mentioned it to his son Henry that month.[44] His own experience of the Aberdeen coalition in the United Kingdom may have influenced him. Be that as it may, he made it his own idea, and in June 1864, he delayed his reply to Taché's advice to dissolve until the possibility of a coalition had been explored and, in particular, he strongly urged George Brown, whom he admired and saw as the key to success, to join the coalition.[45] Although it is cloaked in his customary modesty, his own statement that he had some part in making the coalition must be accepted.[46]

It seems, however, that Monck had no such part in initiating Confederation as he had in bringing about coalition. Confederation seems not to have engaged his attention before June 1864, and then only as an undertaking of his ministers, as one way – "the big plan" – for the reconstruction of the union. In his memorandum of June 30 for the Colonial Secretary on the formation of the coalition, he does not even mention federation.[47] Nor did his concern with defence lead him to take up the project of federation, since the new measures for the defence of Canada were worked out quite separately until the defence agreement of June 1865. It only became apparent to Monck and Cardwell, as Confederation became a possibility with the

44. It seems with present evidence that J. S. Macdonald first suggested coalition: C.O. 42/640, Monck to Newcastle, Confidential, Mar. 31, 1864; Bruce W. Hodgins, "The Political Career of John Sandfield Macdonald to 1864" (Unpublished Ph.D. thesis, Duke University, 1964), p. 423; P.A.C., Letters to Henry, Monck to Henry, Mar. 28, 1864. It may of course have been Monck's own idea returned to him by Macdonald. Monck had mentioned coalition to Brown in May, 1863; J. M. S. Careless, *Brown of the Globe*, II, (Toronto, 1962), 132.

45. P.A.C., Monck Letters, Monck to Taché, June 16, 1864; Monck to Brown, June 21, 1864.

46. P.A.C., Macdonald Papers, Monck to Macdonald, June 21, 1866 and Macdonald's memo on Monck's threat to resign, J. A. Pope, *Memoirs of Rt. Hon. Sir John Alexander Macdonald*, (Toronto, 1944), pp. 710-11. J. C. Brady in an admirable study, "Lord Monck in Canada" (unpublished M.A. thesis, University of Western Ontario, 1964), pp. 153-159: "Had not Monck been the man he was and followed the course he did, it is possible a coalition would not have been formed."

47. P.R.O., C.O. 42-641, Monck to Secretary of State for Colonies, June 30, 1864.

success of the Quebec Conference, that defence had lost its primacy to the creation of a united British North America.[48]

The reason it had done so was perhaps not merely because a larger political unit would aid defence. Monck had during his term of office received letters from C. B. Adderley,[49] that suggest that he was at least subjected to ideas that reached beyond military defence or political union. For example, in 1862 Adderley wrote Monck that he had in the government of Canada "a difficult & important task, perhaps the solution of the problem of our present Colonial Empire". "Is it possible," he continued, "to maintain colonial connexion with great & free Colonies, free as ourselves in Parliamentary conditions, yet hanging on us for protection & refusing to assume the habits [?] of freedom?" The only difficulty in reaching a solution was the "dualism" of Monck's position between the Canadian and the imperial governments. "I believe it possible by wise influence & prudent management, though impossible in theory, and if you can manage as I hope you will, to make Canada see that England cannot do more than re-inforce her arms when danger comes & that she must undertake her freedom to the full in its vigour as well as its enjoyment, we may still go on together & be a great Empire. The present state of things is just inducing England to shake off Canada at the approaching re-formation of Nations in North America. Don't be the last Governor General."[50]

Such a view could grow into the idea that Monck might redeem the situation by helping to create a British-American nationality. As Adderley had written in 1863, "a revision of the Union is indispensably necessary".[51] Coalition in 1864 had opened the way to revision, Confederation would make possible the formation of a new nationality. And a self-governing, an independent nationality would be a better defence against American attack than fortifications and Armstrong guns. So much, of course, is projection beyond any evidence Monck left of his thought, except for a hint in his confidential dispatch to Carnarvon in 1866. What is certain is that the diplomatic,

48. A. B. Erickson, *Edward T. Cardwell, Peelite* (Philadelphia, 1958) makes this point, p. 35, as does Brady, "Monck", p. 197. The agreement of 1865 contained the Godleian concept of "reciprocal obligation".
49. Written enquiry has failed to discover letters from Monck to Adderley in the Norton Papers in Birmingham, as it has failed to find letters from Monck to Godley in the Godley Papers in Canterbury, New Zealand.
50. P.A.C., Monck Letters, Adderley to Monck, Aug. 29 [1862].
51. *Ibid.*, Adderley to Monck, June 12, [1863].

military and political problems Monck faced as governor general
reached a common solution in Confederation. The common solvent
could have been the idea of colonial nationality.[52]

If Monck was not an exponent of Confederation, he was, nevertheless, most active in carrying it into execution. When Tilley was
defeated by anti-Confederate forces in New Brunswick in 1865, steps
had to be taken to recover the ground lost. To all that followed,
Monck was a party, proposing, advising, tempering, in private correspondence with Cardwell at the Colonial Office, Gordon in New
Brunswick, Macdonald and then Sir Fenwick Williams in Nova
Scotia.[53] He did suggest to Cardwell that Williams be appointed to
replace Gordon,[54] but otherwise seems to have initiated little. But he
knew all that was afoot and proved a wise and prudent manager in
matters requiring both delicacy and tact.

Similarly, he was present in 1866 to help the business along during
and after the Westminster Conference in London. He conferred with
Carnarvon and with his advisers, (C. B. Adderley, his friend and
admirer, was Under-Secretary for the Colonies) and he kept in close
touch with John A. Macdonald.[55] He talked with important politi-

52. *Ibid.*, Cardwell to Monck, Sept. 1865; R.G. 7, G12 Governor General's
    Letterbooks, 79, Monck to Carnarvon, Sept. 7, 1867 [*sic*: 66], printed by
    W. M. Whitelaw, "Lord Monck and the Canadian Confederation", *Cana-
    dian Historical Review*, Sept. 1940, p. 305.
53. *Ibid.*, Cardwell to Monck, Mar. 4, 1865 in which he informs Monck that
    Gordon and Macdonnell were now doing their duty and supporting
    Confederation, and that it would be a grave error for Monck to go to
    the Maritimes (as Gordon had suggested he should). Macdonnell to
    Monck, Mar. 20, 1865; Cardwell to Monck, April 1, 1865, Cardwell to
    Monck, July 8, 1865, Cardwell to Monck, July 29, 1865; Cardwell to Monck,
    Oct. 13, 1865, Gordon to Monck, Feb. 7, 1866, in reply to Monck of Jan.
    8, Williams to Monck, March 24, 1866; P.R.O. 30/48/6/39, Cardwell
    Papers, Gordon to Cardwell, Feb. 25, 1866, to say he has seen Monck and
    settled how to carry Confederation in New Brunswick.
        One of the difficulties of research on Monck is that all but two of his
    private letters to Cardwell are missing.
54. Writing to Monck, (*ibid.*, June 17, 1865) Cardwell took up the suggestion,
    but appointed Williams to Nova Scotia when Gordon decided to remain in
    New Brunswick, having been talked to in England by Cardwell, Monck
    and his bride; *Ibid*, Cardwell to Monck, Sept. 15, 1868.
        Monck may have also had some effect in a joint letter to Timothy
    Anglin and Charles Hatheway, ministers who resigned from the Cabinet
    of Premier Smith of New Brunswick, in diminishing their opposition
    about the Quebec scheme; *Ibid.*, Cardwell to Monck, Sept. 9, 1865.
55. *Ibid.*, Carnarvon to Monck, Dec. 31, 1866, a meeting for Jan. 8, 1868,
    Sir Arthur Harding, *Life of Henry Howard Molyneux Herbert, Fourth
    Earl of Carnarvon, 1831-1880*, (London, 1928), p. 303, says Monck, Adder-

cians who had been made uncertain of supporting Confederation by the Repeal agitation in Nova Scotia and the imperial guarantee of the loan to build the Intercolonial Railway, the *sine qua non* of the entry of Nova Scotia and New Brunswick to Confederation.[56] He spoke in the House of Lords, his first appearance there, to support the bill.[57] Monck, more than any other man, was central to the whole intricate process of negotiation that led from the coalition of June 1864, to the inauguration of the Dominion of Canada, July 1, 1867.

The coming of Confederation was itself one of those rare periods of convergence in events when everything combines to produce a result which transforms the pre-existing situation. So it was for Monck's particular concerns. Diplomatic relations with Washington and defence against American attack would be easier, the latter perhaps unnecessary, if British North America were united and on the road to nationhood. The imperial troops could be withdrawn, and the United States, free of the irritation of a British strong point in the north, might be expected to accept a new nation in America. Finally, the relation between the United Kingdom and Canada would become the mature relations of equals as Canada lost the colonial dependence on which observers remarked.[58] It would be, finally, the first step in the "nationalization" of the British Empire of which Godley had written in his exuberant way.

IV

It is not possible to document yet the extent to which Monck accepted the ideas of Godley and Adderley. His acts and attitudes as governor general strongly suggest that those ideas were his guiding

ley, F. Rogers, and John Reilly, the legal draftsman, met on Jan. 26, 1867, at Carnarvon's London house. Also P.A.C., Macdonald Papers, Monck to Macdonald, Charleville, Dec. 23, Dec. 29, Dec. 31, 1866, and Jan. 3, 1867, London, Jan. 18, Mar. 2, Apr. 5, 1867.
56. *Ibid.*, Monck to Macdonald, March 2, 1867.
57. United Kingdom: *Debates, House of Lords*, Feb. 19, 1867, pp. 579-582. He spoke with habitual brevity on this his first appearance to assure the House that the agitation against Confederation in Nova Scotia had been got up by a few energetic people, and the measure would ensure the good government of the provinces other than Canada, and would put relations between the mother country and the colonies on a more satisfactory footing.
58. W. H. Russell, *My Tour of Canada*, (London, 1863), p. 98: "The Canadian mind suffers as the mind of every country which is not a nationality must suffer, and caution takes the place of enterprise."

principles and that so far as circumstances allowed he consciously and deliberately sought to realize them. If this was indeed the background of his thought as governor general at the time of Confederation it helps to explain the intellectual position from which he confronted the still heavy duties of that office in a time of unusual difficulty and extraordinary opportunity.

More than mere endurance was called for, however, if his term of office was to have the results suggested above. Monck in fact had other qualities that served Canada well. One was his personal amiability, even geniality. This ability to win men's liking and respect had much to do with bringing about the coalition of 1864 and holding it together, except for Brown's defection, until its work was done. Monck also possessed unusual sincerity and modesty – the latter may have been one of his political handicaps – and this made it possible for him to win the co-operation and good will of all the politicians with whom he had to work. He left no resentment, no ill-will, behind him among all his Canadian ministers.[59] Finally Monck had beneath all other qualities a certain reserve and independence of mind that made him a man not only of integrity but of an unusual steadiness of purpose and conduct. If indeed he saw his term as governor general as an opportunity to bring Canada up to full self-government and perhaps to independent nationality; if indeed he accepted something of the ideas of Godley and Adderley on colonial policy; he would then make his own what he chose from those ideas, as he had worked out his own liberal principles, and his practical steadiness and amiable knowledge of men would enable him through others to realize as much of those ideas as circumstances permitted. Such a man, with such ideas, could in the circumstances of Confederation have helped bring to birth a new nationality.

59. Unless Galt continued his strong feeling over the Confederation honour he, with Cartier, had declined.

The Oregon Dispute and the Defence of Canada

PATRICK C. T. WHITE

"The means must be vast and the expenses enormous," wrote Sir Charles Metcalfe, the governor general of Canada, if that colony were to be defended against the United States. Indeed, he continued, if Britain were to fight a successful war over Oregon she would have to become "a greater continental power" than the United States.[1] This candid and sombre assessment of the situation by Metcalfe showed both the nature and the dimensions of the dilemma which Britain faced in her dispute with America over Oregon. If negotiations over this contested territory failed and if the United States resorted to force Britain would be put to terrible cost. The staggering extent of the latter had been studied with particular care in the years between 1841 and 1846 and it brought profound concern to those charged with the responsibility of governing. Reasonable men were compelled to ask themselves if the country could afford such an additional expense and even if it could whether Oregon were worth it.

How these questions were answered would determine to a marked degree the course which Britain would follow in her negotiations

1. Metcalfe to Stanley, Montreal, July 4, 1845. C.O. 539/143, P.R.O.

with the United States. It is true, of course, that the government had
other pressing problems on its mind. The tragedy of the Irish famine
and the effect it had upon the Corn Laws dominated much of the
cabinet's thinking. The state of relations with France and the course
of events unfolding in Mexico also drew its attention. These problems
weighed heavily upon the government, and their influence upon
developments in North America have been examined with admirable
scholarship.[2] Less attention has been given to the question of the cost
of defending Canada in a war fought over Oregon. And when one
examines this, it becomes clear that no government was ready to
undertake the enormous expenses required to hold Oregon – an area
which too many thought was of marginal importance to the British
Empire and which too few believed was of strategic value to Canada.

Both the United States and Great Britain had early claims to the
Oregon territory and each had based them upon the traditional principles of prior discovery and present occupation. The United States
argued that Robert Gray had discovered the mouth of the Columbia
River and that Lewis and Clark had travelled its length. Britain
answered that Francis Drake had first visited the area and that Captain Vancouver's exploration had confirmed Britain's claim to the
northwest Pacific coast. The United States countered by arguing that
she had inherited, through the Adams-Onis Treaty of 1819, the
Spanish claims to Oregon and that these pre-dated Britain's. If the
United States held a marginal advantage on the issue of explorations,
the opposite was true when it came to the issue of occupation. It was
true that John Jacob Astor had established Fort Astoria at the mouth
of the Columbia River before the War of 1812, but the North West
Company and later the Hudson's Bay Company had a more extensive
and effective hold upon the country.

The Convention of 1818 had avoided the question of the ownership
of Oregon by simply providing for the extension of the 49th parallel
to the "Stony Mountains" and agreeing that nationals of both the
United States and Great Britain could freely enter into the territory.
This "joint occupation" was to last originally for a period of ten
years and was subject to renewal. In 1825 and 1827 the two governments held discussions over Oregon. The Americans then insisted
upon the 49th parallel to the Pacific coast. This was a position that

2. See in particular Frederick Merk, *The Oregon Question* (Cambridge, Mass.,
   1967) and John S. Galbraith, *The Hudson's Bay Company as an Imperial
   Factor, 1821-1869* (Berkeley and Los Angeles, 1957).

had been held earlier by Monroe and was one from which the United States never budged. Britain, for her part, argued for a line along the 49th parallel to the Columbia River and then down that river to its mouth. Since neither side was prepared to compromise and since each was convinced that time was its chief ally, the Convention of 1818 was renewed.

The vast and rapid influx of settlers into the region and the election of James K. Polk as president in 1844 brought the Oregon crisis to a head. What was really at issue, of course, was not the territory to 54° 40'. In spite of bellicose American slogans to fight for that line, the government of the United States was only committed to the 49th parallel, so that the argument revolved around the area between that line and the Columbia River. It was recognized by the British government that the dispute over Oregon could not be settled by an adjudication of the claim to prior discovery. "We question," wrote the London *Times*, "whether either of the two nations be disposed to settle the matter as one of right merely. The fact of first occupation is obscure; of first ownership nearly as obscure." Therefore, *The Times* continued, "Equality of partition between England and the United States is dictated by the convenience of both."[3] What made this reasonable approach difficult for Peel and Aberdeen was the looming presence of Palmerston, who had denounced in the most violent and vitriolic terms the Webster-Ashburton Treaty of 1842. That had been a treaty of equality of partition and yet Palmerston wrote that "Never was there imbecility like that of Ashburton, if it was nothing worse."[4] And Russell had added that Ashburton had "made about as bad a treaty as it was possible to make . . .".[5] The political consequence of an unfavourable treaty on Oregon was, therefore, always in the forefront of the minds of the cabinet. But this was finally overborne by the size of the military costs of defence and war.

Protecting British North America had always posed difficulties for Britain. The War of 1812 had shown that it could be done, but it had also revealed the capacity of the United States to bring great weight to bear upon Canada. The Duke of Wellington had, after the Treaty of Ghent, suggested that "it was vain to hope for naval

3. London *Times*, January 2, 1846.
4. Palmerston to Russell, Sept. 1842, G. P. Gooch (ed.), *The Later Correspondence of Lord John Russell, 1840-1878* (London, 1925), vol. 2, 59.
5. *Ibid.*, Russell to Lansdowne, Sept. 22, 1842.

superiority upon the Gt. Lakes".[6] Nor could he see any effective
scheme for striking into the United States. "I have never yet seen,"
he wrote, "any Plan of attack upon that Power which was at all
likely to answer the purpose, but I am certain that an attack could
not succeed made from this Frontier...."[7] Indeed, he later observed,
"I have been astonished that the officers of the army and navy employed in that country were able to defend these provinces [in the]
last war."[8] He did suggest, however, that efforts should be made to
secure Canada. The important points to defend were Quebec, Montreal, and Kingston. He proposed that, at the first, an entrenched camp
and citadel be built, while at the last two, the construction of extensive works be undertaken. Facilities should also be created so that all
naval forces could be concentrated on any one of the three lower
Great Lakes. Finally, a fort should be kept at Niagara to provide
visible evidence for the local inhabitants that Britain meant to defend
them.[9] Because of their high cost, these proposals were never fully
implemented. And what stuck in the minds of successive governments was the Duke's conviction that control of the Great Lakes was
impossible to attain. For the next twenty years, Lord Stanley
observed, Britain's policy in Canada was to be "founded on that
notion".[10]

But now there was an apparent threat of war and it was perfectly
clear that new and aggressive measures would have to be taken if
Canada were to be protected. And so the government set into train
the inquiries which would determine whether this different course of
action were either possible or desirable. Sir George Arthur, the lieutenant-governor of Upper Canada, in a memorandum written after his
return to England in 1841, argued that it would be difficult if not
impossible to "carry war" to the United States. The opposite, however, was not true. The United States, he suggested, had "the greatest
facilities for rapidly concentrating on their Frontier opposite to
Canada, Men and Munitions of War from all parts of the States."
Equally grave was the fact that the United States currently enjoyed

6. Stanley to Murray, Sept. 29, 1841. W.O. 80/11, P.R.O.
7. Wellington to Bathurst, March 1, 1817. W.O. 80/11, P.R.O.
8. Duke of Wellington to the House of Commons Select Committee on Public
   Income and Expenditure, April 15, 1828, The Duke of Wellington (ed.),
   *Despatches, Correspondence and Memorandum of Field Marshall Arthur,
   Duke of Wellington* (London, 1867), vol. 4, 394.
9. Wellington to Bathurst, March 1, 1819. W.O. 80/11, P.R.O.
10. Stanley to Murray, Sept. 29, 1841. W.O. 80/11, P.R.O.

superiority over Great Britain on the Great Lakes. Control of the latter was, of course, crucial and Arthur felt that if Britain were to send out steamships she could redress the balance and keep her troop commitments to a minimum. But, he concluded, the difficulties in defending Canada were many and the costs high. This latter was vital in a period when "economy is of the utmost consequence".[11]

Sir George Murray, who had served as the administrator of Upper Canada in 1815, as Secretary of the Colonies from 1828 to 1830, and was now Master of the Ordinance, was equally pessimistic. Canadian defences were in a lamentable state, he said, because of Britain's policy of "Either that of proposing Fortresses on too great and expensive a scale, and which are consequently never accomplished – or that of being satisfied with Wooden block Houses, and such other constructions of so perishable a nature that they fell into ruins before the time has arrived when they are wanted." To rectify these errors would take both time and money. Beyond this, there were two other factors to be considered. Any successful campaign in Canada would require first "an ascendancy, or at least the means of carrying on a balanced contention for ascendancy upon the Lakes", and second the "unanimous and energetic cooperation of the Population of the Province in its defence". On both these counts, wrote Murray, "I fear we cannot place any great reliance".[12]

Nevertheless, Murray was not prepared to turn Canada over to the Americans for the asking. Any war should, of course, be "defensive". For example, the south bank of the St. Lawrence might be lost, but "it should be made as long as possible the seat of a desultory warfare." Further, stabbing attacks should be made upon the United States. "Offensive enterprises of a defined and limited nature" should be encouraged. Attacks upon and the destruction of American naval establishments would suit this purpose admirably. But the demand by George Simpson of the Hudson's Bay Company for troops for Oregon should be rejected. That organization should be required to raise its own forces to defend remote and inaccessible posts. In the last analysis, Murray said, any defence of Canada rested upon two propositions. The first was the control of the Great Lakes. The second was the "hope to make him [the American] tire of the war, if his

11. Sir George Arthur, Memo on the Defence of Canada (undated). W.O. 80/11, P.R.O.
12. Murray to Goulbourne, Sept. 3, 1845. W.O. 80/11, P.R.O.

expectations of speedy conquest are not suddenly realized". In a pre-
scient remark, he added that the American people would soon be
alienated from a war in which their navy was crippled and "their
efforts to conquer Canada ineffectual".[13]

Lord Stanley, the Colonial Secretary, was deeply conscious of the
hazards that a war posed. "I am clearly of the opinion . . . ," he wrote,
"that in such an event, our operations on the Canadian frontier must
be purely defensive." "It must be admitted," he confessed, "that in
Canada as elsewhere, our defensive works are sadly deficient." He
asked the advice of the Duke of Wellington, the commander-in-chief,
who had then referred him back to his earlier proposals. But, as
Stanley admitted, these had been so costly that all governments had
deferred action upon them. Stanley had, however, instructed the
Ordinance to begin work at Kingston and Montreal, but said "the
calls upon them in every direction are so numerous, and the expense
of work of this kind so great" that little headway was being made.
He concluded frankly by saying that "I believe the fact to be that if
a war were to break out, all our colonies are defenceless to a great
extent. None however, except Canada, could be seriously endangered
as long as we maintain our Naval supremacy; and on that we must
rely for the protection of all of them." The monies to defend them by
"military works" would "apal [sic] Parliament".[14]

The unpleasant extent of Canada's vulnerability and the huge
costs involved in defending her had been meticulously laid out by
Metcalfe in a despatch to Lord Stanley. The latter had considered it a
"very wild letter",[15] but it was startling only in its recognition of the
work that had to be undertaken. Metcalfe pointed out that the control of the lakes was essential and that Lower Canada and New
Brunswick would have to be defended by separate forces, for the
passage of troops on the St. Lawrence was impossible in winter.
Further, Lower Canada would have to be protected by an army
"competent to defeat the whole Military Force of the United States,
and sufficient to enable us to take military possession of Maine, New
Hampshire and Vermont. . .". Upper Canada, unless the lakes were
secure, would require equally substantial forces. In fact, Metcalfe
continued, one would need 25,000 troops for each of the Canadas as
well as the militia and local forces. And these troops were only for

13. Murray to Stanley, Sept. 8, 1845. W.O. 80/11, P.R.O.
14. Stanley to Peel, August 12, 1845. Peel MSS, 40468.
15. Ibid.

defensive purposes. If, he suggested, one contemplated "extended operations of offence in the enemy's country a much larger force would be necessary". His judgment here was that an additional 50,000 to 100,000 men would be required.[16] In short one would need up to 150,000 troops. The reaction of the government to this can well be imagined when one recalls that Wellington began his Peninsular campaign against Napoleon with only 26,000 British troops and fought at Waterloo with roughly the same number of his countrymen.

Additional inquiries about Canada only elicited further information designed to confirm the most disheartening assessment of the situation. It was discovered by the Admiralty that the only guns present in Canada that could be used to arm new ships on the Great Lakes had been sent out in the "last War". The report discreetly added that these were hardly of the "calibre" needed to arm the steamships required for defence. The Admiralty also noted that the necessary guns would have to be sent out for ships which had yet to be built. These vessels of the imaginative future would, of course, have to be manned by crews from England, for Canada lacked trained sailors.[17]

The Duke of Wellington's memorandum to Aberdeen completed this dreary story. "God forbid," he wrote, "that this Country should be involved in Hostilities about the Oregon territory, Texas and still less Mexico." "I declare," he continued, "we could not put even five thousand Men under Arms, in case of the occurence [sic] of such a necessity without withdrawing the Foot Guards from all the stations in which they are employed in preserving the Peace and the Lives and Properties of the People of the Country." With that economy of words and that incisiveness of mind that characterized him, he concluded that all the world knew of this weakness and that it would be folly to think that this "knowledge should not have an influence upon our Political Influence and Power in every Question under discussion".[18]

The weight of this evidence drove Peel to despair. The cost of raising the forces and building the facilities for defending Canada were such, he wrote, "that many will think actual war a tolerable evil

16. Metcalfe to Stanley, Montreal, July 4, 1845. C.O. 539/143, P.R.O.
17. Admiralty to Lord Lytton, January 19, 1846. W.O. 1/555, P.R.O.
18. The Duke of Wellington's Memorandum on Oregon and Texas, March 1, 1845. Aberdeen MSS, 43060.

than such a state of burdensome and anxious suspense".[19] It was not the first time in the course of history that a politician has suggested, out of a sense of frustration, that war might be cheaper than peace. But only the foolish act upon such a premise and Peel was not that. The real question was whether the disputed triangle of the Oregon territory was worth either staggering expenses for defence or the terrible costs of war. Of course, the answer on both counts was no. Peel and Aberdeen could add and they both knew what a cost sheet was. It was all said very nicely by the London *Times* which so often put the government's views. "We will not stay to argue which nation could inflict the greatest amount of evil. It is superfluous." War over Oregon would be intolerable and would inflict more damage "than a century of peace could repair".[20] Fortunately, the solution was close at hand. "We are willing to cede the title of sovereignty and dominion over the greater part of the Oregon. We only require that the commercial advantage of the country be continued to us. We will not renounce our right to participate in the navigation of that great river which, if not discovered first was certainly traced first by our people."[21] The *Quarterly Review* shared this view and argued that the time had come to accept the 49th parallel to the Pacific as the boundary.[22]

These were terms that both the government and the country were ready to accept. Indeed, they were very close to the ones that Aberdeen had had in the back of his mind for a long time. He had written Pakenham as early as March 1844 instructing him to endeavour to draw out from the Americans an offer of the 49th parallel to the Pacific "with the Proviso that all Ports to the South of that parallel to the Columbia inclusive, shall be free Ports to Gt. Britain". He added that the navigation of the Columbia should be common to both nations and that the 49th parallel as a boundary should extend "only to *the Sea*; and not to apply to Vancouver's Island".[23] Now two years later he had, with acceptable modifications, got these terms, and it was a source of great and constant satisfaction to him. To have fought a war over Oregon would have been an act of folly. The evidence had shown that neither the Hudson's Bay Company nor a

19. Peel to Stanley, September 5, 1845. Peel MSS, 40468.
20. *The Times*, January 17, 1846.
21. *The Times*, February 26, 1846.
22. *Quarterly Review*, March, 1846, CLIV, 564.
23. Aberdeen to Pakenham, March 4, 1844, Aberdeen MSS, 43123.

host of military and naval experts deemed the disputed territory worth a war involving a Canada so vulnerable to attack and so costly to defend. "I think," wrote Aberdeen, that the Oregon "Convention has given universal satisfaction." And equally important, he added, was the fact that "I am not aware that we leave any question behind us which is likely to grow up into serious cause of quarrel with the United States."[24]

24. Aberdeen to Pakenham, June 30, 1846. Aberdeen MSS, 43023.

Violence
in Canadian History

KENNETH McNAUGHT

The uses of violence and non-violence have become fashionable subjects of historical debate. While the reasons for this are not obscure
the same cannot be said with respect to the terms in which that
debate is carried on. We read about violence steadily escalating in
the twentieth century. Frequently the picture is set against a pano-
rama of violence reaching all the way back to the Thirty Years War
and Hugo Grotius. But all too often the accounts of violent episodes
and trends, of non-violent movements ending in violence, of protests,
revolutions, wars and repression leave us with an almost undifferenti-
ated and abstract concept of violence. In the midst of peace-research
model-making and psycho-historical analyses of the sources of hostility and aggression we tend still further to generalize about violence.

The historian has a distinct contribution to make to the study of
violence. Perhaps for special reasons, American historians and social
scientists have been as quick to seize upon the problem as they have
upon the closely related "new field" of black history. We already
have a *History of Violence in America*[1] and a clutch of think-pieces

1. H. D. Graham and T. R. Gurr, (eds.) A *History of Violence in America*
(New York, 1969).

by such Democratic court historians as Arthur M. Schlesinger Jr., pointing out that violence is a distinctive feature of the American experience and that there are certain long-run conditions for the maintenance of civil peace which have not often existed in American history. These conditions appear to be public acceptance of the legitimacy of governmental authority, consistent and rational employment of the power of the state, and prompt, fundamental government action to eliminate violence-producing grievances. In addition to this kind of analysis, which usually turns out to explain persistent violence in particular aspects of American history, such as race relations, industrial organization and territorial expansion, one finds in American discussions of the subject frequent reference to a still more general violence-factor. This factor is frequently described as a prevailing carelessness towards human life and is attributed variously to revolutionary origins, the cumulative experience of successive frontiers, strong individualistic and anarchistic strains in the American radical tradition and, more recently, to both militarism and "alienation".

Apart from the analytical problems facing American historians as their country careens through a sea of violence comparable only to the storms of the 1850s and 1860s, what do we, as Canadian historians make of all this, and what do we say about violence in *our* country? To begin with, it is clear that we react to contemporary expressions of violence in our country with a good deal of surprise. Academics and political leaders have been as one in their expressions of concern over the events at Sir George Williams University, the incidents of violent student protest and disruption on other campuses, the spreading concept of "confrontation politics" and the recurring violence of the *nationaliste* movement in Quebec. Pierre Elliott Trudeau has said that the threat to Canadian security from a fall-out of American violence was greater than any military threat of the sort that NATO was designed to counter.[2] Professor Ramsay Cook, returning to Canada after a year in Massachusetts has written:

---

2. *Toronto Star*, November 9, 1968. Speaking to students at Queen's University the prime minister said: "In my scale of values, I am less worried about what might happen over the Berlin wall than I am about what might happen in Chicago, in New York – or in our Canadian cities. If, within the next half-dozen years or so there are the beginnings of civil war in the States, it could overflow the borders into Canada and Mexico. . . . Somehow I don't think the Separatists would be involved – but that's another argument."

Mais la violence engendre la violence. A ces les auto-
rités, souvent appuyées par un large public, réagissent
avec des mots violents ou des lois repressives. (L'un
des signes les plus evidents du bouillonnement politique
qui caractérise notre époque est sans doute la violence
verbale qui caractérise de plus en plus la discussion
politique: notre vocabulaire politique est de plus en
plus marqué au coin de l'exagération, de la fantaisie et
de la grossièreté.) La violence dite officielle a été un
phénomène assez fréquent aux Etats-Unis au cours des
dernières années; de nombreaux indices laissent croire
qu'elle est à prendre racine au Canada, spécialement au
Québec.[3]

It is the phrase "prendre racine au Canada" that merits some
reflection, for the assumption that lies behind it is widely held by
Canadian historians, namely the assumption that our history has
been largely free from the violence and extremism in action that have
scarred American history and whose cumulative effect has produced
the not unexpected contretemps of the present day. Within the
corpus of Canadian historical writing since the First World War – a
body of historical research and thought that is far more comparative
in nature than is the case with most national history – it has become
almost a point of consensus that the most significant difference between Canada and the United States is that Canada lacks the tradition of a violent revolution and a shattering civil war, that she enjoyed instead a comparatively peaceful evolution from colony to
responsible government to independence. True, there had been unpleasantness with certain Indians, and even with Americans from
time to time, and there had been several comic-opera rebellions and
some rather nasty strikes but on the whole resort to violence was
pretty clearly an aberration from the norm in the Canadian experience.

There are two aspects to this generalized version of our history
that seem now to deserve reconsideration. The first is that anyone
reviewing even the "bare facts" of our history is likely to conclude
that they do not substantiate the received version. The second aspect
of the widely held views about Canada's peaceful evolution is that
the interpretation based upon those views leaves the present genera-

3. *Le Devoir*, October 30, 1969.

tion of Canadians with a very inadequate perspective when considering the degree of abnormality represented by our contemporary troubles. Any reassessment of the role of violence in Canadian history might well start by considering some of the ways in which our experience has been similar to the experience both of Europe and the United States – rather than by emphasizing only the apparent differences. In a recent essay Charles Tilly advised Americans to consider

> the commonality of collective protest and violence that suggests that it has historically functioned as an integral part of the political process, and as such has been quite normal in most European societies. The American belief that it is abnormal, shared by many Europeans, is a consequence of selective historical recollection.[4]

The editors of a *History of Violence in America* observe that

> collective violence in America has been employed as a means to an end, and that a society that has successfully employed violence to attain such desirable goals as national independence, continental domain, manumission of slavery, domestic order, and international security, will be reluctant categorically to condemn the instrument of their achievement.

It should be obvious that if American historians, looking at their history "from the top down", have managed to minimize the role of violence in that history, Canadian historians should at least be asking themselves whether they have not done the same thing – and the more easily since in Canada violence, both public and private, has usually been less dramatic and less well publicized. What is now billed as abnormal in our society may in fact be very normal. Moreover, violence viewed as a failure of power rather than as an essential function of "power", may present some fresh insights on the nature of our evolution as well as upon our comparative position in the contemporary world. It is in the area of distinguishing the various manifestations and uses of violence, both actual and threatened, that some of the most interesting speculations are emerging in the present

4. "Collective Violence in European Perspective", in H. D. Graham and T. R. Gurr, *op. cit.*, p. 1.

almost frantic discussion of the subject in the United States.[5]

In the Whig version of Canadian history it is assumed that we have been essentially mild-mannered and even "colonial-minded" throughout most of our collective career and that we were thus so "deferential" by nature that force was seldom required. This was particularly true, apparently, when we adopted an essentially British pragmatism and patience in our progress towards independence. If we have in fact been essentially British in our political attitudes and behaviour the most obvious thing to look for is a more central role for violence in Canada than has often been attributed to it. While England, like Canada, has a reputation for non-violence in its domestic affairs, it does not require any great research to conclude that the English reputation rests more upon the quick results obtained by resort to violence and upon the greater "legitimacy" of governmental authority in England than it does upon the actual non-occurrence of violence. If, in fact, our patterns of social-political life have been basically British perhaps we should re-examine the extent to which violence has been an "efficient" part of our social growth, of our constitutional evolution and of our policy-making processes. To the extent that our evolution has been affected by French influences and heritage we might have still greater reason for such a re-examination.

II

Let us test the hypothesis that in Canada not only has violence been applied frequently as an instrument by established authority, by the dispossessed, by special interest groups reacting against social trends or political policies, and by the state in its relations with other states, but that such resort to violence has been so frequent as to be an essential ingredient in our historical evolution.

If we begin by reviewing the use of force either in defence of borders or of "our interests" abroad two thoughts are likely to occur to us immediately. The first is that the quantitative scale of Canadian events has a distorting effect in any comparisons made with the United States. One-tenth of the number of troops employed by the United States during the Spanish-American War, for example, is not very far from the number of troops sent by Canada to help suppress

5. See, for example, the *Journal of International Affairs*, Vol. XXIII, 1969, No. 1, especially Hannah Arendts, "Reflections on Violence".

the Boers. When such scaled-down comparisons are applied to the two world wars they yield even more startling results. The second preliminary thought is that to call Canadians an "unmilitary people"[6] is to minimize not only the frequency of our resort to arms, but the very central place occupied in our politics by military questions. From the period of the American War of Independence down through the Confederation debates, the conscription crises, and the present defence policy review it is clear that questions of military defence have been amongst our major political preoccupations. To argue, as many have, that we have frequently beggared our armed forces, or shown a too heavy reliance upon the military forces of Britain or the United States for our protection certainly does not mean that we place less reliance on military force *per se* than do Americans. In the 1920s and 1930s, for example, the United States was not notably more lavish, proportionately, in its military budgets than was Canada. Prior to the Second World War and the nuclear era, both Canada and the United States enjoyed to some extent what C. Vann Woodward has called an "age of free defence". But whenever a build-up of force has appeared essential, or even useful, neither nation has shown itself to be particularly unmilitary.

In comparisons with the United States it has been argued that Canada is less prone to the use of violence because we have never been caught up in crusades for ideas. There are two sides to this crucial interpretative argument that deserve comment and investigation. The first is the assumption that the major outbursts of American military violence *were* essentially ideological crusading. The infusions in the various American military endeavours of economic interest, regional loyalties, national and racial prejudices, and general patriotism (not to mention the substantial war-resistance movements of which the country may rightly boast) all invite a basic question about Canadian-American comparisons. In any comparison at the level of "ideology" the significant point is not that the United States was more caught up with ideology but that ideology was frequently different from the ideologies which proved effective in Canada.

The other side of the argument is that ideologies in Canada have been at least as effective in justifying resort to violence as has been the case in the United States. Were the reasons for the defence of

---

6. See G. F. G. Stanley, *Canada's Soldiers: The Military History of an Unmilitary People* (Toronto, 1954).

Quebec, of Niagara, of Chateauguay, or for the Papal Zouaves and
the expeditionary forces in South Africa and Europe really so much
more mundane and devoid of ideological and "crusading" content
that they are of a different order from the reasons that have impelled
Americans to battle? It might even be argued that in most cases of
Canadian military action such motives as economic advantage have
been less prominent than in American warfare, while "crusading
ideas" such as the preservation of French and Catholic civilization in
North America, the temporal authority of the Papacy, the "rightness" of Pax Britannica, the survival of Canada, or the "rule of law
under the United Nations" have been at least as important as have
American ideas about a "city on a hill", manifest destiny", "freedom" and "democracy". In 1914 and in 1939 it even appeared that
Canada was prepared to beat the United States to the crusader's cross.
To say that our definitions of ideological purpose have often differed
from those of the United States is by no means to say that we have
shown an historical unwillingness to justify warfare by appeals to
ideology.

While we have perhaps kept a sharp eye out for defence bargains
we have put our faith in military force just as surely as have the
Americans. The raucous naval debates preceding the First World
War and the nuclear arms election of 1963 have much in common.
Both events demonstrated our continuing belief that we must pay
military tribute to whatever imperial power seems best able to
assemble sufficient force to keep secure our way of life – including
our investments at home and abroad. Even a budgetary analysis
(again allowing for the distortions of scale) of the relative weight
attached by the United States and Canada to military and non-
military means of securing a favourable world order shows Canada
placing slightly greater weight on the military side – a point to which
Dean Acheson referred obliquely in his recently published memoirs.[7]
At the same time, as is revealed by such incidents as the imperial
calls for help in the Sudan, at Chanak and in Vietnam, we have
somewhat callously reserved the privilege of contracting out of
particular wars – for reasons both material and ideological – while
continuing to endorse the right of the imperial power itself to engage
in those conflicts and the concomitant right of ourselves to profit
from them.

7. Dean G. Acheson, *Present at the Creation* (New York, 1969).

If our history is to be in any sense philosophy-teaching-by-example it must depict precisely our acceptance of military strength as the chief expression of power in international relations. For it is the question of how the threat of military violence is related to power that lies just beneath the surface of our contemporary defence–foreign policy debates. To understand how deeply and consistently we have always relied on an almost simplistic concept of military force is essential to understanding our difficulties today in adjusting to the revolution in the nature of such force. It is true that we once had trouble deciding whether we would buy some "tin-pots" for our navy or whether we would get better value (in every sense) by buying three dreadnoughts for the British navy, and that we have not always been sure whether we should conform to British or American military patents. But this kind of distinction between the weapons of military violence is virtually meaningless compared to the quantitative and, therefore, qualitative difference between conventional weaponry on the one hand and nuclear or biological weaponry on the other. Because of our deep-grained and persistent reliance on whatever means of military violence we could ourselves afford, or that we could secure through colonial loyalty, we are unprepared for the present and future changes in the nature of international relationships.

In a day when any small country may completely upset "the strategic balance" by acquiring and being willing to use biological or chemical attack, when the major weapons cannot be used by the nuclear powers with any rational hope of victory, and when many poor countries seem less vulnerable in conventional warfare than are great powers, the historical conventions about the use of military violence are clearly in need of revision. Hannah Arendt has recently commented on this question in a way that is very relevant to Canada:

> What all these uncomfortable novelties add up to is a complete reversal in the relationship between power and violence, foreshadowing another reversal in the future relationship between small and great powers. The amount of violence at the disposal of any given country may soon not be a reliable indication of the country's strength or a reliable guarantee against destruction by a substantially smaller and weaker power. And this again bears an ominous similarity to one of

the oldest insights of political science, namely, that
power cannot be measured in terms of wealth, that an
abundance of wealth may erode power, that riches are
particularly dangerous for the power and well-being of
republics – an insight that does not lose in validity
because it is conveniently forgotten, especially at a time
when its truth has acquired a new dimension of validity by becoming applicable to the arsenal of violence as
well.[8]

The disservice performed by an historical interpretation that de-
picts Canada as less committed to the employment of as much
military violence in maintaining her interests as it has been conveniently possible to arrange is obvious. Such an interpretation belies
the facts and thus obscures our historical vision. It suggests that our
post–World War II military spending within a new imperial
alliance system is somehow new in kind as well as new in size. A
history which minimizes the functional role of a major historical
belief-force to the point of distortion and which also fails adequately
to analyse objective changes in conditions that underlay previous
policy assumptions is of little service to the present.

III

Most of our historical writing has prepared us still less adequately to
view contemporary violence in our society as predictable rather than
unexpected. A good case can be made that even the classic violence–
non-violence comparisons within Canada illustrate the distortions
that are at least partly the result of looking at history from the top
down. The late Chester Martin drew a sharp distinction between the
way in which responsible government was achieved in Nova Scotia
by Joseph Howe ("without the breaking of a pane of glass") and in
the Canadas (only after two rebellions and to the accompaniment of
continuing violence, both physical and verbal). Yet the implication
that Nova Scotians were notably more sophisticated and less violent
than the ultras of Upper Canada or the French of the lower province
doesn't really stand up to closer investigation. Nova Scotia "matured"
throughout its pre-1847 history in the midst of almost chronic

8. *Op. cit.*, p. 3.

colonial warfare and threats of war, and produced a turbulent society dedicated to the scarcely peaceful pursuits of the fisheries and privateering and which employed some extremely violent political language. It was Joseph Howe, for example, in the midst of his eminently moderate pleading with Lord John Russell for the blessings of responsible government, who gave vent to a belief in Anglo-Saxon superiority which, for sheer precision, matches anything heard during the tribulations and trial of Louis Riel or the conscription campaigns of the two world wars.[9] If our Canadian history teaches us anything it is that racist doctrine contains more potential violence than any other social-political notion. Nor does post-1847 Nova Scotian history add much credibility to the original comparison. One thinks, for example, of the nearly perpetual industrial warfare in the coal-steel towns from the 1880s to the 1930s, and the major rioting and looting in Halifax during the Second World War.

Beyond such regional comparisons, however, even a selective review of violence in our domestic affairs suggests the thesis that many, if not most, significant constitutional and policy changes have been directly related to and profoundly affected by collective violence, or threatened violence.

Taking as given the context of violence, both private and public, throughout the years prior to 1791 let us recall some of the pivotal points of change after that date. In the decades following proclamation of the Constitutional Act the social growth and attitudes of the Canadas were profoundly affected by war, protests and repressive violence, as well as by the increasingly intemperate language of politics – while in the West, Seven Oaks and Fort William saw the culminating violence of a protracted struggle for control of the fur trade. However one defines "politics" in these years it is beyond doubt that practically every kind of violence was functionally related to it. Regionally-based grievances in Upper Canada, coming gradually to a focus in the capital, produced a nascent radical-reform party,

9. Quoted in J. H. S. Reid, K. McNaught and H. S. Crowe, (eds.), *A Source-Book of Canadian History* (Toronto, 1964), p. 118. It may also be worth recalling that Howe was not present at the pre-Confederation conferences because he thought it more important to ensure the application of imperial violence as fisheries commissioner defending Maritimes rights under the terms of the 1854 treaty. Commenting on Lord Falkland's despatches to the Colonial Office, Howe observed that it was probable that some colonist would shortly "hire a black fellow to horsewhip a lieutenant-governor". See J. W. Longley, *Joseph Howe* (Toronto, 1912), p. 101.

demands for republican independence and an overt, if inept, resort to armed rebellion. The period also produced an almost trigger-happy response by legitimate authority. Punitive jail sentences, parliamentary expulsions, hangings, private assaults on the persons and property of radicals and effective militia action were, so far as can be measured, widely tolerated by a majority of the population. In Lower Canada the violence of the Craig régime, militant confrontations in the legislature, and the abortive rebellion saw the birth of modern French-Canadian nationalism.

While it is unnecessary to recapitulate the intimate relationship between the rebellions and the Durham mission and between Durham's Report and the coming of responsible government, it is worth remembering the aura of violence in which this all happened – for it is in that context that some of our most basic political attitudes and our party system began to take shape. The implications of violence, always hovering in the wings of the political stage, were certainly not overlooked by contemporaries, and were frequently used in succeeding debate. In 1854, for example, when John A. Macdonald was defending the Clergy Reserves Bill against the high church and Orange establishmentarian, John Hillyard Cameron, he made specific the warnings of violence. It might be wise, he declared, in a state where one Christian church enjoyed majority affiliation, to establish that church; such a system had proven beneficial in England. However, it had proven disastrous in Ireland and was no less dangerous in Canada. "I believe," said Macdonald, "it is a great mistake in politics and private life to resist when resistance is hopeless. . . . There is no maxim that experience teaches more clearly than this, that you must yield to the times. Resistance may be protracted until it produces revolution. Resistance was protracted in this country until it produced rebellion." And Macdonald went on to draw the conclusion: resistance to secularization of the Reserves would invite a response similar to that which had been earlier incurred by the Family Compact.[10] Surely the establishment of a party system, the concept of *la survivance*, the 1837 rebellions and their suppression, the enthroning of Sir Isaac Brock as anglophone Canada's only national

---

10. See D. G. Creighton, *John A. Macdonald: The Young Politician* (Toronto, 1952), pp. 214-15. As for violent political language being a new danger sign today, it was on the floor of the legislature in 1861 that Macdonald confronted Mowat with: "You damned pup, I'll slap your chops!" *Ibid.*, p. 310.

hero,[11] the achievement of responsible government and the secularization of the Clergy Reserves all demonstrated an important causal
role for violence (and the apprehension of violence) that has been
very much underplayed and, as a specific historic force, unexamined.

Canada's junior-grade manifest destiny – the acquisition and absorp-
tion of the West – offers several instructive examples of the epidemic
distortions in Canadian-American comparisons. While it is more than
evident that violence pervaded every phase of westward development, no one can mistake the thrust of our general historical interpretation: the two rebellions were largely abortive and proved the
efficacy of Canadian insistence on maintaining law and order; we had
no substantial Indian warfare or vigilante tradition for much the
same reason. In the West, as elsewhere, change came not as a result
of violence, but as a consequence of political debate followed by
legislative and executive action. Violence was not a function of the
political system but an aberration quickly corrected.

If we take account of differences in scale as between Canada and
the United States, and if we ask the question of the relationship of
violence to the process of achieving the goals of "Ontario imperialism" in the West, a very different interpretation is certainly plausible.
The essence of a counter-interpretation is that the use of various
kinds of violence in the post-Confederation West proved, once again,
not only that such means could be successful but that violence and
a readiness to advocate violence were integral to the country's political
system. During the Red River Rebellion Riel and his supporters employed violence to reject an already prescribed political-cultural fate.
The state applied counter-violence. In a very real sense both uses of
violence were successful, and both profoundly affected the future of
the West. Riel's first rebellion was, in fact, a successful revolution,
for it "overturned" one form of prescribed government (territorial)
for another (provincial). At the same time the post-rebellion federal
show of force also satisfied Ontario's view of the West as the proper
patrimony of central Canadian anglophone farmers and businessmen.

Ontario's view of the West had, of course, to be reconfirmed in
1885. The combination of "populist", Indian and Métis grievances
that culminated in the second rebellion and the Regina scaffold did
much more than validate the rapid construction of the Canadian

11. An intriguing evidence of continuing gratitude to Brock is in AMEX: *The
American Expatriate in Canada,* Vol. 2, No. 1 (1969) which bears the
dedication: "Thank you, General Brock Issue."

Pacific Railway. The completely successful application of military force endorsed once again the use of violence to secure across the West the patterns of commerce and agriculture approved by English-speaking Protestantism. As the Superintendent of Methodist Missions in the Northwest at the time observed:

> Many lives were lost in this unfortunate disturbance. On the other hand, much good resulted. Disaffected half-breeds and rebellious Indians were taught a salutary lesson; they learned something of the strength of British rule, and likewise experienced something of its clemency and righteousness.[12]

Clemency, however, was not total. When Louis Riel dropped through the scaffold in the yard of the Mounted Police barracks in Regina the relationship of violence to the Canadian political system was seen most precisely. Legitimate force applied by the state is usually endorsed by Canadians – but so, too, is violent resistance to widely admitted injustice. This ambivalence, complete with partisan overtones, was accurately exhibited in the Toronto *Globe* on November 28, 1885:

> We ask all fair-minded English-speaking citizens to put themselves in the place of the men of Riel's race before charging them with an offensive sympathy for an indefensible rebel.
>
> The man represented a cause.
>
> To deny that the Half-breeds had sore grievances would be futile. . . . They had vainly petitioned for redress again and again. . . . In a like position, men of English blood would have sternly appealed to the sword after their position had been neglected. . . . Riel came to further an agitation not only legal, but proved justifiable by the subsequent concessions of the Ottawa administration. . . .
>
> Riel has died that English blood may no longer cry from the ground for his punishment.
>
> But how shall justice be satisfied while those who are responsible for the shedding of French blood and Eng-

12. James Woodsworth, *Thirty Years in the Canadian North-West* (Toronto, 1917), p. 12.

lish alike – of all the blood shed during the campaign –
still hold up their heads?
    The cry of French Canada is practically for the com-
pletion of the national assizes.

The national assizes dragged on for some time. In the decade
which ended with the party revolution of 1896 Canadian political
debate was shot through with recollections of rebellion, with scarcely
veiled threats of further violence and with a verbal ferocity certainly
not exceeded in the 1960s. Pitched battles between Orangemen and
Catholics, competing lumber interests, competing railway-builders,
striking workers and militia provided the milieu in which anglophone
cultural domination of the West was reinforced and a nascent industrial system nourished. Not much below the surface of Mercier
nationalism, of Nova Scotia's secessionist resolutions of 1886-87, of
annexationism and of Manitoba's resistance to the C.P.R. monopoly
lay the threat of violence. In such a climate few politicians and fewer
editors resisted the temptation to turn the potential of violence to
partisan ends. As part of the Blake-Liberal campaign to woo sufficient
Quebec support to overthrow Macdonald, John Cameron's *Globe*
editorials are a good example of the decade's violence potential. When
Manitoba decided to construct the Red River Valley Railway as a
government work and thus challenged Ottawa directly (after provincial charters to private companies had been disallowed in support
of the C.P.R. monopoly), the *Globe* was unrestrained in its enthusiasm:

> What about the effect of such a lesson [as the rebel-
> lion of 1885] on the people of Manitoba? Their moral
> right to build local railways where they please is abso-
> lute. Their constitutional or legal right is just as
> certain. . . . They have represented their wrongs consti-
> tutionally for now nearly seven years. Nothing has
> been conceded to them. Their peaceable agitation is
> ignored just as that of the Halfbreeds was.[13]

As the Manitoba contractors pushed their grading southward and
encountered serious opposition from the C.P.R. and Ottawa, the
Globe openly advocated armed rebellion:

13. *Toronto Globe*, February 15, 1887.

Everything tends to support the opinion that they will
not submit. And if they do not, if they insist on a passage [of the C.P.R. tracks at Morris], if the forces of
the two companies come into collision, and if bloodshed
occurs, will not the blood refresh the redness now stal-
ing upon the hands of the men at Ottawa, and will not
the whole responsibility for the dreadful troubles that
will probably ensue rest upon that infamous gang of
political prostitutes? . . .

Hence, the country may expect to hear at any day
that the gang at Ottawa have wantonly provoked a
third insurrection. Nay, they have done that already.
The wanton provocation has been given, and the only
question now is whether the white men of Manitoba
are meeker than the Halfbreeds.[14]

The supporters of rebellion and secession got their "better terms",
partly through the additional political assistance of the 1887 Inter-
provincial Conference, when in 1888 the C.P.R. monopoly was re-
scinded and Ottawa inaugurated the subsidy system for the Nova
Scotia coal-steel industry. Yet the use of violence by the state in
support of a budding transportation-industrial system did not diminish, nor did resort to violence and the ambiguity of non-violent resistance by the aggrieved come to an end. Quite the reverse. Between
1876 and 1914 there were at least thirty-three interventions in strikes
by the military and five occasions on which the troops were called
out to control Orange-Catholic rioting.[15] As in the United States
following the railway strike of 1877, when the "gentry" suddenly
coughed up huge donations for local armouries, so in Canada businessmen were prepared to pay the costs of military occupation of
their properties in the interest of law, order, and business as usual.
The political élite was happy to endorse amendments to the Militia

14. Ibid., August 17, 19, 1887.
15. I am indebted to Professor Desmond Morton for references to the opera-
    tion of the Militia Act. It is interesting to note that the creation of a
    permanent force, as opposed to militia, to replace British regular troops
    in Canada was more in response to concern about domestic law and
    order than to worry about external attack. Still later the fundamental
    purpose of a peacetime military establishment in Canada was made
    explicit by R. B. Bennett's Minister of Justice, Hugh Guthrie, who told
    the League of Nations Assembly that we maintained "only such military
    and air forces as are necessary for the maintenance of law and order
    within our own borders". See Debates, House of Commons, 1932, p. 2959.

Act to make it more efficient in the age of industrial and religious conflict. Yet, while the use of both militia and permanent force soldiers on "strike duty" increased steadily in the years immediately preceding the First World War the most dramatic scenes of violence in the twentieth century came, at least in part, as a result of that war.

The first of these scenes was racial with class connotations, the second was essentially class conflict with racial connotations. Both were intimately related to the country's political system and definitive of future policy and political directions. The first, the 1918 anti-conscription riots in Quebec City, saw the assembling of an even larger military force than had been amassed during the previous record occasion of July 12, 1878, in Montreal.[16]

The country weathered that storm. But it is beyond question that the final resort to private and public violence in Quebec City, bringing to an unmistakable peak two decades of francophone resistance to involvement in British wars (and bitter resentment of anglophone Canada's cumulative opposition to the spread of French language and culture), deeply influenced Mackenzie King's policy towards the Empire-Commonwealth, the League and armaments, let alone his Lapointe-based attitude to Quebec politics and provincial rights.

The second instance of violence growing out of the war environment was, of course, the 1919 Winnipeg General Strike. As North America's closest approach to a successful use of the general strike weapon, and as Canada's most significant experiment with massive non-violent social action, that strike needs reassessment in the light of much that has happened in the 1960s. Deeply influenced by the

16. Frequent threats and outbreaks of violence in Montreal prompted Lord Dufferin to write to Lord Carnarvon during the Guibord affair: ". . . I am keenly alive to the danger with which this affair is pregnant. Moreover the affair discloses a lamentable blot in our constitution, as well as in our social organization. There is absolutely no force whatsoever behind the Law. The Military, at all times a bad instrument for dealing with rioters, are themselves a mob inspired by the same fanatical passions as the rest of the populace. What we want is a body like the Irish Constabulary living in barracks, excluded from all contact with the people and disciplined and controlled by the central and not by the subordinate authority." See C. W. de Kiewiet and F. H. Underhill (eds.), *Dufferin-Carnarvon Correspondence, 1874-1878* (Toronto, 1955), p. 159. Through slow stages of expanding the "Dominion Police" and then amalgamation of that force with the R.N.W.M.P., the R.C.M.P. was formed and ready for action in the 1935 Regina Riot and subsequent unpleasantness. The original model of the Irish Constabulary remained influential.

philosophies both of British Labour and the Industrial Workers of the World, the six-week tie-up of Winnipeg's economic life had a profound effect on the Canadian political system. Out of the strike, the trials, and the jail sentences grew an intensified class feeling, a deepened suspicion of élite-controlled state violence, a fresh drive for independent labour politics and thus, a principal tap-root of the C.C.F. – N.D.P.

Besides its basic impact on the Canadian party system the violence in Winnipeg in 1919 had other legatory ramifications. The goals of the strikers and their sympathizers were not merely economic. They were, in a real sense, the goals of participatory democracy, the goals of people who were deeply alienated from a society whose structure and purposes they felt unable to influence. Without specifically describing the furniture of heaven, speakers at the mass strike meetings and at the Labour Church services expressed clearly enough their aspirations for an egalitarian, cohesive society while their newspaper celebrated the new-found method of change: "There is great cause for congratulation during this struggle, in that until the present moment the participants are more orderly than a crowd of spectators at a baseball game. . . . There has been evolved a weapon of great power – orderliness."[17] But non-violence was not permitted to usher in the day of shared power. The response of property was remorseless: an entire police force dismissed and replaced by untrained specials, toughened legal penalties for "sedition", arrest of the strike leaders, and violence-producing intervention by the military and the Mounted Police. The ironic potential of violence in an essentially non-violent mass action as well as the "participatory" goals of the strike will likely provoke further examination by social historians in the 1970s.

The successful application of state violence in Quebec and Winnipeg (as well as the threatened violence of stand-by military force in other western cities) did nothing to diminish the postwar use of violence to enforce industrial discipline. The Liberals, having loudly denounced the Borden-Meighen policies in Winnipeg used still greater military force to settle what Arthur Meighen called the "class war" in Nova Scotia's coal-steel towns.[18] When the miners

17. *Western Labor News Strike Bulletin*, May 17, 1919.
18. Curiously the biographers of Mackenzie King have practically nothing to report on King's assessment of Nova Scotia's labour troubles in the early 1920s – nor of his quick response in 1924 and 1925 to requests for military

struck on the job, giving (as Meighen noted approvingly) two-thirds of a day's work for two-thirds of a day's pay, Mackenzie King denounced "loafing on the job" as one of the worst kinds of industrial warfare known, and his government sent in the troops two years in a row.

In the 1930s, thanks largely to the build-up of municipal and provincial police forces and of the R.C.M.P., the military was not as frequently called out in aid of the civil power, but neither the incidence nor the significance of violence declined. In the semi-police state of the 'thirties, labour leaders and their offices were subjected regularly to police violence, unemployed marchers were dispersed (often, as at Regina in 1935, with excessive violence), sit-down strikers were beaten by hired industrial thugs, and unemployment was finally relieved (as in the United States) by mobilization for war.[19]

During the past twenty-five years, it is the brief periods of relative domestic tranquillity that appear on reflection to be aberrant, rather than the instances of violence. In these years actual violence and the apprehension of violence have been as intimately related to our political-social processes as has been the case in the rest of our history – no less and no more. The most profound shifts in our attitudes to the party method of representative government, to our constitutional arrangements, to the purpose and structure of our universities, to our foreign and defence policies and to the inter-relationship of our two cultures have been deeply affected by the violence factor. The political and intellectual origins of the Quiet Revolution are to be found in the Asbestos strike of 1949 just as the advance of and response to *séparatisme* are impossible to understand without reference to the uses of violence, both private and public. Reports calling for revolutionary changes in university government refer just as pointedly to the critical context of violence as does the Preliminary Report of the Royal Commission on Bilingualism and Biculturalism. And once again, in many areas of our life, we confront the central irony of non-violent reform action generating violence.

support. Although the 1924 request was of dubious constitutionality King nevertheless applied a very strict interpretation of provincial rights when he was asked to intervene with other than the instruments of violence.
19. Nor were campuses free of the heightened vigilance. In 1940 President Cody called out University of Toronto police to prevent a leader of the Oshawa strike from criticizing Premier Hepburn at a meeting scheduled by the university C.C.F. club.

IV

Perhaps the most important conclusion to be drawn from this tentative survey is that today's climate of violence in Canada is no more rigorous than that which we have experienced through most of our history. The other principal conclusion is that the portrait of Canada drawn from American comparisons as a country in whose historical evolution violence has been peculiarly minimal is in need of revision. It seems obvious that a merely quantitative comparison of the incidence of various kinds of violence is misleading – although even this has not been seriously undertaken. From the foregoing discussion one might argue that the official uses of violence in Canada have been more consistent and effective while the "private" uses of violence have been less anarchic and individualistic than in the United States. Both these differences would be consistent with the existence of a comparatively more ordered society in which, as Sir John A. Macdonald once put it, constitutional liberty rather than democracy was to be the guiding light. Yet it seems true, also, that the violence of protest and reform (both actual and threatened) continue to be an integral part of our political processes at least partly because historically our governments and other decision-makers have responded fairly promptly to violence-prone situations. Further investigation may well prove that the apparently strong Canadian attachment to the political method as opposed to other means of protest and change is a function of the efficacy of violence within the system. The most important comparison between the roles of violence in American and Canadian history may be that in Canada public and private violence have been more, rather than less, closely related to the operations of the political system than has been the case in the United States.

Laurier, King, and External Affairs

C. P. STACEY

O. D. Skelton, the powerful civil servant who was the permanent head of the Canadian Department of External Affairs from 1925 to 1941, was in a sense a link between Sir Wilfrid Laurier and Mackenzie King. He was Laurier's biographer and his devoted and partisan admirer; and he was the most influential adviser King ever had.

Skelton first found himself in a position to exercise a direct influence on national policy in 1923. King, who attended his first Imperial Conference in London that year, invited Dean Skelton (as he then was) to accompany him as an adviser, and, as a preliminary, to survey the problems the conference would face and make recommendations as to how the prime minister should deal with them.

Skelton was in no doubt whatever as to the line to take. It is clear that he intensely disliked the procedures in imperial relations that had been developing since the Canadian Conservatives' coming to power in 1911 and particularly since the outbreak of the First World War. The trend represented by the Imperial War Cabinet and the Imperial War Conference, in the direction of a co-operative imperial foreign policy founded on consultation between the United

Kingdom and the Dominions – a trend with which Sir Robert Borden was thoroughly in sympathy – seemed to him an aberration. He told King that an attempt was being made to reverse traditional Canadian policies, and he represented this attempt as primarily a British project, disregarding the extent to which the Borden and Meighen administrations in Canada had encouraged the new developments. It could have been said with at least equal force that it was Skelton who was proposing a reversal of policy – of the policies adopted by recent Canadian ministries to meet the emergencies of the most eventful decade in Canadian history; but Skelton chose to regard himself and King as the conservatives, and the British as the dubious and dangerous innovators. King obviously had no fault to find with Skelton's advice. He followed it in the discussions at London, and the Imperial Conference of 1923 stands in history as the occasion when the idea of a unified Commonwealth policy was defeated by the concept of a variety of independent national policies.[1]

So far as I know, Skelton never defined his conception of Canadian external policy in words like "Back to Laurier"; it would not have been like him to do so. But, essentially, that is what it was. Writing the *Life and Letters of Sir Wilfrid Laurier* was Skelton's specific apprenticeship and preparation for his task in the Department of External Affairs. As for Mackenzie King, he owed much of his political success to Laurier, who took him into his cabinet at an unusually early age virtually straight from the civil service (a procedure commoner in more recent times than it was in 1909); and King convinced himself that Laurier had designated him as his successor – though there is some evidence to the contrary.[2] He prided himself on his fidelity to Laurier, and considered this a major explanation for his own hold on the Province of Quebec; if there is anything in the story that he fell away from his allegiance so far as to let it be known that he was willing to accept office in Borden's Union Government in 1917, he contrived to forget this lapse entirely.

In these circumstances, it is interesting to speculate how far Laurier's external policies of 1896-1911 may have influenced King's in 1921-1948.

1. I have discussed these matters in "From Meighen to King: The Reversal of Canadian External Policies, 1921-1923", *Transactions*, Royal Society of Canada, 1969.
2. R. M. Dawson, *William Lyon Mackenzie King, A Political Biography*, I (Toronto, 1958), 291, 304-5.

II

The general nature of Canadian external problems during Laurier's administration is familiar and can be recalled briefly.

This was the period in British history which Skelton called "the flood tide of imperialism"; the age of Joseph Chamberlain and Cecil Rhodes and the South African War. It was a time of centralizing tendencies, when enthusiastic Englishmen like Chamberlain, better informed about British problems of power than about the nature of Dominion nationalism, tended to think and talk about the British Empire as a nation, and needed from time to time to be reminded by Dominion statesmen that it was in fact no such thing, but a league of nations. In a succession of colonial conferences it fell to Laurier to be the chief remembrancer, a task which he performed with firmness and urbanity. In 1897, in one or two public speeches in England made under the influence of the Diamond Jubilee, he gave some momentary countenance to the idea of organic changes in the constitution of the Empire; but in the conference that followed it was Laurier (as he explained to a French-Canadian friend three years later) who drafted the well-known resolution which the conference approved by a large majority expressing the opinion that the present state of imperial relations was "generally satisfactory under the existing condition of things".[3] This strikes an authentic Laurier note – satisfaction with the *status quo*, and suspicion of proposals for change which had, in the case of Chamberlain's, a strong centralizing flavour.

Laurier as prime minister did not have to deal with the emergency of a great European war, though the increasingly critical state of relations with Germany cast a dark shadow across the last years of his administration. The one war that Canada did take part in under Laurier was that in South Africa; and it is worth remembering that this was a war in which the Dominion undertook participation without parliamentary authority. Laurier, finding himself under pressure as the result of an organized campaign in English-speaking Canada which had developed with great suddenness as war broke out in South Africa, tried to satisfy as wide a segment of Canadian opinion as possible by agreeing to dispatch a contingent without waiting to assemble Parliament, while at the same time seeking to represent the

3. Lucien Pacaud (ed.), *Sir Wilfrid Laurier: Lettres à mon père et à ma mère, 1867-1919* (Arthabaska, P.Q., 1935), pp. 272-74. (April 12, 1900).

contingent as a largely unofficial group of volunteers and asserting that the measure involved no precedent.[4] He later explained the government's action in terms which seem more ingenious than ingenuous:

> . . . If we were to be compelled to take part in all the wars of Great Britain, I have no hesitation in saying that I agree with my hon. friend [Henri Bourassa] that, sharing the burden, we should also share the responsibility. Under that condition of things, which does not exist, we should have the right to say to Great Britain: If you want us to help you, call us to your councils; if you want us to take part in wars let us share not only the burdens but the responsibilities and duties as well. But there is no occasion to examine this contingency this day. My hon. friend forgets one thing which is essential to this discussion, that we did not use our powers as a government to go into that war. . . . We simply provided the machinery and expenses for the two thousand young men who wanted to go and give their lives for the honour of their country and the flag they love. . . .[5]

The South African War, then, was one in which Parliament did not decide the question of Canada's part; but Laurier nevertheless argued that the circumstances were special and that under more normal conditions it would be for Parliament to make the decision. As the German crisis deepened the Laurier administration committed itself more and more to this point of view. At the Imperial Defence Conference of 1909 Laurier's Minister of Militia, Sir Frederick Borden, emphasized Dominion autonomy as the basic principle, while also proclaiming the fundamental community of interest between Canada and the mother country:

> . . . we are left absolutely to ourselves. Under the militia law of Canada the Governor-General in Council has power to mobilise the whole of our forces, and if a war is imminent and Parliament is not in session, Parliament may be called within 15 days, and Parliament

4. Norman Penlington, *Canada and Imperialism, 1896-1899* (Toronto, 1965), chaps. 16 and 17.
5. *Debates, House of Commons*, March 13, 1900 (cols. 1846-47).

will then decide, and Parliament can alone decide
whether we will take any part in that war, whatever it
may be. . . . If . . . we maintain forces which are organ-
ised on a common principle and in co-operation and in
co-ordination with those of Great Britain, then we are
ready, if we see fit, to take part in any war in which
the Empire is interested. That is the whole point, that
we shall be ready if we wish to take part; but we are
not bound to take part if we do not wish to do so. . . .[6]

The following year Laurier stated the same principle in the debate
on his naval legislation: "The position which we take is that it is for
the parliament of Canada, which created this navy, to say when and
where it shall go to war. . . . If England is at war we are at war and
liable to attack. I do not say that we shall always be attacked, neither
do I say that we would take part in all the wars of England. That is
a matter that must be determined by circumstances, upon which the
Canadian parliament will have to pronounce and will have to decide
in its own best judgment."[7]

It is interesting that in 1914 (with a Conservative government in
power) Parliament had no more to do at the outbreak of war than in
1899. The Cabinet committed Canada to participation well before
Britain's declaration of war; the Navy was handed over to Admiralty
control, as permitted by Laurier's Act, on August 4, the day of the
British declaration, by order-in-council;[8] and when Parliament came
together in accordance with the Militia Act on August 18, it merely
provided the means of implementing the decisions already taken by
the executive. Nevertheless, Sir Robert Borden liked to talk as though
Parliament had made all the essential decisions. In his election manifesto of 1917 he said, "Canada, as became a partner nation in the
British Commonwealth, entered the struggle by the decree of her
Parliament."[9] This was magnificent, but it was not fact. Of course,
Sir Robert, and Sir Wilfrid – and Mackenzie King – all knew well
that in any case, under the Canadian parliamentary system, it was
the Cabinet that had to make the decisions; it was its business to
recommend to Parliament what it had to do. The talk of Parliament

6. Department of External Affairs, *Documents on Canadian External Relations*, I, 1909-1918, document 378.
7. *Debates, House of Commons*, Feb. 3, 1910 (cols. 2964-65).
8. *Documents on Canadian External Relations*, I, documents 38-48.
9. *Gazette*, Montreal, November 12, 1917.

deciding was no more than talk; but it was a great political convenience.

It is comical that it should be Sir Wilfrid who gave currency to the phrase, "If you want us to help you, call us to your councils", a phrase which he repudiated in the same breath and which in fact, as Lord Minto told Chamberlain, represented a policy for which he had no use at all. It is not surprising that Chamberlain was bitter and bewildered about it.[10] Passive resistance to involvement in British councils was in practice one of the great themes of Laurier's career. There is a passage in Skelton's biography of him that is worth quoting:

> In forming his policy on imperial relations, Sir Wilfrid did not follow solely his individual preference. . . . More important than personal preferences was the need of preserving national unity, or preventing a division on racial lines. His constant effort was to find a policy and a formula which would keep the country not only moving in what he considered the right direction, but moving abreast. As a responsible administrator, he was more concerned in settling concrete problems than in framing abstract theories of empire. . . . Whether or not he could have been positive and constructive, it is a fact that his most important work in this field was negative, the blocking of the plans of the advocates of centralization, who suffered from no shortage of theories. It is an opinion, but an opinion strengthened by the experiences of later years, that this work, negative though it may have been, was the work his day demanded, an essential stage in the development of Canadian nationality.[11]

This is authentic Laurier again, and authentic Skelton too; but as many readers will instantly perceive, it is also singularly authentic Mackenzie King. The concern for national unity is familiar; but so is the idea that the highest statesmanship consists in preventing evil

10. J. E. Kendle, *The Colonial and Imperial Conferences, 1887-1911* (London, 1967), pp. 36-37. Minto's letter to Chamberlain, April 14, 1900, is quoted at length by Paul Stevens in "Wilfrid Laurier: Politician" (M. Hamelin, [ed.], *The Political Ideas of the Prime Ministers of Canada* [Ottawa, 1969], p. 73).
11. Skelton, *Laurier* (ed. 1921), II, 289.

rather than in creating good. This doctrine King often proclaimed in his later years. After surmounting the greatest crisis of his career in 1944 he reflected, "Over and over again, I have thought of what I said to [Emil] Ludwig that some day the world will know some of the things that I have prevented. . . . I must make increasingly clear to the world that prevention of wrong courses of evil and the like means more than all else that man can accomplish."[12] One wonders how often and how carefully he had read that page of Skelton.

III

The parallel between Laurier's policies before 1911 and King's after 1921 is evident enough to need no laboured exposition. When King and Skelton repudiated the Conservative readiness to participate in a common Commonwealth foreign policy based on consultation they were going back to Laurier – Laurier plus the new autonomy won during the war of 1914-18. The old shibboleths reappear: notably "Parliament will decide", which King used to effect in the Chanak affair of 1922 and which did him yeoman service in the years before 1939.[13] Now, however, it came more and more to be suggested that Parliament might decide whether or not Canada would go to war, not only the extent of her active participation.

Whatever one may think of King's external policy between the wars, its consistency is remarkable. I think it is evident that he always recognized that Canada would have no choice but participation in a major war in which Britain was involved; he gave no hint whatever of this to the public, but he said it pretty frankly to the assembled premiers at the Imperial Conference of 1923, while at the same time leaving no doubt of his hostility to "intervention in lesser issues". He made it clear to at least some of his Cabinet colleagues in 1938 that neutrality in such a war as was threatened had no place in his scheme of things.[14] What he was not prepared to do, however, was to make any public commitment in advance of the actual moment of

12. J. W. Pickersgill and D. F. Forster, *The Mackenzie King Record*, II (Toronto, 1968), 271-72.
13. As we have seen, however, Sir Robert Borden, too, was acquainted with this useful formula.
14. "Imperial Conference, 1923. Stenographic Notes of the Fourth Meeting," October 8, 1923, King Papers, Public Archives of Canada. King Diary, August 31, 1938, quoted in the present writer's *Arms, Men and Governments: The War Policies of Canada, 1939-1945* (Ottawa, 1970).

crisis. At the time of Munich, it is true, he seems to have been disposed to announce that if the Chamberlain approach to Hitler failed Canada would support Britain; but Ernest Lapointe advised against it, and his advice was followed.[15] King's diary for August 24, 1939, reveals that with war virtually certain the Cabinet decided to persevere with the policy of making no public commitment until the guns were actually firing; yet no one spoke for neutrality.

The defence of the *status quo* and the dislike of innovation are quite as clear under King as they were under Sir Wilfrid; and it was not only British centralization that he resisted. Nothing is more revealing about King, it seems to me, than his hostility to a Canadian (Senator Raoul Dandurand) becoming president of the League of Nations Assembly in 1925, and to the election of Canada to the League Council in 1927. In the first case Skelton differed with him; in the second certainly, and possibly in both, it was Lapointe who was the innovator, and it was to placate Lapointe that King finally agreed. People like Lapointe saw in these proposals a new international status and importance for Canada; King saw in them primarily unnecessary responsibilities, commitments, and complications.[16] This is all of a piece with King's obvious reluctance during the Second World War to seek a larger role for Canada in the policies of the Grand Alliance – which led Churchill to congratulate him on having "been so fine about letting England lead". King did not dissent from this proposition, and in replying revealed the fact (for which there is other evidence) that some of his associates were not altogether satisfied with his attitude. "I said it had been difficult to maintain my position at times but that as long as I knew we were being consulted and getting informed on new policies and were able to speak about them before they were settled, I thought it was much better before the world to leave the matter of leadership in the hands of the President and himself."[17]

Churchill had in fact put his finger on an important King inhibi-

---

15. H. Blair Neatby, "William Lyon Mackenzie King", in Robert L. McDougall, (ed.), *Canada's Past and Present: A Dialogue* (Toronto, 1965), pp. 17-18.
16. James Eayrs, "A Low Dishonest Decade", in *The Growth of Canadian Policies in External Affairs* (Durham, N.C., 1960), p. 680; Skelton to King, March 31, 1925, King Papers (I owe this reference to Mr. Donald M. Page); H. Blair Neatby, *William Lyon Mackenzie King*, II (Toronto, 1963), 194-95.
17. *The Mackenzie King Record*, II, 91.

tion. The last thing King ever wanted was to have Canada taking a lead in international affairs. It is worth while to recall the Ethiopian crisis of 1935, when the King government repudiated its representative at Geneva when he proposed the imposition of additional sanctions against Italy. It was made clear to the unfortunate Dr. Riddell at the time that the government's objection was not so much to the measures proposed as to the fact that they were being labelled a "Canadian proposal".[18] Canada was prepared to follow, but not to lead; and the reason, pretty obviously, was that assuming leadership in such a matter was likely to provoke serious divisions within the country.

IV

In framing the policies we have so briefly glanced at, were King and his adviser Skelton consciously following Laurier? Or were they merely following a line natural to a Liberal government much dependent on Quebec support? One might even go further and ask, were they merely following a line which every government in a country divided like Canada must follow within limits? It would be risky to give a dogmatic answer.

However, it is at least interesting to observe how prominent Laurier's name is in the copious record of Mackenzie King's own thoughts that he left behind him. Many people will remember the remarkable passage from his diary concerning his election as party leader in 1919, quoted by MacGregor Dawson:

> . . . my thoughts were of dear mother & father & little
> Bell all of whom I felt to be very close to me, of grand-
> father & Sir Wilfrid also. . . . The dear loved ones know
> and are about, they are alive and with me in this great
> everlasting Now and Here. . . .[19]

Already, it would seem, Laurier was becoming almost a part of the King family mythology. Nor did his position in King's mind diminish with the passage of time. Laurier was one of the characters from the beyond (along with King's benefactor Peter Larkin and members of

18. See, e.g., Acting Under Secretary of State for External Affairs to Canadian Advisory Officer, Geneva, December 1, 1935, King Papers, folio 181225.
19. Dawson, *King*, I, 310.

the King family) who spoke regularly to him in séances in 1932 and 1933.[20] And he constantly appeared to King in the "visions" or dreams recorded in his diary during the Second World War period. Readers of *The Mackenzie King Record* will have noted the number of references to Laurier printed there from King's diary. There are of course many more in the original diary itself. As the question of conscription became more and more insistent King's mind dwelt increasingly on 1917 and the treason against Laurier within the party. When he heard on October 13, 1944 that J. L. Ralston was coming back from Europe to urge a change of policy, his comment was, "It is a repetition of the kind of thing that led to the creation of the Union Government after Borden's return from England. That will not take place under me."[21] This boded ill for Ralston's project. And when on the evening of October 30 King became convinced that there was a conspiracy against him in his Cabinet he wrote that it was plain to him that "in pretty much all particulars my position is becoming identical to that of Sir Wilfrid Laurier's where his supposedly strongest colleagues left him, one by one, and joined their political enemies and became a party for conscription". From this moment, I think, he was determined to expel Ralston from the government.[22] I suspect that anyone who became identified in King's mind with the opposition to Laurier on this question was automatically ticketed as an enemy. Perhaps, however, the mental process worked the other way round: those who came to be regarded as enemies on the conscription issue were tagged as traitors of the sort who had stabbed Sir Wilfrid in the back. As so often with King, the question seems to be one for the psychologists.

It is worth while to remember that in 1945, in the last election he ever fought, Mackenzie King was still emphasizing his connection with Laurier and his fidelity to him, and drawing a parallel between the situation then facing him in Quebec, and that which had confronted Laurier in 1911.[23]

There are two things particularly in the period just before the Second World War which make me feel that it is at least possible that memories of Laurier had some direct influence on King's external policies. One is his own record of a Cabinet meeting on August

20. Neatby, *King*, II, 406-7.
21. *The Mackenzie King Record*, II, 122.
22. *Ibid.*, 174. See *Arms, Men and Governments*, Part VII.
23. *Gazette*, Montreal, June 4, 1945 (speech in Montreal).

10, 1938, which dealt with the vexed question of British air training in Canada. Many would have thought the meeting unsatisfactory, for there was no real decision except not to proceed with a plan which had been worked out between representatives of the British Air Ministry and the Canadian Department of National Defence.[24] But King wrote in his diary,

> I could see quite a division of feeling on the part of those present; Rogers, Ilsley and Power and Howe taking a less critical view of the whole business than Lapointe and Cardin, though all saw the political implications and the danger that this step might seem a commitment of war [sic]. I was glad to find Lapointe and all present agreeable to my taking the view that we should be in a position to co-operate in the event of Parliament deciding we should do so; in other words, follow the Laurier naval policy in relation to air, of having an efficient service in Canada which, if Parliament so decided, could be made a part of one great service in time of war. The meeting lasted over two hours. On the whole, it was a very satisfactory one.

How seriously is one to take King's analogy with Laurier's naval policy? If one takes it literally, one has to face the possibility that the decision of the following year, to set up the British Commonwealth Air Training Plan on a basis of handing the raw human material of Canadian air power over to the British Air Ministry to use as it saw fit, may have been based in some degree on memories of Laurier and 1910. But it would be dangerous to make any such assumption. I do not recall any reference to the Naval Service Act precedent during the 1939 negotiations, and I think the weight of evidence is that the predominant factor in the decision was mere economy.[25] If the mantle of Laurier were used to cover so essentially anti-national a measure as the B.C.A.T.P. agreement of 1939, Sir Wilfrid's shade would have a good deal to answer for. But it is worth remembering that the King government that year declined to place the Navy at Admiralty disposal under the 1910 Act as in 1914,

24. On this incident, see James Eayrs, *In Defence of Canada: Appeasement and Rearmament* (Toronto, 1965), pp. 98-102, and *Arms, Men and Governments*, Part II.
25. *Arms, Men and Governments*, Part I.

though the Admiralty requested it and the Canadian Chief of the
Naval Staff recommended it.[26] (Parliament, of course, had nothing to
do either with this decision or with that to undertake the Air
Training Plan.)

The other incident is perhaps more familiar and also more significant. On January 16, 1939, in the debate on the Address, Mackenzie
King read statements made by Laurier in the Naval Service Bill debate
of 1910. (It is interesting that he said he had come across them in
reading E. M. Macdonald's *Recollections*, though they are well known
and are quoted in Skelton.) King's preface to his quotations is rather
remarkable:

> I should like to read that statement to-night because
> at the time it was made it was expressive of Liberal
> policy concerning the relation of this country to other
> countries at a time of war. It was a statement of the
> Liberal policy which was accepted then, a statement
> which sets forth the Liberal policy as it has been fol-
> lowed ever since. I wish to give it as a statement of the
> Liberal policy as it is to-day and as it will continue to
> be under the present Liberal administration.

King proceeded to read two quotations. The first was, "I am a
Canadian first, last and all the time. I am a British subject by birth,
by tradition, by conviction – by the conviction that under British
institutions my native land has found a measure of security and
freedom it could not have found under any other regime." The other
was the famous utterance quoted above (page 89), beginning, "If
England is at war we are at war and liable to attack", and continuing
with the qualifying sentences that follow down to the words "in its
own best judgment".[27] The prime minister then abruptly passed on to
other matters.

Why did King choose in 1939 to make what amounted to a
declaration that Liberal policy on the question of peace and war in
that year was precisely what it had been under Laurier in 1910? A
generation of constitutional development seemed to have been written
off as if it had never been. The statement must have troubled many

26. *Ibid.*, Part V.
27. Both quotations are from Laurier's speech of February 3, 1910 (*Debates,
House of Commons*, columns 2959 and 2965).

of King's followers, especially in Quebec. On the following March 30 he felt obliged to devote several columns of *Hansard* to complaining of the "obvious misrepresentations or misconceptions" that had arisen from his statement:

> My immediate purpose in quoting the statement, as will be apparent from the context, was to emphasize the continuity of Liberal policy as regards parliamentary control. . . .
>
> Sir Wilfrid Laurier was not a man to set bounds to a nation's growth. . . .
>
> There have been great changes since 1910. . . .

It was surely very unlike King to have omitted to protect himself with qualifications and circumlocutions when he made his original statement on January 16. But perhaps he thought that the great name of Sir Wilfrid was itself protection enough.

V

It is hardly necessary to recall that when war actually came in September 1939 King and his colleagues did not act on the "when England is at war we are at war" principle. The Canadian Parliament was allowed to go through the forms of decision, and Canada was officially neutral for a week after Britain went to war. Nevertheless, perhaps Laurier in 1910 and the momentarily incautious King of January 1939 essentially had the right of it. By 1939, whatever may have been the case earlier, it was clear that if Britain went to war – a war in which national existence was at stake – then Canada would of necessity go to war too. Even Skelton knew that the government could not adopt a posture of neutrality "without suffering immediate defeat".[28] The neutral week was a formality, and everybody understood it.

What I have been doing in this paper is merely suggesting that the relationship between the policies of King and the policies of Laurier is worth thinking about. The link between these two prime ministers was unique in Canadian history. I think it would be accurate to say

28. King Diary, August 31, 1938. See *Arms, Men and Governments*, Part I.

that Sir Wilfrid Laurier became one of Mackenzie King's rather numerous superstitions. At a future day, perhaps, circumstances will permit some earnest student to make a statistical study of the references to departed friends and relatives in the King diary. Offhand, my impression is that Sir Wilfrid's only rivals would be King's mother and the dog Pat. I should add that it is by no means clear that King's public policies were dictated, or even powerfully influenced, by his superstitions. But it is possible that this particular superstition was in some degree an exception. After all, Laurier was not just a myth. His career was a great political fact. He was one of the most successful practitioners in history of the notoriously difficult art of governing Canada. It would not be surprising if a later, and ultimately still more successful practitioner took him for a model.

Fleming and Tupper: The Fall of the Siamese Twins, 1880

ALAN WILSON

On May 22, 1880, an order-in-council from Ottawa announced the termination of Sandford Fleming's services as the government's Engineer-in-Chief for the Canadian Pacific Railway. Newspaper reaction was mixed. The *Globe* condemned the implication that Fleming had been incompetent, especially during the administration of Alexander Mackenzie. The Montreal *Gazette* lamented Fleming's continuance even as a consultant on the C.P.R., for his continued influence "will be detrimental to the interests of the Northwest". The *Halifax Morning Chronicle* concurred.

At 53, Fleming had reached the last major turning point in his life. Many of his old staff wrote sympathetically to him. His closest friend, George Grant, Queen's University's distinguished Principal, protested that "the Government must have been willing to sacrifice you, . . . The whole thing looks very suspicious to me, & I cannot but think you will yet be recalled as a necessity". Sandford's brother, David, staunchly railed against the "Rabid politicians . . . , greedy

99

contractors . . . , or malicious bad hearted Engineers so called". In the House, the Hon. David Mills, late Liberal Minister of Interior, asked the Minister of Public Works, Hon. Hector Langevin, whether all papers relating to Fleming's "dismissal" would be made available. Langevin objected that the proper term was "withdrawal", to which Mills supplied "removal", while T. W. Anglin proffered "dispensed with". Further discussion prompted "superseded", "retired", and "severed his connection".

Canadian historians have reflected the same divergence of views. Two authorities have come closest to the mark: J. W. Longley suggested that either Fleming or Tupper had to go. Fleming "resigned"; G. P. deT. Glazebrook suggests that while Fleming was "removed", he was probably "the inevitable victim of a not very successful experiment in government construction . . . [and of] a party move to throw discredit on a previous administration".[1] But Fleming's difficulties have not been satisfactorily explained, even by his memorialist, L. J. Burpee.[2] Indeed, they require an examination of his professional engineering associations, his survival during three federal administrations, his friendship with Sir Charles Tupper, and of the condition of the Liberal-Conservative party.

Fleming's association with Charles Tupper began in the years before Confederation. Fleming's arrival in Nova Scotia from Canada promised ready action in surveying the Intercolonial railway line; his useful Halifax connections through marriage, and his interest in developing coal and salt resources in Tupper's section of Nova Scotia were natural and mutual attractions. They soon became business partners in Springhill coal and Cumberland salt ventures, for which Fleming assumed much of the modest exploratory costs. Tupper's usefulness to Fleming included his frequent services as family physician and influential friend, prompted partly by the nearness of the two houses each maintained in Halifax and in Ottawa. Tupper also encouraged Fleming in some of his most ambitious railway ventures. In return, Fleming and his engineering colleague, Collingwood Schreiber, assisted Tupper and his supporters in stopping the Nova

1. J. W. Longley, *Sir Charles Tupper* (Toronto, 1926), pp. 179-80; G. P. deT. Glazebrook, *A History of Transportation in Canada* (Toronto, 1938; reprinted in the Carleton Library, 1964), II, 72.
2. L. J. Burpee, *Sandford Fleming, Empire Builder.* I wish to acknowledge my gratitude for the steady support of my research assistant, Mr. Ronald Hotchkiss.

Scotia Anti-Confederates, and in working with the former New Brunswick Liberal, S. L. Tilley. In the 1870s, when Fleming became the Engineer-in-Chief for construction of the Intercolonial Railway, his association with Tupper was extended. Tupper, who had now joined Macdonald's federal cabinet, vigorously supported Fleming's proposals for the Intercolonial at the expense of Fleming's *bête-noire*, Charles John Brydges of the Intercolonial Railway Commission and the Grand Trunk Railway.

In the Intercolonial venture, moreover, Fleming advanced his reputation as an effective leader of those often bibulous, undisciplined engineering forces that built the great trunk lines of Canada and the United States in this period. Two men – Collingwood Schreiber and Marcus Smith – became his chief assistants. Fleming's great strength as chief engineer – and a particularly vulnerable point – rested in his close personal relations with his staff. Railroad engineering on such a vast scale put special demands of discipline and endurance upon all who engaged in it. Further, the anxiety of local interests and of private capitalists made such ventures – particularly those by government and public servants – especially controversial. In the Intercolonial project Fleming faced an awesome task, but his labours were dramatically increased when he accepted simultaneously the chief responsibility for the Canadian Pacific Railway. Moreover, the reduced economic circumstances of the nation, public scandal in high places, and the bitter political rivalries of the 1870s compounded all of his problems. In these circumstances, Fleming's reputation as a crony of Charles Tupper had a decisive effect upon their careers.

Their troubles in 1880 were a direct consequence of the Pictou Railway controversy of 1865-67. Fleming, then the Chief Railway Engineer of Nova Scotia, had been charged by the premier, Tupper, to advise on the building of a spur line to connect Truro, an obvious Intercolonial junction, with the North-shore port of Pictou, fifty miles away. Amid the stalled negotiations over the Intercolonial, building intra-colonial lines may have been appropriate, but the Pictou line was open to several objections. To the people of Cape Breton Island, it did not reach far enough; Yarmouth in the southwest broke sharply with Tupper, and became a centre of the Anti-Confederates; advocates of the Intercolonial protested against what they deemed was a needless draining of resources from the main line. But the chief objection arose over Tupper's decision to relieve his government of the critical problems of faltering Pictou contractors

by releasing Sandford Fleming from his government post and giving
him a fresh contract to complete the line himself as a private
engineer-contractor. Fleming compounded the criticism by employing unorthodox, though apparently successful, building and sub-
contractual methods, and by turning an undetermined profit on the
undertaking. By May 31, 1867, when the work was finished, the
partnership of Tupper and Fleming had been bitterly debated in the
legislature, the Antis had added to their armament, and the loyalty
of many Tupper supporters had been put to the test. A Conservative
of such loyalty and probity as Sir John Thompson remembered the
Pictou affair years later in writing to Sir John Macdonald, "that in
twenty three years observation of Fleming – beginning with his
robbery of Nova Scotia to the extent of his whole fortune by breach
of trust, . . . I have never been able to regard him otherwise than
as the great example which Canada presents of successful dishonesty
and conceit. . . . I will send you the particulars of Fleming's connection with the N.S. Railways. . . ."[3] In the 70s, Fleming and
Tupper were persistently linked in attacks by Liberal critics such as
A. G. Jones, Mackenzie's chief political adviser on the Maritimes, by
Conservative supporters such as C. J. Brydges, and by Conservative
stalwarts such as Senator David Macpherson, railway contractor and
a man as critical of Quebec and the Maritimes as was George Brown.
The ghost of the Pictou affair – whatever its substance – would haunt
the two old allies with disastrous consequences for both.

Sandford Fleming's relationship with Sir John Macdonald was
never cordial, although Lady Macdonald held the Flemings in great
affection. Sir John had given to C. J. Brydges and his co-commissioners
for the Intercolonial the task of melding efficiency and patronage in
that great undertaking, and Brydges regularly left Macdonald in no
doubt of his opinion of Fleming:

> Rose gave me Fleming's letter to you. I think it is a
> very weak document. . . . Howe told me that he and
> his party were exceedingly afraid of Fleming, and that
> they had the greatest difficulty in bringing themselves
> to consent to his position, arising out of what they felt
> were gross errors – to use mild terms – in the Pictou
> matter. I was somewhat surprised to hear that Mr.
> Schreiber (Fleming's head man on the Intercolonial)

3. Public Archives of Canada, Thompson Papers, Thompson to Macdonald,
30 July and 11 August, 1889.

> had resigned . . . , for the purpose of tendering for the
> construction of some portions, at any rate of the
> work . . . he would have enormous advantage . . . and
> to my mind this opens questions which I may think
> about but would rather not express a definite opinion
> upon at present.[4]

Similar views regarding Tupper, Fleming and the perils of the Intercolonial came to Macdonald from Senator David Lewis Macpherson: "I see part of the Intercolonial is located. I suppose practically given to the Maritimers. I imagine the Lower Canadians will claim the balance. . . ."[5] Although Macdonald's confidence in Tupper remained strong – by the end of the 70s Tupper was still the heir-apparent – the political difficulties involved in Fleming's activities must have been apparent to Macdonald.

In 1871 there arose the question of appointing a chief engineer for the C.P.R. project. Macdonald preferred Walter Shanly, but being preoccupied in treaty negotiations at Washington, he wired his consent to Langevin's nomination of Fleming. Significantly, Langevin would have relieved Fleming of the Intercolonial, and it was this arrangement to which Macdonald had agreed. Macdonald's doubts and Fleming's responsibilities were amplified, however, when no successor could be found for the Intercolonial, and Fleming was forced to continue for five years the superintendence of both enterprises.

Sandford Fleming had his own reservations about Sir John Macdonald, however, and a great faith in Sir Charles Tupper's prospects. Fleming had dealt regularly with W. P. Howland and William Macdougall, both as Reformers and following their translation to Macdonald's Great Coalition in 1864. Their interest in the West and in railroad expansion carried him back to his own days with the Northern Railway, his survey of Collingwood harbour, and to the *Globe*-inspired dreams of western development. By the late 60s, when the coalition spirit of Macdonald's government was waning, Fleming linked his conversations with these two associates with his recognition of Charles Tupper's genius for adapting to changed circumstances. Had Tupper not brought men and ideas from Nova Scotia Reform ranks into his Conservative party in the late 50s? Had

4. P.A.C., Macdonald Papers, Brydges to Macdonald, 14 January, 1869.
5. *Ibid.*, Macpherson to Macdonald, 8 July, 1867.

Tupper not disarmed the Nova Scotia Antis and helped to bring
Joseph Howe into the federal cabinet? Had Tupper not formed an
important new federal association with the former New Brunswick
Liberal, S. L. Tilley?

On April 26, 1869, Sandford Fleming wrote to Tupper making a
slightly veiled proposal:

> When you reach Ottawa you will find the Govern-
> ment very strong, in my mind too strong; it will
> stand a fair chance before long of breaking in two. . . .
> There is no opposition . . . , but you will find amongst
> conservatives and reformers from Ontario and perhaps
> other provinces an undercurrent of dissatisfaction . . .
> if at any time in the future you may see it expedient
> to strike out on an independent line you may safely
> calculate on winning a great many friends and sup-
> porters from Ontario. . . . Do not however be at all in a
> hurry, . . . you have only had one Session to cultivate
> it and that may be insufficient.[6]

Thus, the chief engineer of the Intercolonial saw himself as a king-
maker. The new combination would bring together men of enterprise
from both of the old parties and from all sections. In a period of
speculation, he had grossly miscalculated John Macdonald's political
durability, and imperilled his own position as a senior civil servant.

In the subsequent events that led to the downfall of the first
Macdonald administration, Fleming found another source of disen-
chantment with Sir John. Fleming had hardly entered upon his new
role as government engineer of the C.P.R. when a conflict arose
between two private groups intent on securing the contract: the one,
led by Senator David Macpherson, and representing Ontario banking
and railroad interests; the other, led by Sir Hugh Allan, and representing Montreal interests, including Allan's Merchant's Bank, and
some controversial American backers. On Macpherson's withdrawal,
a new board was struck in co-operation with Sir John Macdonald
in an attempt to strengthen Canadian and provincial representation.
Subsequently Allan headed a delegation to England to look for support from imperial financial interests. But in the late winter of 1872-
73 Sandford Fleming had become alarmed over Pacific affairs; on March
18, he wrote to Tupper:

6. P.A.C., Tupper Papers, Fleming to Tupper, 26 April, 1869.

I am not by any means satisfied with Pacific Railway matters . . . , particularly with regard to the unlimited powers taken by the Delegates to England. . . .

I have refrained from troubling Sir John hoping that the difficulties . . . might be counteracted in some other way. I am at last constrained to ask you to speak to Sir John . . . and press upon him the importance of Gov^t interfering before any mischief is done. I think I have some right to claim the attention of Sir John to this. I was induced, reluctantly & contrary to the advice of my nearest friends to become a Director by him. I have made myself liable for a very much larger amount than I ever dreamed of when I consented to go on the Board. I am led to believe that the Gov^t would hold a controlling influence over all that was done, but I now learn from Hon. Mr. Campbell that the Gov^t decline to interfere, thus leaving the Delegates to bind the company & Govt to any terms they may claim to make however extravagant.

I do not wish to embarass in any way but it is due to the Gov^t, the Undertaking and to myself to try to avert disaster where I can.[7]

Thus, on the eve of Macdonald's loss of office, Fleming had enlisted Tupper's assistance in registering his protest against Macdonald's policies. In Macdonald's mind, thereafter, Fleming must be associated with the painful memory of the Pacific Scandal, and his relations with Macdonald's successor, Alexander Mackenzie, might well be taken as an indication of Fleming's real colours.

On November 14, 1873, following the news of the Conservatives' resignation, Fleming wrote to his father-in-law, "I don't suppose the recent changes will affect me much one way or another. I have only seen Mr. Mackenzie for a little time one day. He appeared quite friendly disposed. . . ."[8]

Alexander Mackenzie remained "quite friendly disposed" for the next three and a half years. As Minister of Public Works, he doubly asserted his responsibility for general policy in railway matters. Fleming's role in establishing policy was not greatly significant. In Inter-

7. P.A.C., Fleming Papers, Fleming to Tupper, 18 March, 1873.
8. *Ibid.*, Fleming to Hall, 14 November, 1873.

colonial matters his greatest battles with C. J. Brydges had ended
triumphantly.

In Pacific railway affairs, Fleming acted virtually as a personnel
manager – content to let Mackenzie nominate minor patronage appointments, while Fleming's choices and many of his old Intercolonial subordinates acted as district chiefs and assumed other key
roles. Fleming had accepted the Pacific post only reluctantly, and he
was receiving no added salary for the further charge. Thus, he gave
only peremptory attention to the broad Pacific policy. After his
famous "Ocean to Ocean" expedition of 1872, he made virtually no
personal inspections of the western operations; he made little attempt
to centralize and co-ordinate them; he placed his faith, probably often
unwisely, in his loyal subordinates' capacity to administer policy for
each section; he accepted Mackenzie's policy of slow piecemeal exploration and construction. Moreover, like Mackenzie, he accepted
the necessity of patronage appointments. Indeed, Mackenzie's activity
as Minister of Public Works in distributing Pacific railroad posts has
not been sufficiently recognized. Fleming saw that need, and survived.
He liked deliberate preparation for railway ventures, but he had not
been responsible for Mackenzie's adopting a schedule that might
serve this end. Their affinity in this regard was one more of tempera-
ment than of mutual agreement on policy. Policy was Mackenzie's
preserve; supplying most of the teams and the details fell to Fleming.
Whatever the attempt of Fleming's later critics to link him with
Mackenzie, Mackenzie's own description of their relationship held
until at least the end of 1877:

> As you have fairly acknowledged I not only placed en-
> tire confidence in you but I endeavoured to be always
> frank and open with you and often reached decisions
> in conversation where, if I had the least suspicion of
> your not acting fairly and loyally to me I could have
> put them on paper as your recommendation. . . . Indeed
> I never had the slightest difficulty with any one of the
> Chief Officers in the Dept. I endeavoured to treat all
> as high minded gentlemen whose technical and scienti-
> fic knowledge removed their opinions in most matters
> beyond my criticism except in matters of govern-
> mental policy where of course, I expected my views
> to prevail.[9]

9. P.A.C., Mackenzie Papers, Mackenzie to Fleming, 26 July, 1877.

From the middle of 1877 this cordiality and high-mindedness were to be put to severe strains. In early 1878, Mackenzie would tell the House in exasperation that he was "no great admirer" of Fleming, but their names continued to be linked by hostile Conservatives until Fleming had been as effectively removed from office as had Mackenzie. As early as 1875, in the "Wallace Scandal", rumours had developed of a rift between them. Fleming's too casual placing of money to the credit of Wallace, his commissariat officer for the eastern division of the C.P.R., had left $40,000 unaccounted for, and had outraged the methodical Mackenzie. But by the spring of 1876 a graver situation had developed.

The previous winter had been one of great anxiety for Sandford Fleming. His brother John had died, and his wife had been near death for weeks. Fleming had only recently suffered the loss of his favourite child, and the strain of nursing his wife through her perilous three-month illness had severely taxed him. By the summer, with the Intercolonial Railway finally in operation and heavy Pacific Railway construction still comfortably remote, Fleming undertook an extended leave for recuperation for himself and his family in England. His correspondence with Mackenzie affirms their good relations and Mackenzie's genuine sympathy with Fleming in his present difficulties. But the opposition press thought otherwise – or affected to do so – and Fleming's journey was proclaimed as evidence of a serious rupture between Fleming and Mackenzie.

Mackenzie denied the rumours but his friends were less convinced of Fleming's good faith. Alfred Jones, always a bitter enemy of Tupper and a consequent critic of Fleming, wrote from Halifax to Mackenzie:

> The Papers here are discussing Flemming's [sic] leaving for England. . . . I thought it queer his going away just now. . . . I thought he was leaving to get out of the way. I don't trust him a bit. He's too intimate with Tupper & all his gang and you may depend you will have to keep your eyes open & watch him closely. He & Tupper were connected with the Pictou road & will always pull together.[10]

Similar cautionary advice came to Mackenzie from Oliver Mowat regarding the situation among the C.P.R. crews at Prince Arthur's

10. *Ibid.*, Jones to Mackenzie, 25 May, 1877.

Landing: ". . . every engineer and employee of the Pacific Railway almost to a man are warm sympathizers with the enemy".[11] In addition, Mowat warned, Senator Macpherson and two other Conservative railroad promoters had planned a trip in that area to gather information with which to attack the government. To these Liberal strategists it seemed apparent that Fleming was moving aside to let the opposition do its work with impunity for him. If such had been the understanding, then, Fleming's removal in 1880 by the *Conservatives* must be classed as a gross betrayal; but the story is not so simply told.

When Fleming took his leave in July 1876, certain arrangements were made to ensure the superintendence of his office and the discharge of his responsibilities as chief engineer of the Pacific surveys. Collingwood Schreiber assumed responsibility for the Intercolonial, and another old Intercolonial lieutenant, Marcus Smith, was advanced from charge of the British Columbia District of the C.P.R. to the added post of Acting Chief Engineer. Thereafter, Marcus Smith became a chief actor in the events leading to Sandford Fleming's departure from the public service.

Marcus Smith had gained experience as assistant to the engineers-in-chief of the Hamilton and Toronto Railway in the Great Western system and of the Canada Southern line. After further service in the Cape of Good Hope, where he had himself been a chief engineer, he returned to Canada to superintend the Intercolonial's Restigouche section. In March 1872, Fleming turned to him as his "principal Resident Assistant" in the difficult and hazardous British Columbia section of the C.P.R. In recommending Smith, Fleming commented:

> Mr. Smith is an Engineer of long standing and wide experience. . . . I am very glad we have secured his services for although he has some little peculiarities of temper he is most reliable and no one could possibly take a deeper interest in the work in hand.[12]

For five years Fleming's reliance on Smith was well repaid. Smith's capacity to organize his subordinates, his passion for accuracy in accounts, his willingness to keep a close watch on rapacious purveyors, and his forthright manner – encouraged partly by the circum-

11. *Ibid.*, Mowat to Mackenzie, 24 July, 1877.
12. Fleming Papers, Fleming to Joseph Trutch, 10 May, 1872.

stance of his enjoying independent means – these gave reassurance to Fleming who could find little time for inspections in this most remote, difficult and controversial region of the C.P.R. construction program. Smith was constant in filing detailed reports to Fleming; in Ottawa during the winters he was clearly Fleming's most talented adviser. But Smith was not drawn into the warm personal attachment to Fleming that so characterized the spirit and morale of the rest of the engineering and survey teams. Marcus Smith's independent, ambitious nature had brought forth from his fellows the half-amused dub, "The Marquis". He knew his powers; he believed himself at least Fleming's equal in experience and engineering judgment, and his superior in logistical and administrative talent. Moreover, Smith was contemptuous of Fleming's too intimate, even unprofessional relations with his staff, of his willingness to accept the role of the civil servant, obedient in policy decisions to his minister, and particularly of Fleming's apparent readiness to submerge his Conservative convictions and to work in such harmony with the Liberal railway policy. Given an opportunity, Smith would operate very differently. His chance came in July 1876.

Soon after Fleming's departure for England, with Marcus Smith's more professional approach, there seemed little chance of survival of the relaxed camaraderie of the C.P.R. engineering staff. Smith was preoccupied with administrative and technical considerations, and his peculiar sensitiveness and growing contempt for Fleming and Mackenzie soon led to strife and to the prospect of his building a counter-force within the railway department.

One large source of conflict lay in the choice of a Pacific terminus. Marcus Smith's residence and associations in British Columbia had largely centred upon Victoria and the Island, where he had been drawn into the self-interest of the two opposing factions in the new province, those of Victoria and of New Westminster. Both accepted the Yellowhead; the difference arose over the terminus. To the Victorians Macdonald's policy of adopting the more northerly Bute Inlet terminus and linking the Island with the mainland by a bridge to Nanaimo offered the hope of restoring the Island's prosperity through the combination of patronage, purveying, and contracting that must fall to Victoria with the adoption of that route. Mackenzie's proposal to bring the railway from the Yellowhead Pass by the more southerly Fraser River route, near New Westminster and to a terminus at Burrard Inlet, was taken as an open threat by the Islanders.

In Smith's view, moreover, Fleming had become a mere lackey of Mackenzie. Fleming was at fault on two levels – one a grander dimension; the other more partisan. In the first place, Smith argued, it was not a political matter by what route the C.P.R. should be built, for only a professional engineer should make such decisions. The route of a transcontinental line should not be determined by immediate political and economic considerations. An access railway geared to the most direct approach to its terminus was not enough; it must also be judged by its potential to develop new areas along the route of access – a colonization line, not a mere access line. But these broader, more professional, and more high-minded objections of Smith were complemented – and to some extent contradicted – by his more immediate partisanship and ambition regarding the route and terminus. Smith accused Fleming of pandering to the Liberals, while he himself adopted tactics calculated to assist the opposition and his friends in Victoria. It was a nice question of the responsibility and loyalty of the senior civil servant.

Marcus Smith's tactics soon gave the lie to much of his elevated professionalism. There is evidence that Smith was allied with his old Victoria cronies in buying up speculative lands in the Bute terminus area. Consequently, early in the surveying season of 1877, Smith took his first covert action when the Conservative opposition revived the prospect of a more northerly route via the Pine River Pass and Bute Inlet.

In a confidential letter of May 15, 1877, Smith instructed Joseph Hunter, one of his new engineering staff, to make preliminary surveys of the more northerly route:

> I don't think the Govt. want me to go, but the opposition do want information about it – and it is generally supposed they will get in power at the next election – so that you would have to do this as it were on the sly – and with a very small party so as not to increase expense . . . and I want to place you on vantage ground for the future.[13]

Smith knew that a general election must be held before the close of the next year's surveying season. Fleming would concur from engineering considerations that sufficient time hardly remained to explore

13. P.A.C., Smith Papers, Smith to Hunter, 15 May, 1877.

adequately the Pine River–Bute Inlet route and, if appropriate, to alter government policy with all the necessary explanations and political manoeuvering. The Yellowhead–Burrard route had the approval of the governor general, the concurrence of the chief engineer, and the prospect of proceeding through the most populous voting areas in British Columbia. Although Smith had already called to his attention the usefulness of exploring the Pine River–Bute route, Mackenzie could see no advantage in adopting the suggestion. Marcus Smith would have to adopt other means.

John Robson, then a Liberal British Columbian, described to Mackenzie why his party had suffered so badly in British Columbia during the 1878 election:

> And to these efforts must be added the influence of Marcus Smith, who, in passing through the District in the fall of 1877, everywhere and most industriously spoke of your railway policy as shuffling humbug, declaring that you had really not the slightest intention of going on with the work in B.C. and predicting very positively the return to power of the Conservatives, the only men, he said, from whom Columbia could hope for a railway – statements which, coming from such a source were *bound* to have considerable influence. . . .[14]

The fall of 1877, then, was marked by steadily worsening relations between Smith and Mackenzie, climaxed in December by a confrontation over routes that inevitably involved the absent Sandford Fleming. Their differences finally led to Smith's effective removal as engineer-in-charge of the British Columbia division and his replacement by Henry J. Cambie, one of Fleming's closest advisers. Thus, although Smith remained nominally Acting Chief Engineer, Mackenzie had effectively assumed even that post. This act, and Mackenzie's resort to Cambie for corroborative opinions favouring the Burrard route, brought to a head the question of the subordinates' loyalty to Fleming. To whom should they be loyal: Mackenzie, Smith, or Fleming? The department's clerks and those engineers directly embarrassed appealed in vain to Fleming to return. Cambie manfully appealed to Smith to understand the position he had been

14. Mackenzie Papers, Robson to Mackenzie, 26 September, 1879.

placed in through the premier's action. The Marquis could find no understanding, however, and feeling more isolated than ever he complained bitterly to Fleming while continuing his intrigues in other quarters. The situation in the department had become intolerable: Mackenzie was not speaking to his acting chief; the control of accounts, even the office mail, had been removed to the premier's office; Fleming's absence was contributing to the uncertainty. Morale had plummeted when, in March 1878, in the midst of a last difficult parliamentary session before a spring election,[15] Mackenzie sent for Fleming.

What prompted the premier directly, however, was the appearance of Marcus Smith's draft report on the results of the surveys of 1877. What was remarkable in the report was the attention given to the merits of the Pine River–Bute route which had, ostensibly, received so little attention in actual surveying. Indeed, the Fraser route was so scantily reviewed that Mackenzie called once more upon the hapless Cambie to furnish an appendix correcting the emphasis of the proposed report. In the midst of these agitations, however, the premier first learned of Smith's steps in sending the secret Hunter expedition into the northern territory. Matters had reached an impasse.

Joseph Hunter was sent for, and emerged in tears from an interview with the premier. Smith's report was held back until Fleming could arrive and offer his opinion. But by that time an election must inevitably be called within three months. Sandford Fleming must face the dilemma of being candid and loyal to his immediate political superior while knowing that Marcus Smith had nicely calculated his position to coincide with the established policy of the party that would almost certainly prevail in the forthcoming contest.

On Fleming's return in May he was immediately closeted with Mackenzie, who instructed him not to consult with Smith but to prepare his own report independently. His immediate reaction, however, was reported to the department in a letter in late May in which he questioned the reliability of a map prepared by Smith in which soil types had been distinctively coloured, a device he thought

> ... a mistake and apt to mislead, as we have not acquired information at all sufficiently accurate, to enable anyone to make such marked distinctions over wide

15. By Mackenzie's preference, but he was forced later to postpone it until fall.

areas, portions of which no one has ever visited, without drawing very largely on the imagination ... if the
Pacific Railway is put under one Contract, serious
difficulties may arise hereafter with the contractors,
who will be paid partly in land and who possibly may
... establish claims against the Government founded
on these very maps, by which they may say they were
grievously misled.[16]

The deputy minister was prepared to burn Smith's map, and the
premier concurred. Fleming attempted to reach a compromise by
which the offending descriptions might be obscured. The decision to
suppress the map was taken by Mackenzie, however, and the map
did not appear with Fleming's formal report in July. In the meantime, it was reported to Fleming by Malcolm McLeod, the noted
pamphleteer "Britannicus", that Joseph Hunter had reported to him
that the Pine River Pass was "utterly unfit for a railway route".
Whatever Hunter's purpose, the news must weaken Smith's position,
and in his report Fleming stood firmly with the Fraser route.

Sandford Fleming had seemingly been forced into a political align-
ment with Mackenzie, and he might well fear the consequences of a
Conservative victory in September with John Macdonald's long-standing commitment to the Bute Inlet. With Macdonald's decision to sit
for Victoria when his party's triumph was declared, Fleming's dis-
comfiture appeared to be complete. The Marquis might well antici-
pate his speedy re-assumption of his old office on a more permanent
basis.

But there was one hitch in store for the Marquis. As a reward for
his role as opposition critic on railways, Charles Tupper was to be
Minister of Public Works. Moreover, Fleming's good friend Alexander Campbell, Macdonald's old law partner, was the senior Ontario
member of the new cabinet. In despair, Smith began a correspondence
of recrimination with Fleming in November, marking their final
break, and indicating the more general nature of the attacks that
Fleming could expect to be directed toward him in the future:

But I have felt for some time that you have not exerted
yourself to maintain the honour and high character of
the staff which is becoming rapidly demoralized in con-

16. Smith Papers, Fleming to W. B. Smellie, 24 May, 1878.

sequence of the encouragement given to time serving
persons or having political backing regardless of merit.[17]

Smith had completed the breach with those whom he accused of
mere pandering to the Liberals, and he would have to turn to factions
within the Conservatives to carry further his attack upon his old
chief.

Charles Tupper's reaction to Smith's increasingly hostile attacks
upon Sandford Fleming was predictable. He stalled for time, tried to
placate Smith, and agreed that Fleming should not resume his full
title and duties until he could complete a report on the controversy
over the routes. In the meantime Smith might regain his composure
if he were not peremptorily removed from the position of acting
chief. Such a politic course, however, did nothing to divert Marcus
Smith.

Throughout the winter Smith badgered Tupper constantly to
recognize the strengths of the Pine–Bute route, to preserve the Conservatives' long-declared policy of adopting the more northerly route,
and to avoid the pitfall of being drawn by Fleming into a mere acquiescence in Mackenzie's plans. By early February it was obvious
that Smith would not be content to confine the battle to departmental correspondence. On February 12, 1879, the *Globe* commented
that a ministerial journal had revealed a new phase in the struggle:

> The Hamilton *Spectator* returns to its charge respecting
> the 'suppressed' railway map, a copy of which seems to
> have reached it. . . . All we know about it is that the
> . . . "suppression" took place at the instance of the
> Engineer-in-Chief. . . . If the *Spectator* thinks it knows
> more about these matters than Mr. Sandford Fleming
> does it is quite welcome to argue the matter with him,
> but it has no right to impute sinister motives either to
> him in a matter so purely professional, or to Mr.
> Mackenzie, who could hardly be expected to issue a
> map in Mr. Fleming's name which that gentleman re-
> garded as inaccurate.

If the article in the *Spectator* indicated Smith's hand in encouraging
a nascent factionalism among Conservatives, Smith was not one to
hide it, for four days earlier he had told Tupper that "Some of your

17. Fleming Papers, Smith to Fleming, 26 November, 1878.

best friends are not a little alarmed . . . they think you are treading on dangerous ground . . . and would thus acknowledge the policy of the Mackenzie Govt. to be the best."[18]

Charles Tupper was in a quandary. After his years as opposition railway critic, he and his old associate, Sandford Fleming, had now both returned to active duty. Moreover, Fleming remained firm in his advice that Mackenzie's policy for the Burrard route had been correct. But could the Conservatives move to adopt that advice without awkwardly denying their past position? It was no longer possible to reach a decision by quiet departmental discussion. The issue had been made public and the press was asking questions. It was virtually certain that Smith had won recognition from the *Spectator* with the support of Senator David Macpherson. Further, Macpherson had long ago been embittered over Conservative Pacific Railway matters at the time of the Pacific Scandal, and Macdonald knew him to be a bitter critic both of Tupper and of Fleming. Macpherson was too strong in Ontario to alienate a second time. Late in March, acting as chairman of the Senate Public Accounts Committee, Macpherson opened a public investigation into all matters relating to the survey, location, and construction of the Pacific railway and telegraph. His first witness was Marcus Smith.

While the *Globe* commented very critically upon Smith's evidence and his insinuations about the lack of competence of his chief and most of his colleagues, the *Spectator* persisted in its earlier line and was joined by another government journal, Thomas White's Montreal *Gazette*. Meanwhile, Marcus Smith wrote at length to Sir Hector Langevin, Macdonald's Quebec lieutenant, recounting his version of events in all their detail – including the Cambie incident – and encouraging Langevin to "drop a line to your colleagues". By early May Macpherson's enquiry had carried the criticisms of the railway office well beyond the question of routes, and had encouraged in the public debate reservations concerning the efficiency of the minister and of his chief engineer. The Montreal *Gazette* warmed to the task and displaced the Hamilton *Spectator* as chief governmental dissident. Marcus Smith must have drawn new courage from the support of these important government organs, but his satisfaction would be short-lived. Almost immediately, it was announced that new surveys were to be undertaken during the approaching season in the area

18. Smith Papers, Smith to Tupper, 8 February, 1879.

favoured by Smith, but lest the Marquis feel any sense of triumph they were to be in the general charge of Sandford Fleming, with direction in British Columbia in the hands of Henry J. Cambie. Already, without Smith's knowledge, the survey parties had been formed, and plans were advanced to provide the new government with the kind of detailed comparative knowledge that would eclipse any charge that they had capitulated and had accepted the Mackenzie route *carte blanche*.

For Marcus Smith the announcement came as a tremendous blow, and on May 12 he addressed his first letter directly to Sir John A. Macdonald. The message was fairly moderate in tone but clear in its implication that Fleming was drawing Tupper into a plot "to suppress all information adverse to the views expressed in his Report". Moreover, Smith suggested, he had "no predilection for any route . . . [and] no desire whatever to injure Mr. Fleming's position but . . . I am well informed that Mr. Fleming is using every means in his power to injure me." To Tupper on the same day, he spoke more directly: "It is well known in the Office that Mr. Fleming is bitterly opposed to this [Bute Inlet] route, not from its defects, but because it was not suggested by himself and he is consumed with an unworthy jealousy of the labours of others."[19] And to another potential Conservative dissident, he wrote on May 16:

> I have addressed a strong letter of remonstrance to the Minister . . . against putting money on *sham* surveys to mislead the public. I believe Dr. Tupper wants to do what is right but *unfortunately* Fleming seems to have a power over him which he is unable to resist and which is causing scandal and discontent in the conservative party and he has been told that Fleming must be dismissed or he will ruin both the minister and the party.[20]

Here was the crux of Smith's strategy. The difficulty rested in achieving a delicate balance between forcing Fleming out and not appearing to threaten Sir John's heir-apparent. The solution rested in professing a readiness to save the minister from himself.

But Marcus Smith's new friends were not all as solicitous for

19. Macdonald Papers, Smith to Macdonald and Tupper, 12 May, 1879.
20. Smith Papers, Smith to D. McCulloch, 16 May, 1879.

Charles Tupper's security. Senator Macpherson had little respect for Tupper and less for the section of the country he represented. Moreover, Thomas White, who was co-owner of both the Hamilton *Spectator* and the Montreal *Gazette*, had other important Montreal connections, all of them associated with the fortunes of the Conservative party. The Merchant's Bank group who had been so bitterly denied in 1872 their opportunity to build the Pacific Railway because of the importunities of their leader, Sir Hugh Allan, had regrouped in 1877. Among their numbers were several men who held important posts both as executives and directors of the Bank and of the Grand Trunk Railway: James Ferrier of the Grand Trunk, John McLennan, Vice-President of the Bank, and C. J. Brydges, Vice-President of the Bank and former Grand Trunk General Manager. Further, White, Ferrier, and McLennan were also Conservative M.P.s, and their alliance with Sir David Macpherson provided the initiative in and out of Parliament for the anti-Tupper and Fleming forces. Their interest in opposing the minister and his chief engineer jointly probably arose from Tupper's known preference that the Pacific Railway should soon be put to private contract, and from the knowledge that Sandford Fleming was friendly with some of their chief Montreal rivals who were bidding for the Pacific contract. Indeed, as Fleming admitted later to Sir John A. Macdonald, he had been invited in May 1879, "to accept an equal share with four others (present proprietors) in the fortunes of the St. Paul, Minneapolis and Manitoba Railway".[21] Two of the four were George Stephen, President of the Bank of Montreal, and Fleming's good friend Donald A. Smith, who had been estranged from Sir John A. Macdonald since the Pacific Scandal. Should Sandford Fleming recommend to Tupper this highly successful railway group, or any other combination that George Stephen could create, the hopes of Montreal's Merchant's Bank group might be dashed again.

On October 27, 1879, Marcus Smith made a further appeal to Senator Macpherson against the cost of the Fraser works: "I am afraid if Sir John's friends don't bestir themselves, the Tupper–Fleming combination will run his Gov't. to the ground";[22] on the following day, he repeated these words to C. J. Brydges, "The friends of Sir John must interpose *at once* or he will be swamped. I wish I could see Mr. T. White M.P. and some other stauncher friends of his. I hope

---

21. Fleming Papers, Fleming to Macdonald, 15 February, 1882.
22. Smith Papers, Smith to Macpherson, 27 October, 1879.

you will do what you can to prevent this enormous waste – it is an outrage against the common sense of the public."[23]

The appeal to Brydges would fall on ready ears. Only seven months had passed since he had been peremptorily dropped by Charles Tupper as General Superintendent of Government Railways, learning the news through the newspapers two days before he received official notification from Tupper.[24] In vain, Senator Macpherson had written to Tupper on January 16 deploring Tupper's "apparent intention to decapitate Brydges. . . . I shall regard it as a grievous error from every aspect – unjust to the Civil Service, unjust to the victim, unjust to the party – exposing it to the taunt of being influenced primarily by vengeance and unjust."[25] Tupper's decision ensured that Brydges, who moved within months to Winnipeg as the Hudson's Bay Company Lands Commissioner, would prove a ready western correspondent for Macpherson on Pacific railway matters. The Montreal–Toronto axis was completed when Brydges played host to Thomas White in an inspection tour of western railway construction in September.[26]

C. J. Brydges would have preferred to have supplanted Sandford Fleming as engineering chief of the Canadian government railways. He was not alone in that ambition, however, for another notable Canadian with western land interests soon put in his bid. Writing to Sir John A. Macdonald in October 1879, Alexander Tilloch Galt offered these observations:

> You will neither obtain speedy nor economical construction under Fleming's management. If you could appoint me Railway Commissioner with plenary powers for one year I am certain with my old Railway experience I would save millions of money and months of time. I should get rid of Fleming and all his expensive paraphernalia. . . . I would like to control the land matters. . . . I apprehend Tupper might not like my suggestion. . . .[27]

A fortnight later Galt carried his suggestion a step further, after reporting to Macdonald that he had reviewed matters with Brydges,

23. *Ibid.*, Smith to Brydges, 28 October, 1879.
24. Macdonald Papers, Brydges to Macdonald, 25, 27, 29 January, 1879.
25. Tupper Papers, Macpherson to Tupper, 16 January, 1879.
26. P. A. C., John McLennan Papers, J. Ryan to McLennan, 9 September, 1879.
27. Macdonald Papers, Galt to Macdonald, 18 October, 1879.

> Fleming seems incapable of grasping the idea of what
> the country wants and what its reserves enable it to do
> and . . . his continuance in the direction of the Pacific
> Railway will defeat all our plans for the development of
> our country. . . . How would it suit your ideas to ap-
> point a Commission to report on the subject of the
> Pacific Ry. If you could induce our friend Gzowski to
> act, and place Brydges and myself on it I believe you
> could be sure of such a report as would be extremely
> useful.[28]

The Montreal group was growing. The list of Fleming's and Tupper's opponents would also grow, and meanwhile a new consideration threatened to bring matters to a critical point.

On June 26, 1879, after a decade of relatively good health, Sir John A. Macdonald had been struck down by a sudden bout of cholera. The attack and its after-effects had been so severe, and they continued so long, that Macdonald began to consider very solemnly his retirement from public life. By the late fall, while he had improved in health, he remained low in spirit and still uncertain of his future.[29] The succession had become a matter of concern; another such attack and the party would face a decision of gravest moment. Yet it had only just returned to power, and Charles Tupper, long considered most suitable by Macdonald as his successor, was implicated in one of the fiercest internecine wars the party had endured. To Senator Macpherson, C. J. Brydges, A. T. Galt and their Montreal associates the prospect of Tupper's ascendancy was frightening. Thus, the quarrel over Sandford Fleming's continuance in office threatened to assume a new character as a test of strength in another contest: if Charles Tupper persisted in backing Fleming, and did so successfully, there might be no stopping him in any ambition.

On October 2, the cabinet concluded a comprehensive review of the reports from the new surveys undertaken in May. Sandford Fleming was in attendance, and it may be presumed that his advice was in accord with his report written five days earlier to Charles Tupper. On October 4, an order-in-council calling for preparation of tenders by mid-November, heralded the cabinet's acceptance of Fleming's long-standing recommendation for the Yellowhead–Burrard route.

28. *Ibid.*, 30 October, 1879.
29. D. G. Creighton, *John A. Macdonald, The Old Chieftain*, pp. 265-66, 275.

But this decision came as an anti-climax, for in his report of September 30, Fleming had changed his mind! The new evidence – more thoroughly prepared than Marcus Smith's – suggested to Fleming that neither the Burrard nor the Bute inlets should be adopted at the moment, for there were even more promising lands and gradients in the Peace River country!

The members of the cabinet, Macpherson and White and their colleagues who deplored the continued pouring of money into "Fleming's paraphernalia", must have been incredulous. How long could a start on the Pacific Railway in B.C. be delayed? As recently as April, Amor de Cosmos had moved British Columbia's separation in the Commons, and a B.C. petition to the same effect had been sent to London. The Conservatives could not run the risk of repeating Mackenzie's follies in the Edgar mission. In despair, Brydges wrote from Winnipeg to Macdonald of his joint tour with Thomas White:

> You are throwing away your opportunities in the North-West. . . . You can have no idea of how your popularity there is sliding out of sight, . . . Tupper may perhaps say that I am interfering . . . [but] I cannot refrain, out of personal regard for you, from telling you the truth. . . . I am very glad indeed Schreiber is coming up here. . . . The engineering staff wants cleaning out terribly. The right thing to do would be to give every man notice to go, and let Schreiber select such as he really wants. . . . The hotels here are overflowing with the staff under pay and nothing to do. It is the town talk here and if the Government do not act promptly there will bye and bye be an explosion that will do you no good.[30]

With such warnings before it, the cabinet could not afford to permit Winnipeg's disaffection over delays and waste to spread. On October 4, they chose the Fraser route, Fleming received his orders, and the preparation of specifications for the B.C. program was swiftly undertaken.

When the tenders were called for, in late October, Marcus Smith seized upon them immediately:

30. Macdonald Papers, Brydges to Macdonald, 26 September, 13 and 25 October, 22 November, 1879.

> Fleming and Tupper have everything now their own way. They suppress maps and Reports and everything else that does not suit their views and set Members of the House and Senate at defiance. Look at the enormous quantities of 1st class masonry for which there is not the slightest necessity in these [B.C.] sections. If it is ever allowed to be carried out then the members of Parliament and the people must be as insane as the Chief Engineer.[31]

Similar letters giving comparative figures which favoured the Bute route went to Brydges and Macpherson. "I have a strong impression that Tupper is the only member of the Gov't. who is pushing this matter – to save Fleming – and that the latter is wilfully misleading the Govt."[32] Once the choice of the Burrard route was no longer an issue, Smith had only shifted the grounds of his criticism to questions of Fleming's engineering competence and of the Tupper–Fleming combination. These letters were having their effect, for Macpherson and Brydges in their turn raised the same points as frequently in a barrage of letters to Sir John A. Macdonald. Matters moved toward a head in late October, when Smith wrote to Macpherson and Brydges a detailed criticism of the proposed B.C. works, concluding with his own proposals for "a *cheap* railway" and with a stern warning about "the Tupper, Fleming combination".[33] On November 2, Senator Macpherson wrote urgently to Macdonald,

> I wrote you a hurried note yesterday covering one from Brydges. . . . I fear it will devolve on me as the "Candid Friend" to expose the whole mismanagement & waste of time & money. . . . I said in my note of yesterday that if the mismanagement of the Ry. Dept. continued unimproved it would destroy your Govt. I might have gone further & have told you that it has already seriously honey-combed it. It is not strengthening to hear the Minister & Chief Engineer spoken of as Siamese Twins & that it is futile to contemplate a change of Eng. [*sic*] although disastrous mismanagement is rampant.[34]

31. Smith Papers, Smith to Macdonald, 31 October, 1879.
32. *Ibid.*, Smith to Brydges, 4 November, 1879; Smith to Macpherson, 19 November, 1879.
33. *Ibid.*, Smith to Macpherson, 27 and 28 October, 1879.
34. Macdonald Papers, Macpherson to Macdonald, 2 November, 1879.

Macdonald had no reason to protect Sandford Fleming, and much cause to wish to protect Charles Tupper from what appeared to be his own folly. The chief victim of 1872 could not risk another great railway scandal. Tupper might soon succeed him, and Tupper must be persuaded to drop Fleming immediately.

Sometime in late November, Sir John A. Macdonald met with Charles Tupper to lay the decision before him. Tupper's reaction was immediate: shock and distaste. Early in December he confronted Macdonald with a diversionary issue: a promise had not been fulfilled to his son, Stewart Tupper, of certain legal business in Winnipeg in connection with western lands; Macdonald was asked to intercede. It was their last letter for sixteen months. Sir Joseph Pope recorded this fact in the Macdonald Papers immediately following the letter concerning Stewart Tupper: "During this period (1880-1) there was an interruption of personal intercourse between Macdonald and Tupper owing to a difference in no way connected with public policy. Sir C. Tupper told me this in 1893."[35] Writing to his second son, Hibbert, in 1889, Tupper had this to say about Macdonald on an occasion when Hibbert was at odds with Sir John over Sandford Fleming's successor, Collingwood Schreiber:

> He [Sir John] has his faults I grant you, but who has
> not? If I was compelled to sacrifice my chief engineer
> in my own department & submit as I did in opposition
> to my own opinions and wishes, ... I do not think that
> you should desert the important post you hold. . . .
> [consider] the great responsibility involved in leaving
> a ministry except for some grave difference upon an
> important question of public policy. I am very glad
> that I did not when strongly tempted make that mis-
> take.[36]

But Charles Tupper was not so philosophic in 1879-80, and he immediately put strong pressure upon Fleming to force his staff into greater efficiency. As Fleming observed to one of his wavering, alcoholic subordinates: "Do let me know what is going on. . . . The Minister is very exacting & impulsive & I find it hard at times to keep matters moving smoothly."[37] But the demands from Brydges and

35. *Ibid.*, p. 129367.
36. Tupper Papers, C. Tupper to C. H. Tupper, 7 & 8 July, 1889.
37. Fleming Papers, Fleming to J. Rowan, 11 December, 1879.

Macpherson continued, Thomas White was unrelenting in publishing scathing letters and editorials in the Montreal *Gazette*, and Sir John Macdonald must have remained equally insistent. On January 12, a breach between Tupper and Fleming arose in an interview, abruptly terminated by Tupper, in which they reviewed the prospects of reduced costs, particularly in British Columbia. Later in the day, Fleming wrote a fifteen-page letter of self-justification, but it could not rescue a broken friendship and association. As Tupper recalled in a letter to Macdonald nearly twenty years later, "it must not be forgotten that Mr. Fleming was so hostile to the construction of a cheap road that a quarrel took place between us on that point and he only yielded when I told him in so many words that I would get another Engineer to take his place."[38] But Charles Tupper had been brought to this course only under the greatest pressure. That pressure had come, however, not only from John Macdonald but also from rumours reaching Tupper of Fleming's readiness to work with the Liberals during the Mackenzie era in ways quite outside his official duties. On at least two occasions during the mid-70s, Fleming had been active in entering into private railroad ventures with known Liberal supporters.[39] Neither arrangement amounted to much, but to Macdonald, and to a lesser degree to Tupper, they must have raised questions.

Tupper's slow response to Macdonald's instructions to disown Fleming, however, and his failure to see the threat to party unity must have greatly weakened his power and his claims to the succession. Consequently, while there appeared no indication that Fleming would be toppled or that Tupper himself had been eclipsed, Macpherson, White and their colleagues persisted throughout the late winter of 1879-80 until their objectives were accomplished.

In March 1880, the House opened debate on the spiralling cost of the C.P.R. project. Immediately, discontent in government ranks concerning Sandford Fleming was dramatically revealed. The Liberal-Conservative member for Glengarry, John McLennan, undertook an exacting examination of the government's railway policy, specifically the expenditures on two contracts which were in excess of the estimates by 32 per cent and 80 per cent.

McLennan had drawn his information from the earlier Report of

38. Tupper Papers, Tupper to Macdonald, 30 September, 1889.
39. For example, his negotiations with D. Blain in Fleming Papers, 1874.

the Macpherson Committee. But he repeated certain charges against Sandford Fleming, and the object of the debate shifted significantly from Pacific Railway contracts to the question of Fleming's competence. The question of Fleming's "very long holiday" was resurrected, as was the "singular want of harmony between the Chief and the subordinates" left in charge. Yet the anomalous question of the chief engineer's salary provided McLennan with his most controversial material:

> The Chief Engineer states he had drawn no salary, that no salary was fixed, but that he expected to be rewarded for his work. This, I think, may be assumed to indicate a lack of control. I can hardly conceive how a Government could control an engineer, who was merely an amateur at his work. The only other position that could be assumed is that he occupied the position which an architect occupied, and with which I dare say many hon. members of this House are familiar, the position which an architect occupies who leads one on in an expenditure beginning very moderately and going higher and higher.[40]

When Sir John A. Macdonald interjected, "Led on by a towering ambition", the coalition against Fleming was complete.

The spectre of rapidly snowballing expenditures haunted McLennan, for he considered that the object should have been to construct a "rapid route" in preference to "a first-class road". Yet he was bothered even more by Alexander Mackenzie's statement in the House in 1878, to the effect that Fleming had had an influence upon matters of policy. McLennan argued:

> . . . I think this House will agree with me that the proper adviser of the Government upon all questions of policy in connection with that undertaking is not the Chief Engineer, or any body of engineers, but this House. This, I hope, would be conceded by the present Government, otherwise I could hardly support them.[41]

McLennan thus revealed how far Fleming had become a bone of contention within the Liberal-Conservative party. Fleming was de-

40. House of Commons Debates, 1880, vol. 1, pp. 381-82.
41. Ibid., p. 383.

scribed by McLennan as the "great power behind the Throne" within the Mackenzie administration.

McLennan, White and their colleagues, however, had for some time feared that Fleming had become a power behind Macdonald's throne through his connection with Charles Tupper. This alarm had greatly increased with Macdonald's attack in 1879, but on March 21, 1880, soon after the new session had begun, their mood turned to one of near panic. On that day Macdonald had been struck down once more while in church, and within forty-eight hours he had advised his ministers of his decision to retire immediately. The issue of the succession could not have come at a more difficult time for Senator Macpherson, who was himself still recuperating at home from an illness of his own. In despair he wrote to Macdonald that his resignation now would cause such consternation in Conservative ranks as "that which reigned at St. Petersburg on the occasion of the explosion in the Winter Palace."[42]

On March 25 Macdonald met his cabinet, which was as Professor Creighton described it, "a company of Macphersons". Macdonald yielded, but if his spirit was willing many of his colleagues knew how frail was his health. Tupper's succession had yet to be put down by his enemies, and Charles Tupper in rising in the House to reply to John McLennan's criticisms knew that he spoke not only in defence of Sandford Fleming, but also of himself.

The minister began in a conciliatory tone, expressing pleasure that McLennan had taken an interest in the railway question. Yet he did not agree with his colleague:

> . . . I cannot go as far as the hon. gentleman had done in intimating that the hon. Minister should accept the advice of any hon. gentleman in this Chamber as more entitled to consideration on this subject than that of the Chief Engineer. If that were done I am afraid we would not make rapid progress with the construction of the Canadian Pacific Railway.[43]

Tupper then recounted how Fleming had been chosen chief engineer of the Intercolonial at a salary of $4,800. Because ministers only received $5,000 per annum at that time, it had been thought inap-

42. Creighton, *The Old Chieftain*, pp. 281-82.
43. House of Commons Debates, 1880, vol. 1, p. 386.

propriate to pay a civil servant more; as a result, Fleming had received no salary for his work on the C.P.R. He had continued in
this capacity until 1876 when he asked for leave of absence on
grounds of ill health from overwork. In Tupper's eyes the chief engineer had carried out his duties competently and had done nothing to
compromise his position. The minister admitted that great expenditures had taken place, but that they had been unavoidable given the
distances and nature of the terrain. Further, he objected to the "somewhat severe strictures of the hon. member for Glengarry in reference
to the administration of the Department", maintaining that the
Ministry of Railways and Canals had been conducted in "the most
expeditious and economical manner".[44]

In effect, however, the statements made by Tupper in defence of
Fleming and himself did nothing to resolve the questions existing
in many members' minds concerning the C.P.R. and its chief engineer.
Indeed, they contributed to a hardening of feelings within government ranks. Within two months the Minister for Railways had again
to defend Sandford Fleming from the criticisms of his fellow Conservatives.

Early in May the Conservative caucus, spurred on by its Ontario
members, determined to face the crises over railway policy and party
unity. Galt's earlier proposal for a Royal Commission on railways
would be adopted; Sandford Fleming would be deposed. Tupper
fought loyally before the caucus on Fleming's behalf; his attitude toward the proposal for a commission was charged with suspicion and
a grudging acquiescence. But on May 22, cabinet passed the appropriate order-in-council establishing Galt's commission, and inviting
Sandford Fleming to accept a demotion to the position of consulting
engineer on the Canadian Pacific and a return to his older position
of chief engineer on the Intercolonial.

Fleming declined the proposals. His departure from the C.P.R. took
place by default, not by resignation. His career as a public servant
was at an end, but his ambitions as a private entrepreneur and pub-
licist had just begun. It was the turning-point of his life, and it was
the climax of his long, intimate association with Charles Tupper.

For Tupper it had been a dramatic test of strength, and he had
lost. Within months he succumbed to exhaustion, and illness. His
departure from active participation in cabinet came about soon after

44. *Ibid.*, p. 388.

Senator Macpherson joined it as Minister without Portfolio. Tupper's role as heir apparent was ended. While his relations with Macdonald improved after their sharp break in 1880-81 – Tupper's later useful-ness as High Commissioner was defended by Macdonald against party critics – he was never again the party's great electoral strategist or Macdonald's close adviser and confidant. The problem of the proper relationship between the senior civil servant and his political chiefs, as revealed in the Fleming crisis, had left its legacy for Macdonald and for the Conservative party.

Canadian Opinion and Foreign Policy

G. P. deT. GLAZEBROOK

It is an assumption in this paper that, in a democracy, public opinion should be brought to bear on foreign policy as on other matters for which Parliament and government are responsible. To some extent this particular field has, in older countries, been regarded as different to others. Such matters as taxation, education, transportation facilities, or agriculture have immediate application to the everyday lives of the people of a country. Foreign policy, however, has been a victim of two contradictory extremes.

On the one hand it has been thought of as esoteric, designed and conducted in secrecy by men initiated into its mysteries and speaking a special language. There is a modicum of truth in the point of view. In relations between governments, as between private persons or business organizations, some degree of secrecy is necessary. It should not and need not follow, however, that a parliament or a people is prevented from discussing and influencing the trends in the government's policy on this as on any other subject. On the other hand the second extreme may then be reached, leading individuals to suppose that they can pronounce on every detail of foreign affairs without the study due to any complicated question.

Such general considerations as these have been relevant in Canada as elsewhere, but others have given abnormal slants to the Canadian approach. The Dominion of 1867 was made up of colonies which had long been involved in various aspects of external affairs, such as trade, immigration, defence, and finance. One of the arguments in favour of Confederation was that it would facilitate the pursuit of these subjects. It was not, however, a part of the union plan that Canada should be a sovereign state; and international custom dictated that only sovereign states might conduct diplomatic relations with each other. The Dominion, like its component parts, was a unit in the British Empire, and although it was suggested in general terms that its status in the world would be higher than had been that of the separate colonies, no effort was made to translate that ambition into constitutional terms. Thus Canada was a colony, if an advanced one, and its international relations could proceed only through London.

A peculiarity of a different kind lay in Canada's juxtaposition to a country likewise made up of former British colonies but born in a revolution that left scars which healed slowly. Relations with that other new country, the United States, have constituted a main theme in Canadian history, so that "Canadian-American relations" have formed a major subject for study, and at times have seemed to be a national obsession. Nearly every aspect of human affairs has been involved in these relations, including war, trade, finance, migration, literature and the arts. The old provinces had suffered military invasions, and many of their inhabitants feared and a few desired political annexation. Americans came to live in Canada and Canadians moved to the greater economic opportunities in the United States. The similarity between the two countries was as great an irritant as the dissimilarities, and of the latter perhaps the dominating one was the disparity in power.

It can never be easy for a minor country to live next door to a great one, but if they are of different background, race, and language neither may expect the other to conform to its code. As these two countries grew up side by side having, apart from the slavery issue, similar social conditions and an intermixture of people, the one grew so rapidly in population and wealth that it need have little concern for the struggling dominion next door. Canadians, on the other hand, could never be oblivious of their great neighbour. Sometimes apprehensive of its power, commonly, if secretly, envious of its success, they consoled themselves by criticism of its domestic and foreign policies, a habit which time only accentuated.

The other great power which chiefly influenced Canada was the centre of the Empire and, for the majority of Canadians, the mother country. For those of French descent there was no comparable pole of attraction. For them there was no constitutional link with their own mother country, and further, nineteenth-century France had traced paths along which the descendants of her sons who had settled on the Atlantic coast and the banks of the St. Lawrence had no wish to follow. They could not be expected to have the same feeling for the United Kingdom as their fellow citizens of British extraction. Although that was a situation which could be divisive, and to some extent was, it by no means led to a neat distinction between those who supported and those who opposed British foreign and imperial policies.

The principal arguments of those who favoured backing Britain in days of need were two: because it was Britain, and because its continued power was important for Canada. The first has sometimes been described as "sentiment", a dangerous word in view of its several meanings, but in this connection usually intended to imply an emotional rather than a rational approach. Such a contrast is in itself subjective, whereas many of those people were thinking in terms of common traditions and objectives. They and others might also be putting weight on another consideration, the maintenance of British strength. If there were enough evidence (which there is not) or if an historian could identify the motives governing individual Canadian responses to such crises as the Indian Mutiny, the Crimean War, the Boer War, or the German threat to British naval supremacy, it would throw a great deal of light on Canadian thinking. All that is certain is that Canadian opinion, while far from unanimous, effectively favoured the imperial cause.

Because of the constitutional position prevailing for some fifty to sixty years after Confederation, Britain held the door to other capitals of the world, so that any Canadian foreign relations had to be indirect. Trade arrangements were worked out satisfactorily under a procedure by which British ambassadors cast no more than a formal mantle over negotiations substantively conducted by Canadian representatives; but political questions – high policy – were not similarly devolved. Thus Canadians, not in the driver's seat, tended to become back-seat drivers; developing strong views about the operation of the vehicle without much direct experience of road hazards. Without authority or immediate responsibility they had little chance to learn the governing principles of foreign policy: to establish priorities, accepting losses in the less essential matters; adjusting the intransigence of their position to the sanctions they could command.

The Treaty of Washington and the Alaska boundary dispute illustrate weaknesses from both the British and the Canadian points of view. In the first case the governing British objective was to reach an over-all settlement that would lead to more than nominal peace between themselves and the Americans. Although this was to their advantage, Canadians had their own axes to grind and protested that the treaty was reached by sacrificing their interests. It was true that the Canadian prime minister was a member of the British team, but he seems to have seen his responsibility not as taking part in the general bargaining but in securing the best results in those subjects, such as the fisheries, which directly affected Canada. Given the fact that the instructions to the delegation came from London and not from Ottawa, he may well have been right.

Canadians were even more indignant about the conclusion of the Alaska arbitration. They assumed that their claim was just, and that therefore justice should and must triumph. They seem to have given little attention to the chauvinistic stance of the American government or to have weighed the relative advantages of a strip of land on the one hand and the risk of armed conflict or at least strained relations on the other. Whether the British representative on the arbitration commission threw in the sponge for political reasons was a matter of opinion, but no one in Canada seems to have expressed at that time any doubt that the Canadian representatives were guided by evidence alone.

One cannot altogether blame adults for back-seat driving if they were excluded from the front seat, but two comments on their role may be relevant. One is that they were, inevitably, suggesting courses which they could not themselves pursue and for the results of which they could not be called upon to accept responsibility. The other is to recall that on a number of occasions Laurier and others announced that it would be better if Canada conducted her own foreign relations rather than leaving them to the British to mishandle. Perhaps it would have been better, but there is no evidence that this is what the Canadian public wanted even if the constitutional difficulties could

be overcome, far less that they were prepared to pay for it. Neither
Liberal nor Conservative governments showed for many years a
desire to get any nearer to the establishment of a foreign office than
the maintenance of a better filing system.

Given the fact that Canada neither designed nor operated its own
foreign policy there was, unavoidably, utter confusion between
foreign and imperial relations. Ideas on the proper nature of the imperial structure were influenced by considerations of foreign policy. If
the fact of empire might draw Canada into the vortex of European
militarism would it not be better to cut the links of empire? When
Britain's sea power came to be no longer unquestioned and Canadian
majority opinion favoured maintaining a favourable balance by sup-
plementing that power, what followed politically? Should there be
some sort of political integration for the direction of defence or, on
the contrary, a kind of allied relationship? One would tighten the
bonds of empire, the other loosen them. Those whose minds were set
on maintaining an integrated empire tended to want foreign and defence policies that would express that objective; others who were
looking forward to independence, or some modified form of it, objected to any commitments abroad that they considered to be of an
imperial character.

Amidst this criss-cross of imperial and foreign factors it is not easy
to detect the identification of national objectives, other than trade, in
foreign affairs. Indeed there is here the appearance of a negative
quality in the outlook of many Canadians because of their concern
that they would be drawn into some undesired course by British
policy. Certainly Canadian participation in the War of 1914 was
robustly positive, but the negative or indirect trend showed again in
the constant references to supporting Britain and France. Only a
handful of people attempted to define the Canadian interest in the
war, to assess the kind of world in which Canada would find herself
if Germany were triumphant and Canada's closest friends were
rendered helpless. The reply to the call to aid the mother country
evoked the question: why help other people?

In the latter part of the war a *modus vivendi* for intra-imperial
relations on foreign affairs was worked out that was something between an alliance and the otherwise obsolete plan of imperial federation. Sir Robert Borden's point of view on imperial questions was in
fact more elastic and less formalized than would appear from his lectures and public statements. In this case he was being purely prac-

tical, dealing with an immediate situation. Canada was heavily involved in the war and he was not satisfied (nor was Lloyd George) with the way in which it was being conducted by the British. Borden therefore demanded a voice in decisions on strategy, and the machinery evolved to meet that demand worked well during the remainder of the war, at the peace conference in Paris, and in the conference at Washington on the Far East.

There is no indication that Borden conceived of continuous consultation as providing a permanent solution; and in fact it could have done so only if the foreign interests of the United Kingdom and the various dominions had remained essentially the same. Two test cases soon revealed that their interests were not identical. In the discussions at London on the renewal of the Anglo-Japanese alliance the Canadian prime minister, satisfied that American opinion was markedly hostile to renewal, set himself to make that impossible. It is indicative of the state of Canadian opinion at the time that, while almost no attention was given to the contrary views of Australia and New Zealand, the success of Meighen in turning the decision against renewal was depicted as a triumphant defeat of British intentions only. Nor does it seem that in arriving at a position on the alliance the Canadian government took into account the effect that termination of the treaty might have in the Far East. Unlike the British, Canadians were not obliged to take a global view; and unlike the New Zealanders and Australians, they lived in North America. From the point of view of Ottawa the London meeting was a great success; whether it was a success in the wider world pattern is less certain.

A similar situation arose in 1922 out of the crisis in the Near East. After the failure of an ambitious Greek campaign into the heart of Asiatic Turkey the Nationalist Turks advanced toward the Straits and the British found themselves in danger of being the sole defenders of that strategic area. Lloyd George, who had backed the Greeks, looked around for help and telegraphed to the Australian, New Zealand, and Canadian governments, asking if they would associate themselves with Britain on the issue and would wish to send contingents if war broke out. The Australians and New Zealanders, to whom the control of the Mediterranean was important, agreed on both points, but in Ottawa there was consternation.

It is typical of the confusion between imperial and foreign affairs that at the time, and since, the Chanak affair should be represented as an episode in the constitutional history of the Empire. Mackenzie

King wrote in his diary that Lloyd George's cable was "drafted designedly to play the imperial game, to test out centralization vs. autonomy as regards European wars". Since the British had no power, even if they had the will, to force Canadian participation, and since it had long been recognized that the despatch of troops abroad was entirely for Canadian decision, it appears that what King was nervous about was Canadian opinion. Not even his own cabinet was unanimous, and the cry of "Britain in danger" would have divided the public, although in what proportions no one can say.

The Near Eastern problem faded out so that no such test of Canadian opinion was called for; but its real significance for Canada lay in the revelation that an imperial foreign policy was no longer possible since the various parts of the Empire had different problems and consequently wished to pursue different paths. In any discussion of these two incidents, it has been the tradition among Canadian commentators to assume that Australians and New Zealanders were more amenable to British requests. But it is well to remember that their interests, like those of Canada, were influenced by the imperatives of their geography. They were Far Eastern countries, and had to think in terms of balance of power there, and of communications with Europe. Perhaps, therefore, the distinction between their points of view and those held in Canada were not so great as might appear. A growing number of Canadians were feeling their way toward a policy of limited liability on the basis of their geographical position. That in itself, combined with the progress of Canadian nationalism, suggested that they should direct their own foreign affairs.

The private and public debates of the nineteen-twenties and thirties offer a rich mine of opinion on what Canadian foreign policy should be. An obvious limitation lay in the lack of interest shown by Parliament, for the members – perhaps rightly – did not regard foreign policy as a subject of general interest to constituents. A characteristic of the discussions, as a distinguished Canadian soldier angrily pointed out, was that they were so much directed to war. A weakness came perhaps from lack of experience, which resulted in devotion to fixed formulas, disregarding the cumulative effect of small daily steps on the one hand and the possibility of unexpected international situations on the other.

Of the many views advanced[1] two were at extreme poles. It was

1. For an analysis of opinion see R. A. MacKay and E. B. Rogers, *Canada Looks Abroad* (London and Toronto, 1938).

held by some Canadians that the Empire (or the Commonwealth as it was coming to be called) should be a unit in foreign affairs; but that, as has been suggested, could obtain only if the foreign interests of the United Kingdom and the dominions were identical. At the other end of the line were those who urged isolationism. They claimed that Europe should solve its own problems and that Canada should mind its own business in North America. Such a point of view found more support in the Province of Quebec than elsewhere, but it had obvious objections. The Canadian economy depended so heavily on its export trade that Canada could not be wholly detached from world affairs. An even more compelling factor was that Canadian isolation would not necessarily be accepted by other countries.

Between these extremes a series of compromises were examined. Collective security through the League of Nations was thought by some contemporaries to be not only a means of maintaining international peace but also of solving the problems of intra-Commonwealth relations. The difficulty with this approach, however, was that little support was found in Canada for the enforcement of League rule through economic and military sanctions. Even those who most earnestly protested their faith in collective security were likely to add in small print that Canada could not be committed to action except by its own Parliament. In practice that meant that the League could be assured of a role no greater than the peaceful settlement of international disputes, any sanctions being applicable only in the unlikely event that all the governments concerned quickly agreed to put them into force.

Neutrality in the event of war was discussed in two different connections. One was the argument that Canada should, whatever the circumstances, be neutral in a war in which Britain was involved. It was a point of view which had limited support and had the obvious disadvantage of inflexibility. The other argument was, somewhat misleadingly, known as "the right to neutrality" although what in fact it meant was the achievement of a constitutional position in which a Canadian declaration of neutrality would be recognized by foreign states: or, more exactly, that if that position did not already obtain (and that was arguable) it should be attained. The two conceptions of neutrality inevitably became confused, leading some people to oppose the second on the ground that it implied the first.

However faulty the discussions of this period about the right foreign policy for Canada, at least they did show an adult desire to think out the national interest. But a time lag put limits to the progress that was being made. Although it had long been obvious, even before the Balfour declaration of 1926 and the Statute of Westminster in 1931, that Canada was free to pursue whatever paths it might choose (to the extent that it could), too many Canadians failed to think in terms of the mechanics of doing so. Instead of equipping themselves with the civil and military establishments needed for an independent role, and learning the game of diplomacy as quickly as possible, they kept turning their eyes to British policy, on which they were more than ready to pontificate. No separate minister of external affairs was appointed until 1946; the department was far too small for the specialized knowledge needed; few missions were set up abroad; and the armed services were starved.

Sometimes it seemed that the staunchest opponents of what they called "imperialism" were determined to think in colonial terms, to judge by their reluctance to concentrate on formulating Canadian foreign interests rather than commenting on British policy. J. W. Dafoe, editor of the *Manitoba Free Press*, was one of the few who followed in this respect a clear line of thought (even if he painted cloudy pictures of those who did not happen to agree with him). Writing to Borden at the beginning of 1923 he expressed his firm opinion that the Empire should not be a unit in world affairs although "there can be a moral unity of the Commonwealth which will insure common action on all occasions when it is necessary". Canada should not be committed to British policies, "on the other hand the British government's freedom of action should not be limited by a supposed necessity for consulting with Canada on matters of policy affecting her own interests. . . . Canada, for instance, is not competent to determine British policy with respect to the United States."

In defining his own position to Sir Clifford Sifton in 1921, Dafoe distinguished between it and that held by the Ottawa lawyer, J. S. Ewart:

> The time has come for Canada to become in the face of the world an independent and sovereign power, attaining such status she will feel herself free and willing to co-operate with other British peoples in matters of common concern so far as the methods of co-operation which are worked out meet with their approval. That strikes the average Canadian as an entirely proper pro-

> position. But Ewart's line of urging Canadians to secure
> their entire independence in order that they may have
> nothing to do with Great Britain which he represents
> as a wholly reactionary Imperialistic nation will not
> get him anywhere.[2]

No doubt Dafoe was right in his estimate of the public reaction to Ewart's point of view, but whether the "average Canadian" – if there was one – agreed with his own is much less certain. A powerful body of Canadian opinion would go less far than he, advocating a close relationship with Britain in foreign affairs. Henri Bourassa's position was somewhat different from Ewart's and Dafoe's. He cherished, he said, a continuing connection with what he called the "true England" but was entirely opposed to Canada being drawn into support of "imperial England".

Whatever other criticisms may be levelled against Mackenzie King's imperial and foreign policies he did at least retain freedom of action. His support of the League of Nations was lukewarm, he used supposedly imperialistic plots as makeweights in domestic policies, for years he did nothing to advance the growth of the armed forces or the Department of External Affairs (of which he was minister). At times he applied to foreign affairs his remarkable capacity for confusing an issue, but he never committed himself to any fixed course as some of his countrymen would have done. Thus the war of 1939 could be judged according to the circumstances of the day. Although King was meticulous in placing responsibility for participation on Parliament he failed to emphasize that his government advocated entry on grounds of Canadian interest, although an obvious case could have been made. It was the same mistake as that of 1914 and with less excuse. The old theme of being at Britain's side appealed, of course, to a great many Canadians but failed to convince others.

The state of mind in Canada after the Second World War was, up to a point, similar to that after the First in that a general consensus existed in favour of taking steps to avoid a repetition; but there was a difference in that no sense of finality marked the second postwar period. Once bitten twice shy, perhaps. The lessons of the thirties were more convincing later than at the time. The United Nations organization was seen as an improved version of the League; and it,

2. Ramsay Cook, *The Dafoe-Sifton Correspondence, 1919-1927* (Altona, Manitoba, 1966), p. 72.

together with related agencies, was to look after reconstruction and security. Soviet policy, however, rendered the UN helpless in political security (the Korean case being an example rather than an exception); and it was the Soviet Union that came to be regarded as the threat to peace. Hence it became necessary to plug the hole in the UN by creating the NATO military alliance as protection against that new danger. Later the North American Air Defense Command was agreed to with the United States in the light of the strategic situation in the continent.

The Canadian government took an active part in the development of these postwar policies, which, according to all the indications, were generally acceptable to the Canadian people. The communist danger was considered to be amply demonstrated by, for example, the revelation of Russian espionage in 1946, the Berlin blockade of 1948, the Korean War of 1950, suppression of the Hungarian nationalists in 1956, propaganda – considered seditious – conducted throughout Canada, and what was deemed to be a generally hostile attitude of Moscow towards the West. For a time, however, such military adventures ceased while the message of Moscow to capitalist countries was skilfully rewritten: The régime in the Soviet Union, ran the new version, has defects but these will be cured in time. Western countries admittedly offer present advantages to the individual. The Soviet Union, on the other hand, is devoted to the cause of humanism. Thus, while capitalism can lead only to a dead end, communism opens the way to a positive future. That the Russian application of humanism in Czechoslovakia in 1968 was of a strictly old-fashioned Russian nature (whether pre- or post-revolution) had curiously little effect on Canadian opinion. The destruction of budding liberalism and independence was not regarded – as it would have been ten years earlier – as a warning. The pendulum had already swung, apprehension of communist hostility had waned, and other influences were at work.

In the nineteen-sixties the consensus on the main lines of Canadian foreign policy dissolved; and hosts of politicians, academics, and journalists expressed opinions on the subject with a confidence that in other circumstances would have suggested deep study and expert knowledge. After some twenty years during which even the competing political parties had found it difficult to differ on foreign policy the field was open to debate. Whether or not because of increased public interest, Parliament devoted more time to foreign affairs: no longer in the form of a handful of members listening with respect but limited interest to ministers, but in vigorous exchange of conflicting points of view.

Civil servants responsible for different aspects of foreign affairs have been placed collectively under the public microscope with conclusions not always encouraging. It is an excellent British tradition that experts should be kept in their place, that war is too serious to be left to generals; but the recent grounds for criticism of civil servants, while not new, are somewhat puzzling and contradictory. One is that the civil servant has too much influence on policy, that he is, in contemporary jargon, a member of the "establishment" (a word which seems to apply to any influential group of which the user of the word is not a member). It would be odd if men and women paid to acquire and make use of specialized knowledge offered no opinions to their minister. If the latter allows himself to be overruled after due discussion he is ill-equipped for his role.

No one is more conscious of the danger of bureaucracy than the trained civil servant, but the other main public comment urges him to be a bureaucrat. This, as applied specially to the diplomat, takes the form of a demand that he be "moral" in the performance of his duties; and this proves to mean that he should follow his own subjective views of morality, confident of his own rightness. Oblivious of his immediate employer, the government, and of his ultimate employer, the public, he is asked to revert to a sixteenth-century concept of absolute right and wrong. If, in his wisdom, he concludes that his instructions are not moral he is presumably called upon to resign his position. How to follow both these precepts at once may well be the main challenge to the civil servant.

While the public may rightly concern itself with administration of policy, its main focus will be directed to the policy itself. From that point of view no one could do other than welcome the growing volume of expressed opinions, the open debate on what foreign policies should be followed by Canada. In a brief essay it is out of the question to attempt anything like a comprehensive account of the many views put forward in recent years; it is possible only to draw attention to some which have been conspicuously advanced. Their wisdom may in due course be tested in the ballot box. The adjective game has many adherents, but the description of foreign policy as, for example, "effective", "meaningful", "progressive", or "dynamic" is intelligible only to the speaker and one must await his translation.

To one adjective, "independent", however, more attention must be given since it touches on so many questions fundamental to Canada.[3]

It has been argued that we should have an "independent" foreign policy, which indeed has been the ambition of virtually every sovereign state since time immemorial, but one seldom realized. At its height the Roman Empire succeeded in having one; Napoleon did not. From Trafalgar to the end of the century Britain could rest virtual independence on absolute sea power combined with financial and commercial strength. But that power did not last, and Britain joined the long list of countries which had to adjust their policies to the exigencies of the world scene. Perhaps, therefore, by "independence" is not meant complete freedom of action without regard to national power and the restrictions created by conflicting intentions of other states. The word might, alternatively, refer to a policy of non-alignment, as professedly followed by a number of states, including India. If so, that would assume that a careful analysis of Canadian foreign interests and capacity to secure them produced the conclusion that Canada could act by itself; that it needed no allies in attaining its objectives; needed neither to give nor to receive commitments to joint action in defined eventualities. Non-alignment would not, of course, preclude membership in the United Nations.

A third meaning attached to "independent" in recent writing appears to relate in various ways to the United States. The occasional implication that Canadian policy should be different to that of the United States only for the sake of being different can hardly be taken seriously. A view which has been more commonly expressed is that foreign policies have been forced on Canada by the United States, a situation comparable to that in parts of Eastern Europe. To some extent the argument seems to be based on the *post hoc propter hoc* fallacy, by which it could equally be deduced that Canada downgraded NATO and moved to recognize Communist China because France had done the same. A little further stretch of the imagination would have the United States twice declaring war on Germany because Canada had already done so.

Some writers, however, claim the application of undue pressure in conversations and negotiations even if the evidence is presumptive and the accounts unrecognizable to those who had participated. It

3. Various views are expressed in a recent collection of essays, Stephen Clarkson (ed.), *An Independent Foreign Policy for Canada?* (Toronto, 1968).

would be abnormal if, between two friendly governments, each did not attempt to influence the other. At times suggestions and inter- pretations may be welcomed, and Canada has in fact gained from its ready access to the information and thinking in the Department of State, as it has long gained from close contact in London, Canberra, Wellington, and other capitals. It remains true, of course, that Canada should not allow itself to be induced by the United States (or any other country) to follow policies or take action in particular cases which are not, in the judgment of its government and parlia- ment, in Canada's best interest. The difficulty, however, is that "best interest" may be – and indeed is – disputed among Canadians; and therefore any parallels between American and Canadian policies may be judged desirable or undesirable according to personal views of what Canadian foreign policy should be.

Some cloudiness of thought is caused by the presence of ghosts breathing down the necks of speakers and writers (if ghosts may be allowed metaphorical breath). Some of these unwelcome wraiths bring the message of anti-Americanism, that is, emotion rather than rational argument. Sometimes this deplorable Canadian weakness is attributed to the United Empire Loyalists. Some of them, no doubt, had reason for such a state of mind but others were on the wrong side in the War of 1812. Perhaps anti-Americanism is inherently due more to the defensive attitude of a smaller power in relation to a great one, which at its worst can be the political and economic equivalent of inverted snobbery. Other ghosts are those of the back- seat drivers. In their mortal form some half-century ago they had at least the excuse of having nowhere else to sit, but that is not a condi- tion applying to their successors. No Canadian has been more per- sistent and more influential in demanding an "independent" Cana- dian foreign policy than was J. W. Dafoe; and no one was more clear-headed on one of its corollaries, that other countries should equally be allowed independence in designing their own. It is normal for one country to dissociate itself from the actions of another, even to express disagreement, as for example, the Canadian government did when the Indians invaded Goa. No doubt other countries think at times that some Canadian foreign policies are ill-advised and have every right to say so.

And yet some Canadians who most vocally demand an "indepen- dent" policy for themselves are not prepared to concede the same freedom to others. One would have thought that the problems of settling Canadian policy were enough without demanding action on the part of others for which you should then logically take a share of responsibility. Some Canadians have been prepared to tell the British how to resolve the Rhodesian problem or the Americans that of south-east Asia. Perhaps they are right and all would go well if only they heeded Canadian advice, but if not, should Canadians then resign any responsibility?

In recent years much has been said and written on what Canadian foreign policy ought to be, and it is appropriate that opinion should differ regarding a subject on which no one will wisely lay down simple formulas. There are, too, many silent Canadians. What kind of foreign policy appeals to the farmers of southern Ontario and Quebec, the lumbermen of British Columbia, fishermen in the outports of Newfoundland, immigrants from eastern and southern Europe? Perhaps from the diverse thoughts of Canadians in different areas and circumstances may come a consensus of the national interest. It is probable, however, that foreign policy will never be examined in detail by more than a relatively small number of individuals, those with the advantages of advanced education, travel, and taste for continuing study. Such men and women may, it is hoped, feel called upon to widen the circle of informed opinion, so that the factors in world affairs and Canadian interests in relation to them may be understood. Only by such means can an educated Canadian opinion on foreign affairs be developed.

Macdonald's Conservative Successors, 1891-1896

LOVELL C. CLARK

The four Conservative leaders following Sir John A. Macdonald are surely Canada's forgotten prime ministers. Some students of the nation's history might feel inclined to add that they deserved this fate. Yet the obscurity in which they have languished is unjust, since during their terms of office they had to face important national issues and certainly at least two of them were men of considerable stature. Perhaps the neglect of the period is less of a commentary upon the forgotten prime ministers than upon the propensity of Canadians to gloss over contentious problems. In any case, both the men and events of 1891 to 1896 deserve closer scrutiny than they have yet received.

The Old Chieftain had left a varied legacy. This included national policies which were proving their worth as a blueprint for the country's development, impending scandals in several departments of government, a growing rift between French and English, and a leadership problem which was to recur a number of times in the next

five years. As a final bequest he left his government and party a
renewed lease on political office. Although it is not possible to discuss
here each aspect of this mixed inheritance, some comments are called
for in a general way before isolating the more significant details.

Macdonald's Conservative successors continued with the national
policies and sought to complement them in various ways which, if
space permitted, could readily be shown to have served Canada well
during a difficult period. Moreover, in spite of the disheartening
depression and the heavy emigration to the south, the country was
making creditable economic progress. In particular, it could be shown
that total Canadian trade rose to record levels during the severe
depression of the early 1890s, with exports accounting for most of the
increase. Also, contrary to what recent strictures on the national
policies of Macdonald Conservatism would lead one to suppose, the
Gross National Product per capita and manufacturing per capita were
both rising at a more rapid rate in Canada during the period 1880 to
1900 than in the United States. As regards the G.N.P. per capita, the
increase during the two decades was 54 per cent for Canada (66 per
cent using the Hartland estimate for G.N.P.) compared with 45 per
cent for the United States. In manufacturing per capita the per-
centage increases were 79.6 for Canada and 67.6 for the United
States.[1] These and other results are a striking vindication of the
National Policy of 1879.

That neither the depression nor the scandals caused the defeat of
the Conservatives seems clear from the results of the 84 by-elections
which took place between the general elections of 1891 and 1896. Of
these the Conservatives won 62 (for a net gain of 11 seats from the
Liberals), the Liberals 21, and an Independent 1.[2] If the Liberals
could not gain seats during years of acute hardship, especially from
1892 to 1895, their economic policies in the view of the electorate
apparently had little to commend them. No doubt the hard times
cost the Conservatives some votes in 1896 (particularly those gar-
nered by the Patron candidates), but their victory over the Liberals
outside Quebec and their defeat in that province suggest that it was

1. Calculated from the data in J. H. Dales, *The Protective Tariff in Canada's
   Economic Development*, p. 136. Professor Dales views the National Policy
   as a "dismal failure".
2. N. Omer Côté (ed.), *Political Appointments, Parliaments, and the Judicial
   Bench in the Dominion of Canada, 1867-1895* (Ottawa, 1896), pp. 285-95;
   ibid., 1896-1917 (Ottawa, 1917), pp. 126-28.

the Manitoba school question which toppled them from power. These considerations justify the major emphasis given here to the leaders and their manner of dealing with this overriding issue.

II

The first of Macdonald's successors was the wealthy Montreal lawyer and businessman, Senator John J. C. Abbott. The position had come to him very much by default. Sir Hector Langevin, who for some years had been the acknowledged heir, was of course ruled out owing to the impending scandal in his Department of Public Works. Sir Charles Tupper, Macdonald's long time comrade-in-arms, and now High Commissioner in London, declined to be considered and instead urged his son, Charles Hibbert Tupper, to give his "hearty support" to Sir John Thompson. He wrote his son that "I need not tell you how glad I will be if our mutual friend Thompson should be the man. His great ability, high legal attainments, forensic powers and above all his personal character all render his choice one of which our party and country should be proud."[3] Thompson was invited by the governor general, Lord Stanley, to form a government, but he too declined, knowing as he did that his being a convert to Roman Catholicism from Methodism had rendered him suspect with some Protestant elements of the Conservative party, especially the Orangemen of Ontario. He recommended that Abbott be sent for. The latter, in spite of his extreme dislike of politics and his ailing health, reluctantly accepted the post, and solely from a sense of duty to the country and the party. Abbott was (to use his own term) a "stop gap" prime minister, until such time as the party could bring itself to accept its first Roman Catholic leader.

The interim arrangement whereby Abbott led the government from the Senate while Thompson led in the House of Commons, worked out fairly well in spite of Abbott's reluctance to assume the leadership and his modest disclaimers as to his qualifications. The government survived the scandal session of 1891, at the price of jettisoning Langevin from the cabinet, and apparently displayed sufficient willingness to probe the allegations of wrong-doing to allay any misgivings which the public may have entertained. In the

3. Public Archives of Canada, Tupper Papers, 9, Tupper to C.H.T., June 4, 1891.

numerous by-elections held shortly afterwards the Liberals were decimated, particularly in the controverted elections, nearly every one of which resulted in the Liberal incumbent being unseated. This was not so much a testimony to the government's newly found purity as to the folly of the Liberal trade policy, which had aroused apprehensions that no amount of scandal or other shortcomings of the government could quell. The opposition policy was stigmatized as disloyal. Negotiations which the Abbott government conducted with Secretary of State James G. Blaine in February 1892, revealed that the United States would consider no treaty except one which required Canada to grant unlimited reciprocity to the United States and to discriminate in her tariff rates against Britain and other countries.[4]

In the meantime Abbott and others hoped that the Ontario wing of the party was gradually coming round to an acceptance of Thompson as prime minister. The reluctance of many Ontario members to accept a Roman Catholic as leader was a symptom of the malaise already weakening the party at the time of Macdonald's death, and which was later to render it incapable of dealing satisfactorily with the Manitoba school question. As Abbott's health deteriorated throughout the summer and autumn of 1892, Thompson received many letters assuring him of the support of the Protestant Conservatives of Ontario. The very protestations were ominous. Sam Hughes, newly elected M.P. and a prominent Ontario Orangeman, informed Thompson that the "boys" now found him acceptable. "What! the pervert? the ultramontane? the roman catholic? the defender of Mercier's Jesuit Estates Act? *Yes*, all say yes."[5] Nathaniel Clarke Wallace, M.P. for West York and Grand Master of the Orange Lodge of British America, wrote that: "No remedial legislation and Sir John Thompson for premier will be my standing ground and tho' you know that there will be strong opposition to both these propositions I shall do my very best with my friends in every emergency."[6] Abbott, when urging Thompson to accept the leadership, advised him "to strengthen yourself by taking in a strong Protestant in Ontario. . . ."[7] When Abbott's health finally compelled him to retire in November 1892, and Thompson was called to the post which was

---

4. P.A.C., Thompson Papers, Letter Book 30. This contains Thompson's minutes of the conferences.
5. *Ibid.*, 160, Hughes to Thompson, August 20, 1892.
6. *Ibid.*, 164, Wallace to Thompson, October 7, 1892.
7. *Ibid.*, 166, Abbott to Thompson, November 10, 1892.

rightfully his, it was clear, in spite of all the assurances, that the dissident elements in the Ontario wing remained strong. It was then, indeed, that the rift with D'Alton McCarthy and the Equal Rights faction within the party widened into open revolt. It also appears that because of Thompson's accession the ranks of the Protestant Protective Association were swelled by disgruntled Conservative Orangemen.[8]

Thompson had won the position by sheer ability and character. His parliamentary addresses and state papers were masterpieces of lucidity and intellectual force; his honesty and integrity were unquestioned. Whether he could have rallied the party and brought the malcontents back to a genuine understanding of Liberal-Conservatism is at least doubtful. Thompson was perhaps too judicial and impartial, when firmness was required as much and perhaps more so than these admirable qualities. His attempt to cater to the ultra-Protestants by bringing Wallace into the ministry proved to be a mistake, for, in the words of one of his colleagues, Wallace was chiefly concerned to "go one better than McCarthy", and did not have the "art of making his Yahoos cheer without putting his foot in it".[9]

Thompson made few other mistakes in his conduct of the government. He continued the prosecutions arising out of the McGreevy affair and eventually laid the scandal issue to rest in a final embarrassing parliamentary debate over the activities of Sir Adolphe Caron. His Liberal opponents were later compelled to admit that politics were cleaner because of Thompson. He "lopped the mouldering branches" off the tariff, to use his own phrase, in a timely concession to the widespread desire for tariff reform. His government negotiated a reciprocal trade treaty with France in 1893, subsidized a regular steamship service to Australia, sent trade missions to the West Indies and to Australia, and appointed the first Canadian trade commissioners abroad. Thompson also took important and imaginative steps with respect to imperial relations and convened the Colonial Conference of 1894 in Ottawa, a distinction which Canada's capital did not achieve again for nearly forty years. That the conference made little immediate progress in its goals of promoting imperial preferential trade, improved Atlantic and Pacific steamship service, and

8. James T. Watt, "Anti-Catholic Nativism in Canada: The Protestant Protective Association", *Canadian Historical Review*, March 1967, pp. 49-50.
9. Thompson Papers, 179, J. J. Curran to Thompson, March 22, 1893.

joint action on a Pacific cable, was due to the extreme difficulty
during these years of attracting capital for the steamship and cable
projects, and, so far as imperial preferential trade was concerned, to
the reluctance of the British government to abandon its free trade
policy. Amidst all these achievements, Thompson successfully met
the preposterous pretensions of the United States with respect to
sealing in the Bering Sea. His selection as one of the members of the
International Tribunal which met in Paris to arbitrate that dispute
was a further proof of his pre-eminent stature. His sad death at the
age of fifty, leaving his family virtually penniless at a time when his
brilliant career was far from having attained its zenith, once more
confronted the government and party with a leadership crisis.

The selection of Mackenzie Bowell as Thompson's successor proved
to be an unrelieved disaster. That Sir Charles Tupper should have
been summoned without delay was apparent to all, except to Lord
Aberdeen, the prejudiced and partisan governor general. It was even
apparent to the jealous and feuding members of cabinet, but their
very division enabled the Earl (and the Countess) of Aberdeen to
foist Bowell upon them as prime minister. It has been suggested that
the Aberdeens performed a service for the Conservative party in 1894
by doing for it what it could not do for itself, namely choose a
leader.[10] Aside from the fact that they performed this dubious service
before the cabinet and party had had scarcely any opportunity of
making a selection of their own, the Aberdeens did so after deliberately excluding from their consideration the most able (as well as the
senior) Conservative leader – on the ground that they thought him
dishonest! How they acquired this notion remains unclear, but presumably their partisanship for Laurier and the Liberals rendered
them susceptible to improper and unfounded charges against Sir
Charles Tupper. At all events, instead of the choice falling upon one
of the leading Fathers of Confederation, an able and dynamic man of
almost unparalleled experience in government, the Aberdeens chose
as the new prime minister (to use their own words) the "rather
fussy & decidedly commonplace" Mackenzie Bowell.

Bowell, who was Minister of Trade and Commerce and acting
prime minister at the time of Thompson's death, had been an M.P.
from 1867 to 1892, when he moved up to the Senate. He was the
senior cabinet member, having held a portfolio since 1878. Editor

10. John T. Saywell (ed.), *The Canadian Journal of Lady Aberdeen, 1893-1898*,
    p. xli.

and proprietor of the Belleville *Daily Intelligencer*, he was also an Orangeman, having at one time been Grand Master of the Order in British America. Yet his Orangeism, like that of Macdonald, was of an older, more tolerant variety. Free from bigotry, he was undoubtedly acceptable to the Roman Catholic populace, including that of Quebec. Bowell had a quality of bluntness and a somewhat choleric temper, but was basically kindly in nature and fiercely loyal to his friends. As time was to show, he could also be extremely vain and stubborn.

Under Bowell's leadership the government began an "unerring path towards disaster".[11] Quite aside from his handling of the Manitoba school question, which was appalling, Bowell was unable to make decisions even upon routine matters of government. Almost at the outset, the Bowell regime committed the greatest blunder in many years by its failure to bring Newfoundland into the Union early in 1895. It was a failure which certainly would not have occurred if Tupper had been at the helm, but which Bowell (and Foster, the Minister of Finance) managed to make possible at a time when the bankrupt colony had scarcely any alternative but to join Confederation. It may well be that completion of the Union would not have struck a very responsive chord in the hearts of parochial-minded Canadians, but the Bowell administration could ill afford to miss any opportunity to bolster its prestige. After staggering from crisis to crisis, Bowell was at last dislodged, but not until the governor general had managed to keep him in office for four months longer, just as he had inflicted him upon the party in the first place. In the end, with all expedients exhausted except the *coup d'état* on Laurier's behalf which he had contemplated earlier, Aberdeen was reluctantly compelled to call upon Tupper.

Sir Charles Tupper was now entering upon his seventy-sixth year. Ahead of him lay two strenuous months as prime minister and nearly five years as leader of the Conservative party in opposition. To both tasks he brought a vigour and boldness that were conspicuously lacking in his three predecessors, and a political astuteness equalled only by that of the Old Chieftain. With less than two months remaining to him before the electorate was to pronounce its verdict, he effected an impressive reconstruction of the cabinet and then went on to wage a vigorous and worthy campaign. His per-

11. Saywell, *op. cit.*, p. liii.

formance is suggestive of what he might have accomplished had he been given time enough.

Tupper's new cabinet was an attempt to break with the hesitancy and temporizing of the Bowell era, and particularly to strengthen the Quebec representation. The resignation of A. R. Angers during the cabinet crisis of July 1895, had cast grave doubt upon the sincerity of the government on the school question. Angers was now brought back and Sir Adolphe Caron and J. A. Ouimet were dropped. Alphonse Desjardins, who had joined during the crisis of January 1896, was retained. Tupper also secured a surprising acquisition in Louis Ollivier Taillon, premier of Quebec, and another notable addition in Senator John Jones Ross, a former premier. Angers, Desjardins, Taillon, and Ross were all men of unimpeachable character and integrity. If not a collection of all the political talents, they certainly comprised one of all the virtues.

Tupper had sought to induce J. A. Chapleau to join his cabinet, but Chapleau preferred to remain lieutenant-governor of Quebec. He gave as his reason for declining that he had given personal assurances to Archbishop Taché early in 1891 "in the face of which, I could not, in honour, re-enter the Cabinet before the remedial Bill was put through".[12] The exact nature of the pledge remains obscure. Chapleau had been a cabinet minister early in 1891, when the prospect of his leaving the government could scarcely have arisen. He construed the pledge to mean that he could not "in honour" re-enter the cabinet in 1896, but it seems clear, on the face of it, that the pledge could equally well make it incumbent upon him to enter and support an administration which had committed itself to remedial legislation. His interpretation of the pledge thus appears conveniently elastic, permitting him to accept the renewal of his appointment as lieutenant-governor, which J. Israel Tarte is alleged to have promised him if he remained aloof from the campaign of 1896.[13] In Chapleau's defence, however, there remains the other possibility, to which he alluded, that he so questioned the sincerity of certain members of the cabinet as to regard the commitment to remedial legislation as valueless. If so, this, rather than the one he gave, should have been the ground of his refusal.

Sir Charles Tupper was undoubtedly sincere in his support of remedial legislation. His negotiations to persuade B. B. Osler, a pro-

12. P.A.C., Bowell Papers, 15, Chapleau to Bowell, May 9, 1896.
13. Tupper Papers, 23, (Journal), n.d.

minent Toronto businessman, to enter the cabinet, broke down because Osler would not agree to support such legislation. Again, the lengthy correspondence which, since January 1896, Tupper had conducted with Hugh John Macdonald in order to bring him into the cabinet provides further proof of the leader's sincerity. He managed to bring Macdonald to the point where he agreed, in spite of his dislike of politics, to "place myself and my services at your command if we can hit upon any means by which I can do so without sacrificing my self respect". Macdonald went on to say that he regarded separate schools as "a curse to the country", and that he had long favoured "national schools". In a surprising reversal of priorities, he considered the school question to be "not only of greater consequence than any question relating to our fiscal policy before the country, but also of far greater importance than any question which can arise, barring only such as affect British connection and our loyalty to the Crown".[14] Holding these views, Macdonald did not see how he could honourably enter Tupper's government.

Tupper's reply took the high ground of constitutional duty which he had always insisted was the real issue in the school question.

> More than forty years ago [wrote Tupper] your father expressed himself very much as you have done on the same question. Yet he did not consider it inconsistent with his undisguised preference for a national system of schools to support, and not merely to support, but to extend and amplify, the separate school system of Upper Canada. You are not called upon to go so far. Our policy is not to devise anything new, but merely to maintain an arrangement to which the national honour and good faith of the country are pledged.
>
> It matters not what our individual views upon the merits or demerits of separate schools may be. It is a fact that years before you took any interest in such matters they were grafted upon the Constitution under which we live.
>
> No one can read the Debates which led up to Confederation without perceiving that without this concession Union would have been an impossibility, and that

14. *Ibid.*, 11, Hugh John Macdonald to Tupper, April 3, 1896. (This, and the letters cited in footnotes 15, 16, and 17, are recent acquisitions).

> such determined opponents of separate schools as
> Brown and Mackenzie surrendered their private opin-
> ions to the public good. Legal technicalities apart, every-
> one knows that in 1870 the same system was guaran-
> teed to Manitoba, and if there is any trouble today it is
> due solely to the unskilfulness of the draughtsman of
> the Manitoba Act in failing to give legal effect to the
> intentions of the Imperial authorities and the Canadian
> Parliament. . . . I cannot state too clearly my convic-
> tion that this is not a question of the establishment of
> separate schools at all, and that no ideas which you
> may have upon the subject need conflict with the duty
> of giving effect to the decision of the highest tribunal
> in the land.[15]

Hugh John Macdonald, who seems to have had few of the generous
instincts of his father, was not very much impressed with Tupper's
argument that there was a constitutional compact to be maintained.
Indeed, he confessed that his preference for "national schools" was so
strong that he "would be willing to take advantage – perhaps un-
fairly – of what you call a draughtsman's mistake".[16] He was compelled to admit, however, that the decision of the Judicial Committee
of the Privy Council in the Brophy case entitled the Roman Catholic
minority of Manitoba to some alleviation of its plight. He did not
agree with the provisions of the Remedial Bill and wished to consider
the particulars of future remedial legislation an open question. On
this condition he agreed to enter the cabinet. J. Stewart Tupper,
Macdonald's Winnipeg law partner, assured his father that he need
not attach too much importance to this stipulation, as he would not
find Macdonald an "unreasonable man" when the time came to settle
the details of the relief to be accorded to the minority.[17]

In the ensuing weeks Sir Charles Tupper sought the support of the
electorate for his reconstructed government. His forthright declara-
tions on the school question in all parts of the country left no doubt
of his sincerity. *La Presse* commented that one could not ask for more
explicit or courageous language from an English Protestant. It was to
the eternal honour of Tupper, the Montreal journal maintained, that
he disdained peril and vindicated right and justice without regard for

15. *Ibid.*, Tupper to Macdonald, April 10, 1896.
16. *Ibid.*, Macdonald to Tupper, April 15, 1896.
17. *Ibid.*, J. Stewart Tupper to Tupper, April 15, 1896.

the consequences. It also lauded him for the vigour of his strenuous election campaign. In spite of his seventy-six years, "sir Charles Tupper est encore le plus solide au poste; M. Laurier est éreinté, M. Montague morfondu, M. Taillon enrhumé, tous sont á bout des forces. Seul, le vieux Tupper parcourt le continent en train-éclair."[18] Tupper deserved the praise. That victory was denied him was no fault of his. The malaise that afflicted the party could not be cured overnight.

III

The problem of the leadership quite evidently had an important, perhaps fatal, bearing on the fortunes of the Conservative government and party. Thompson's premature death, and Tupper's exclusion from office until it was too late, were disastrous blows. When to these reverses there is added the challenge of one of the most controversial of issues, further explanation of the fate which overtook the Conservatives seems superfluous. That Bowell, the weakest of prime ministers, should have been confronted with the most difficult of problems, is surely one of the ironies of Canadian history. But the crisis over the Manitoba school question was not only a crisis of leadership; it was also a crisis within the party, and here it was a symptom rather than a cause of Conservative ills. What the Manitoba school question made apparent was the sickness which had affected the Ontario wing of the party to the point where it had quite lost touch with the facts of political life, the recognition of which had been the very founding principle of the Liberal-Conservative party.

Those facts were, simply, that the country could not "be governed by a totally unfrenchified government", as Macdonald had observed long ago,[19] and, as a corollary, that any political party which hoped to hold office must have the support of both French and English. The Liberal-Conservative party was a partnership between a conservative Quebec and a tolerant Ontario Toryism designed to work for common objectives of mutual benefit. The terms of the bond were not explicit, but they made clear that French-speaking and English-speaking Canadians would create and share a transcontinental Dom-

18. *La Presse,* 17 juin, 1896.
19. Donald Creighton, *John A. Macdonald: The Young Politician,* p. 227.

inion on something like terms of equality. This dualism, which
was definitely but not precisely indicated in the B.N.A. Act, was
spelled out in the Manitoba Act of 1870 and the North-West Territories Act of 1875 as amended in 1877. School and language rights
gave both French and English an equal right of way throughout a
vast empire which was one of the first fruits of their co-operation.
When the bill for honouring the bond between the two partners was
presented in the form of the Manitoba school question, the Ontario
wing of the party refused to pay it.

The Ontario wing was not, however, merely reacting. An important segment of it had in fact been responsible for starting the
agitation which, as one of its consequences, gave rise to the Manitoba
school question. It had become infected in the late 1880s with an
English-Canadian nationalism in which the chief ingredients appeared to be an aggressive Anglo-Saxon racialism and a militant
Protestantism. Whatever the causes of this nationalism, and whatever its positive attributes, it was anti-French and anti-Catholic.
Under the ironic name of the Equal Rights Association this group
proceeded to attack and destroy the institutions of dualism wherever
they were to be found – in the West, in the federal Parliament, in
Ontario itself. In a few short years it had drastically altered the
nature of the Canadian Confederation. Throughout a vast domain,
which French and English had agreed to share, English-Canadian
nationalism had triumphed. In Manitoba, the attack on the school
and language rights of the minority had been completely successful.
In the North-West Territories, only the dual school system had
survived, and that in attenuated form. In Ontario, it was only with
difficulty that the government of Sir Oliver Mowat withstood repeated attacks on the constitutional and acquired rights of Roman
Catholic and French-speaking Canadians.

Although this racial and religious bigotry was not an exclusively
Ontario Conservative phenomenon, it found its most congenial home
there, particularly among the Orangemen. It was D'Alton McCarthy
and the "Equal Righters" who carried the torch westward to the
prairies; it was other prominent Conservative leaders and newspapers
who applied it to the readily combustible tinder of Ontario preju-
dice. When the Equal Rights Association disappeared, its spirit lived
on in the form of "McCarthyism" within the Conservative party of
Ontario. If McCarthy and Lt.-Col. William E. O'Brien are regarded
as renegades who were no longer within the party, plenty of others

within the fold were their counterpart and concerned themselves chiefly to vie with them in arousing racial and religious passions. The list includes such prominent Ontario Conservatives as N. Clarke Wallace, William R. Meredith, William F. Maclean, John Ross Robertson, Alexander McNeill, Dr. Thomas Sproule, James P. Whitney, Thomas Dixon Craig, E. F. Clarke, George Taylor, F. C. Denison, Sam Hughes, Lt.-Col. Richard Tyrwhitt, and G. R. Cockburn; and, among Conservative newspapers, *The Mail, The World, The Telegram,* and, to a lesser extent, *The Empire.* These were the spokesmen who aroused Manitobans to the discovery of previously unknown grievances which unscrupulous provincial politicians were quick to exploit. It was they who repeatedly assailed the Mowat government for allegedly enhancing the school privileges of the Roman Catholics and French Canadians of Ontario. It was they who inspired the legitimate mistrust which Quebec entertained of the sincerity of Conservative pledges of remedial legislation. In short, these were the authors not only of the Manitoba school question but of the defeat of the Conservatives in 1896.

The virus which infected the Ontario wing of the party had taken hold in the closing years of Macdonald. *La Presse* said long afterwards that he had left a "héritage de procès", and that it was "en soudoyant et en encourageant en sous-main les McCarthy, les Wallaces et les autres fanatiques, qui sir John A. Macdonald a compromis l'avenir de son parti. . . ".[20] It was true enough that the Old Chieftain had left a "héritage de procès", but the rest of the charge was grossly unfair. His own views were well known, and there can be little doubt that he disapproved of what was happening. Far from countenancing the activities of McCarthy, he had implored him to desist from his harmful agitation.[21] In the Ontario general elections of 1890 he had refused to help W. R. Meredith because of the anti-Catholic and anti-French course adopted by the provincial Conservative leader. He said to those about him that if he were to vote in that election it would be against Meredith and his candidates.[22] His failure to take stronger action against those who were disrupting the party was unquestionably dictated by his assessment that the racial and religious cleavage was not the most serious of the problems facing him at the close of his career.

20. *La Presse,* 28 avril, 1896.
21. Creighton, *op. cit.,* p. 518.
22. Thompson Papers, Letter Book 26, Thompson to J. J. C. Abbott, July 17, 1891.

McCarthy had told him that the fundamental problem confronting the country was not whether it was to be annexed to the United States, but whether it was to be English or French. For Macdonald the latter question was settled – the country was to be both; but the former was precisely the all-important issue of the moment. Given the precarious circumstances in which his national policies were placed, owing to the depressed times and the considerable amount of annexationist sentiment, he could ill afford to alienate any support in the crucial contest of 1891. By his final election victory he had won for his party and its national policies yet another mandate. Time and the return of commonsense might be trusted to take care of the other issue. Unfortunately, this did not turn out to be the case.

From what has been said thus far the malaise within the Ontario wing of the party was clearly one requiring treatment. Granted that Macdonald and his colleagues failed to arrest or treat that condition, how did they fare in their efforts to treat one of its symptoms, namely, the Manitoba school question? Were errors of a political (or legal and constitutional) nature committed here? The first important decision was of course that of Macdonald not to disallow the Manitoba Public Schools Act of 1890. The wisdom of this cannot seriously be questioned. The futile experience with Manitoba railway legislation of a few years before indicated that disallowance would simply create demagogic opportunities for Premier Thomas Greenway and his ruling spirit, Joseph Martin, to exploit. As Macdonald noted at the time, they probably would have dissolved the Legislature, won an election on the issue, and then reintroduced the school legislation. Again disallowance would have to be employed, and the cycle of excitement would be repeated.

There can be no great quarrel with the course adopted by Macdonald and his Minister of Justice, Sir John Thompson. The main criticisms are that instead of reserving the Act, pending a reference to the courts as to its constitutionality, they allowed it to go into operation, thus subjecting the Roman Catholic minority to serious financial disabilities; and that they left the initiative to take court action to the minority, with the result that it was some time before a valid case (Barrett v. City of Winnipeg) was under way. This had not even reached the Supreme Court, let alone the Judicial Committee of the Privy Council, by the spring of 1891, when the period for disallowance expired. Aside from the dilatory nature of the proceedings, and the temporary inconvenience to the minority, however, it must have seemed certain to Macdonald and Thompson that all would come right in the end. The Act was clearly unconstitutional and would surely be struck down.

That it was not struck down is another of the unfortunate accidents which the Conservative governments of these years seemed fated to encounter. The failure to engage Edward Blake as counsel (for which Thompson must be blamed, and for which he paid dearly), the further failure to retain Sir Horace Davey, and the last-minute acquisition of Sir Richard Webster, were all disastrous episodes in the sequence of events. Even Webster's wretched mishandling of the minority case, however, does not excuse the incredible judgment of the Privy Council declaring the Public Schools Act of Manitoba *intra vires*. This judgment, which reversed a unanimous decision (three Protestant justices, two Roman Catholic) of the Supreme Court of Canada, has been described by a recent authority as "difficult to justify, to say the least", and as "probably the most extreme example of judicial amendment of the Canadian Constitution".[23] The ultimate responsibility lies, of course, with those Canadians who insisted upon having their constitution interpreted by men on the other side of the Atlantic who knew little or nothing of Canada, its history, its circumstances, or its needs. Ironically enough, Macdonald had been one of these. At the time of the establishment of the Supreme Court he had argued for the retention of appeals to the Privy Council, on the ground of maintaining the British connection, and had thereby helped to undermine his life's work.

The damage had been done, and the question of what to do now had to be faced by Sir John Thompson. It was obviously difficult for a Roman Catholic prime minister to act in a situation which by now had become enmeshed in sectarian passions; for Thompson, with his agonizing concern to be impartial, it was also a pitiable dilemma. It is arguable that in his desire to avoid even the appearance of favouring his co-religionists he did them less than justice. In spite of the judgment of the Privy Council that the Public Schools Act of Manitoba was *intra vires*, the federal government was clearly empowered to frame, and the Dominion Parliament to pass, remedial legislation rectifying the grievances of the Roman Catholic minority of Manitoba. Subsections 2 and 3 of section 22 of the Manitoba Act of 1870, which confer this power, are obviously designed to deal with provincial legis-

23. D. A. Schmeiser, *Civil Liberties in Canada*, pp. 160-62.

lation which, although constitutional, may nonetheless create a grievance. A case can easily be made out, therefore, that Sir John Thompson should have acted forthwith on the petitions of the minority for redress of grievance.

Such action would have been little short of heroic on the part of a government and party already torn by racial and religious dissensions, and especially on the part of a prime minister who was almost daily being attacked (by such prominent individuals as Dr. Albert Carman, the Superintendent of the Methodist Church of Canada) as a "Jesuit" and a "Papist" who was not to be trusted. That the situation was such as to inspire caution and timidity is easily understandable but, quite apart from this, Thompson's course can be defended on constitutional as well as political grounds. When no less a person than D'Alton McCarthy, whose reputation as a constitutional authority was esteemed by many, could contend that the Barrett decision had ended the matter and that the federal government must decline to entertain the appeal of the minority, then it is evident that here was a "grey" area of the constitution which would have to be illuminated before there could be further action. It was Thompson's hope that the Brophy case, by providing clear answers to a number of pertinent questions, would finally allay all doubts, and that fair-minded men, irrespective of their creed or personal opinions, would feel obliged to submit to the findings of the courts. It was a vain hope in view of the climate of the times, but Thompson can scarcely be blamed for harbouring it; had he not sought the clarification provided by the Brophy case, he would have been blamed all the more.

The answers when they came were clear enough. The Barrett decision had not ended the matter; the Roman Catholic minority had a well-founded grievance, the particulars of which were more than adequately spelled out; and the Dominion Parliament had the power to pass remedial legislation. The mandatory implications of the Brophy judgment are also clear. The government and Legislature of Manitoba were duty bound to remedy the grievance promptly, and, failing this, the Governor General in Council and the Dominion Parliament were duty bound to enact remedial legislation. The honour of the Crown and Parliament required that the constitution be upheld and that the obligations which it imposed upon them as guarantors of minority rights be fulfilled. On any other view, constitutional government ends and revolution begins. The arguments of David Mills in the debate on the Remedial Bill are irrefutable in this regard.

The government's procedure in the Manitoba school question thus far had been well-nigh impeccable. The much more difficult task of political action still lay ahead, however, and by another of those malign twists of fate which seemed to dog Conservative fortunes it fell to Sir Mackenzie Bowell, the well-intentioned but inept successor to Thompson. Armed as he was by the Brophy decision, Bowell's course should have been clear. The formal hearings by the Governor General in Council of the minority's plea, and any counter-plea by the Manitoba government, should have been conducted, as was done. The request to Manitoba to make the necessary amendments to its school legislation should then have been promptly and courteously made, as was also done, and when, after a decent interval, Manitoba had declined to act, remedial legislation should have been pressed through Parliament without delay. In the meantime, a vigorous effort should have been made to educate the Conservative party and the country generally to the necessity of seeing to it that the constitution was maintained.

Bowell took the first two steps, but on the third one he wavered in hopeless irresolution until it was too late, and he did virtually nothing about the last. The hearings before the Canadian Privy Council in late February and early March, 1895, were derided by many at the time as a farce in which the cabinet tried to hide its political responsibility behind a judicial façade, and it is possible that the government thus weakened the position which it later took – that it was duty bound to enforce the Brophy decision. The holding of the hearings can be reconciled with the mandatory implications of the Brophy judgment, however, if it is assumed that it was incumbent upon the government to hear from the minority the precise extent of the redress which it claimed (or with which it would be content) and also from the Manitoba government any arguments why such redress should not be granted, or should be granted only in modified form. As it was, the government was subsequently accused of having dealt with Manitoba in peremptory fashion.

With the quasi-judicial hearings over, and the Remedial Order in Council issued, the Bowell government now vacillated over the question of whether or not to dissolve Parliament and seek a mandate from the electorate for its policy of remedial legislation. It was Sir Charles Hibbert Tupper's contention that such action, promptly taken, was essential to the success of remedial legislation. In view of the limited time remaining in the life of the Seventh Parliament, he was undoubtedly right. Furthermore, if its record of successes in the by-elections up to that time is any guide, the government probably would have won. Out of 71 by-elections up to March 1895, the government had won 56, for a net gain of 17 seats from the Liberals, while the Liberals had won only 15. Instead of such resolute action, however, the Bowell government staggered through two more parliamentary sessions and two disastrous cabinet crises.

Having decided against dissolution, Bowell's only hope was to proceed with remedial legislation once Manitoba declined to act. Yet, when the almost insolent reply of Manitoba was received during the session of 1895 Bowell did not act, nor did he take up the perfectly insincere proposal for a commission of enquiry contained in that reply. Others had suggested the appointment by the federal government of a royal commission to investigate and publicize the facts of the school question, and if this had been done it would have strengthened the government's hands by helping to educate and prepare the public for what was to follow. Almost the only valid point made by Laurier, during a year or more of evasion on the school question, was his contention that while Roman Catholics might not consider further investigation to be necessary in view of all the facts brought out by the litigation, Protestants were in need of such an aid to understanding. But Bowell took no constructive steps in this regard whatever. F. C. Wade's scurrilous tract on the school question was industriously circulated by the Manitoba government, while John S. Ewart's devastating reply and his earlier book appear to have gone almost unheeded. Although Bowell was undoubtedly sincere in his desire to see justice done to the Roman Catholic minority, he did not even dismiss N. Clarke Wallace from the ministry in spite of months of blatant declamation against the government's school policy.

In short, Bowell frittered away nearly a year in indecision. When remedial legislation was at last introduced, well on in the special session of 1896, neither the public nor his Conservative followers were adequately informed on the school question, the life of Parliament was short, and the opportunities for obstruction infinite. The Remedial Bill was doomed to failure.

It was an inglorious end to the first and only attempt to enforce the remedial clauses which the constitution contains for the protection of minority rights. In the course of nearly six years the appeal of the minority had dragged its way through the courts to the court of Parliament itself. Now that the time had come to carry the issue to the electorate, the accumulated weight of mistrust as to the government's sincerity was too great to be shouldered even by such a stalwart as Sir Charles Tupper. His position that the government was duty bound to see justice done to the Roman Catholic minority of Manitoba was forthright, and his efforts to rally his party and the country behind that policy were unflagging. Yet Quebec turned its back on the Conservative government in what seemed to be a betrayal of its compatriots in Manitoba and a rebuff to its ecclesiastical leaders. Both the betrayal and the rebuff were more apparent than real. Ontario Toryism had taken the path of intolerance, with the result that the Liberal-Conservative alliance between it and a conservative Quebec came to an end. Quebec's faith in its long-time Ontario allies had been exhausted; in a political re-alignment it sought new allies whose record, as exemplified by the Liberal government of Sir Oliver Mowat, augured a more satisfactory partnership.

IV

Sir John A. Macdonald and his Conservative successors had provided the national policies by which a transcontinental dominion might hope to grow and flourish. The material foundations had been soundly conceived and well laid, but the vision of an expanded household in which both French and English would dwell on terms of mutual respect had become blurred. In the late 1880s and early 1890s the Ontario wing of the Liberal-Conservative party, succumbing to what was apparently an English-Canadian nationalism, proceeded to assail all the provisions for dualism which the Founding Fathers, in a more generous age, had written into the B.N.A. Act, the Manitoba Act, and the North-West Territories Act. The assault was a challenge not only to dualism, but to the principles and practices of constitutional federalism. At the local level it posed the problem of a just balance between majority rule and minority rights; at the national level it raised the question of the relationship between the federal government, as the guarantor of minority rights, and the local legislatures which override those rights. The failure to cope with these twin challenges signified not merely a failure to recognize the limits beyond which majoritarian rule becomes tyranny, or to accept the duties and obligations which federalism imposes; it represented a loss of that largeness of vision with which the nation-building project had commenced. It stunted and warped the spirit of the young Dominion at the very time when its physical well-being seemed all but assured.

In the long run the turn of events proved to be disastrous for the prospects of the federal government's ascendancy and of a dual Canada. Laurier's "sunny ways" ended in the betrayal of the Roman Catholic and French-speaking minority of Manitoba and in the rebuff of the hierarchy. The clear pledge of remedial legislation if necessary, which he had made in Quebec during the election campaign of 1896, he discarded in favour of some niggardly concessions for the minority wrung from the Manitoba government in return for a cabinet post for Clifford Sifton. The federal government abandoned its role as the guarantor of minority rights. It is only now, after more than seventy years, seeking to repair in some measure that dereliction of duty.

Stephen Leacock and the Age of Plutocracy, 1903-1921

RAMSAY COOK

The first two decades of the twentieth century witnessed the transformation of Canada from a predominantly rural and small-town country into an industrial and urban society. The 1921 census revealed that for the first time more Canadians lived in urban than in rural settings, and that that point had been passed in Ontario and Quebec almost a decade earlier. Lorne Murchison's Elgin, Ontario, "a thriving manufacturing town", was increasingly typical of central Canada, though Abe Spalding's Morley, Manitoba, remained representative of the prairie West.[1] Both Elgin and Morley symbolize what was happening to the country in the years before the Great War: industrial growth and agriculture settlement. Large-scale population movements accompanied both developments. Most striking was the influx of immigrants from the British Isles, Europe, and the United States. But no less important was the internal migration from coun-

---

1. Sara Jeannette Duncan, *The Imperialist* (1904; reprinted in the New Canadian Library, Toronto, 1961), p. 25; Frederick Philip Grove, *The Fruits of the Earth* (1933; reprinted in the N.C.L., Toronto, 1965).

try to city. Both movements profoundly altered the character of the country. Ralph Connor's *Foreigner* (1909) challenged the traditional dominance of English and French in Canada, while rural depopulation struck some as the country's most debilitating social problem.[2] The change from rural to urban living has seldom been more nostalgically described than in the concluding chapter of *Sunshine Sketches of a Little Town*. Stephen Leacock knew what was happening to Canada; he made it the subject of his two finest books, *Sunshine Sketches* and *The Arcadian Adventures of the Idle Rich*.

The age of the great transformation was also the age of the great barbecue. The men behind the rapid economic development of the period accepted the challenge of a vast, underdeveloped domain: mines to be opened, electricity to be harnessed, transportation systems to be built, steel to be rolled, land to be parcelled out, grain to be milled, textiles to be woven, forests to be felled, and pulp to be crushed. Corporate enterprise was the new business form of the period, the merger a frequent event.[3]

In these opening years of the century great fortunes were made – some very great – and the concentration of economic power fell into the hands of a relatively small number of men. One careful examination of the Canadian business community in 1909 concluded that "at the base of the financial structure in Canada is to be found a triangular formation consisting of twenty-three capitalist financiers upon whom depend, in a very large measure, the type and direction of material prosperity".[4] This was the age of Sir Wilfrid Laurier and Sir Robert Borden. It was also, perhaps pre-eminently, the age of Senator George Cox and Herbert Holt, Sir Henry Pellatt and Senator L. J. Forget, H. M. Molson and Sir Donald Mann, Zebulon Lash and R. B. Angus. These were but the most prominent of the men who changed the face of the country, and who met at the local Mausoleum Club to discuss the usefulness of troops in labour disputes, the selfishness of farmers, and the incompetence of politicians.

"Permit me to congratulate you on your prompt action in sending troops to Cape Breton," Sir Edward Clouston of the Bank of Montreal told the prime minister, during the 1909 miners' strike. "It is un-

2. Rev. John MacDougall, *Rural Life in Canada* (Toronto, 1913).
3. L. G. Reynolds, *The Control of Competition in Canada* (Cambridge, Mass., 1940).
4. Nathaniel S. Fineberg, "The Canadian Financial Triangle", *Moody's Magazine*, VIII, 5, November 1909, 381. I am indebted to Mr. J. M. Bliss for this reference.

doubtedly saving riot, bloodshed and much destruction of property, and as we have large interests in that section of the country, we have reason to be thankful."

"The attitude of the West regarding elevators, freight rates, free trade, etc.," Sir Edmund Walker of the Bank of Commerce told a newspaperman, "is quite natural when one remembers that agricultural people are both selfish and ignorant."

"I intrude upon the lofty utterances of your chief character," wrote J. W. (later Sir Joseph) Flavelle, of William Davis Co., about J. S. Willison's *Laurier*, "his grace, dignity, catholicity, and poetry, with the vulgar common sense, commonplace of everyday things – with the workingman's view of trade – with the robust man's standard of active development in a young country of exhaustless resources yet undeveloped – with an active, energetic practical man's scarcely concealed contempt in strenuous business life, for the grasp of a Blake, a Cartwright (whom you barely mention) or a Laurier – who when brought into contact with the actual realities of business life, talk wisely, but do nothing."[5]

In the same circle the "imperial question" also came up for frequent discussion, for it suffused so many other issues of the day, social, political and economic. From the outbreak of the South African War to the close of the Great War, the problem of Canada's relations with Great Britain and the future shape of the Empire was the great national question. Few were satisfied with the existing undefined, but clearly colonial, relationship. But even fewer had concrete ideas about paths to the future. A businessman might rejoice in the imperial preference that brought him a knighthood; he might even favour closer political union for the members of the Empire.[6] But imperial preferences that would have admitted British manufactured goods into the Canadian market were another matter, as Sara Jeannette Duncan explained as early as 1904 in her novel, *The Imperialist*.

Everywhere, then, in the early decades of the twentieth century, the businessman's imprint was plain. This new power did not pass

5. Public Archives of Canada, Laurier Papers, E. S. Clouston to Laurier, July 15, 1909; University of Toronto Library, Walker Papers, E. B. Walker to C. F. Hamilton, July 29, 1910; Queen's University, Flavelle Papers, J. W. Flavelle to J. S. Willison, April 25, 1903. Professor Peter Oliver drew my attention to this letter.
6. James Eayrs, "The Round Table Movement in Canada", *Canadian Historical Review*, XXXVIII, 1, March 1957, 1-20.

unobserved. At the very beginning of the period the position and power of the successful businessman was remarked upon by that prolific chronicler, J. Castell Hopkins. He observed that in English Canada the old "loyalist" élite had suffered a noticeable decline in status. "Successful merchants, well-to-do manufacturers and prosperous professional men have succeeded to its social place and traditions . . .".[7] The acerbic Colonel George T. Denison, police magistrate, who disliked businessmen nearly as wholeheartedly as he did Americans, made the same point rather graphically. "Parvenues are as plentiful as blackberries," he told his poet friend Charles Mair in 1911, "and the vulgar ostentation of the common rich is not a pleasant sight."[8] Two years later the young English poet, Rupert Brooke, having just completed a lengthy cross-country tour, wrote home that he looked forward to resuming his travels in the United States. "Canada is a most horribly individualistic place," he complained, "with no one thinking of anything except the amount of money that they can make, by any means, in the shortest time."[9]

This was undeniably the age of enterprise. Accompanying the great strides in material development was the "boom mentality". Virtually every foreign observer of Canada in the period wrote something similar to J. A. Hobson's comment in 1906. "The poor relation has come into her fortune," he noted, "a single decade has swept away all her diffidence, and has replaced it by a spirit of boundless confidence and booming enterprise."[10] The nation was vibrant; the century was clearly Canada's.

Not everyone happily accepted this new materialistic yardstick that was part of these boom years. A few, like J. S. Woodsworth, wondered whether quality might not be as important as quantity in immigrant selection.[11] Small pockets of radicals and socialists began to appear in various parts of the country, often quarrelling as much among themselves as with the capitalist enemy, but nevertheless questioning the dominant values of the age.[12] Then there were the

7. J. Castell Hopkins, *The Progress of Canada in the Nineteenth Century* (Toronto, 1900), p. 573.
8. Queen's University, Mair Papers, Denison to Mair, December 31, 1911; cited in Carl Berger, *The Sense of Power* (Toronto, 1970), p. 182.
9. Geoffrey Keynes, *The Letters of Rupert Brooke* (New York, 1968), p. 509.
10. J. A. Hobson, *Canada Today* (London, 1906), p. 4.
11. J. S. Woodsworth, *Strangers within Our Gates* (Toronto, 1909).
12. Martin Robin, *Radical Politics and Canadian Labour, 1880-1930* (Kingston, 1968).

increasingly powerful farmers' organizations, denouncing the tariff, preaching the virtues of the family farm, and exhorting the rural hosts to revolt against the "new feudalism".[13]

Yet there was no movement of criticism directed against Canadian materialism comparable to the muckrakers in the United States. Indeed the two major muckrakers in Canada, Edward Porritt, the crusading Cobdenite, and Gustavus Myers, the radical socialist,[14] were imported. For the most part Canadian intellectuals appear to have rejoiced in this first age of affluence. But there were exceptions, and of these the most notable because of his later emimence as a humorist was Stephen Leacock. His very fame as a humorist has meant that his role as social critic has been ignored or misunderstood. But without some consideration of his political attitudes,[15] his career loses a whole dimension. Indeed that missing dimension provides an important element in an understanding of Leacock the humorist. He was more than just a funny man; at least some of the time he was a funny man with a serious purpose.

13. Edward Porritt, *The Revolt in Canada Against the New Feudalism* (London, 1911).
14. Gustavus Myers, *The History of Canadian Wealth* (Chicago, 1914). Myers' second volume, which would have dealt with the twentieth century, never appeared.
15. Ralph L. Curry's *Stephen Leacock: Humorist and Humanist* (New York, 1959) almost totally ignores Leacock's social and political views, as do most literary critics. Robertson Davies insists that "Leacock's importance to Canada rests solely upon the body of his work as a humorist", though it is not clear from the essay that Professor Davies has read Leacock's non-fiction (Robertson Davies, "On Stephen Leacock", in A. J. M. Smith, *The Masks of Fiction* [Toronto, 1961], pp. 93-114); F. W. Watt, "Critic or Entertainer? Stephen Leacock and the Growth of Materialism", *Canadian Literature*, 5, Summer 1960, 33-42, touches on some of Leacock's political ideas. Donald Cameron's essay, *Faces of Leacock* (Toronto, 1967), follows in the traditional path but occasionally shows some awareness that Leacock had something to say as a political commentator. Still, it is difficult to understand why Mr. Cameron chose to write a chapter on Leacock as a novelist, which he was not, and failed to write one on Leacock as a political economist, which he was. Finally, H. A. Innis' "Stephen Butler Leacock, 1869-1944", *Canadian Journal of Economics and Political Science*, X, 2, May 1944, 216-26, has some interesting comments on Leacock as a social scientist but is so hostile to Leacock's "imperialism" as to fail to understand it.

II

In 1903, having been "pronounced completely full"[16] and awarded his Ph.D. by the University of Chicago, Leacock took up a permanent teaching post at McGill. Lord Minto, who had recently had a long stay in Montreal, remarked that "the leaders of English society in Montreal are nouveaux riches."[17] It was also a city where the cause of Empire was raised high by such luminaries as Sir William Peterson, principal of McGill, and Hugh Graham, editor of the *Montreal Star*, and denounced with equal vigour by Henri Bourassa and his young friends in *La Ligue nationaliste canadienne*. It was in this atmosphere that Leacock resumed his career as a humorist, started writing academic books, and launched himself as a commentator on current political events.

One of Leacock's teachers at Chicago had been Thorstein Veblen; indeed Leacock arrived in Chicago in 1899 – the very year that Veblen's most famous book, *The Theory of the Leisure Class*, was published. Leacock took at least one class under the Chicago iconoclast – the economics of the Navajo Indians, if the 1937 account is to be taken seriously, and it is the only reference that Leacock ever seems to have made in print to Veblen.[18] He does not even include him in the bibliography of his *Elements of Political Science*. Nevertheless his writing is full of Veblenesque features: "pecuniary emulation", "conspicuous consumption", "devout observances", to say nothing of "the higher learning as an expression of the pecuniary culture". In an early essay, "Back to the Woods", Leacock gave an example of "conspicuous leisure" that would surely have pleased the sardonic Veblen:

> Every day there move northward trains, packed full of lawyers, bankers, and brokers headed for the bush. They are dressed up to look like pirates. They wear slouch hats, flannel shirts, and leather breeches with belts. They could afford much better clothes than these,

16. Stephen Leacock, *Sunshine Sketches of a Little Town* (1912; reprinted in the N.C.L., Toronto, 1960), p. xiv.
17. P.A.C., Minto Papers, Lord Minto to King Edward VII, January 18, 1903.
18. The only direct reference to Veblen that I have come across is in Leacock's *My Discovery of the West* (London, 1937), pp. 171-73, where he offers a witty and reasonably accurate description of Veblen and his theories.

but they won't use them. I don't know where they get
these clothes. I think the railroad lends them out. They
have guns between their knees and big knives at their
hips. They smoke the worst tobacco they can find, and
they carry ten gallons of alcohol per man in the bag-
gage car.[19]

Veblen seems to have influenced Leacock in a general way, perhaps reinforcing the impact of Adam Smith whose work Leacock
examined for his doctoral thesis, on "The Theory of Laissez-faire".[20]
But it was not so much the theories of Smith or Veblen that influenced Leacock as their iconoclastic approach, their effective writing
style, and their concern with "the effects of machine industry and
the industrial revolution".[21] Moreover, Veblen the outsider and the
son of Norwegian immigrants was concerned about the new plutocracy that set the tone of the pecuniary culture in the United States.
Leacock, though much less an outsider, being the son of British immigrants, found a similar plutocracy setting the tone of Laurier's
Canada. Here is Leacock's description of that Canada, written in
1917:

The rise of the great trusts, the obvious and glaring
fact of the money power, the shameless luxury of the
rich, the crude, uncultivated and boorish mob of vulgar
men and overdressed women that masqueraded as high
society – the substitution, shall we say, of the saloon for
the salon – all this seemed to many an honest observer
of humble place as but the handwriting on the wall
that foretold the coming doom.[22]

It was against these conditions and against this plutocracy that
Leacock, like Veblen, was to direct his most biting criticism. Yet Leacock's attack on the "leisure class" was never as systematic as
Veblen's, and he was far too sceptical to follow Veblen along the
road to "technocratic socialism" – a precursor of Social Credit, Leacock later christened it. Indeed one of Leacock's *Nonsense Novels*,
"The Man in Asbestos", while obviously a satire on Edward Bellamy,

19. *Literary Lapses* (1910; reprinted in the N.C.L., Toronto, 1957) p. 121.
20. Innis, *op. cit.*, pp. 218-19.
21. H. A. Innis, "The Work of Thorstein Veblen", *Essays in Canadian Economic History* (Toronto, 1965), p. 23.
22. "Democracy and Social Progress", in J. O. Miller, *The New Era in Canada*
(Toronto, 1917), p. 17.

could just as well have been directed against Veblen's technocracy.[23]

Two themes run through all Leacock's discussions of social, economic and political questions during the age of plutocracy: a critique of individualism and a plea for imperial unity. In fact, Leacock had much in common with those social-imperialist thinkers who are often associated with the name of Joseph Chamberlain and whose influence reached a peak between the Boer War and the Great War. He would almost certainly have agreed with Austin Chamberlain's contention that "democracy wants two things: imperialism and social reform", and for Leacock the two were integrally united. Just as *laissez faire* and anti-colonialism had gone hand-in-hand, so now collectivism and the new imperialism were closely associated.[24]

In his political science textbook, Leacock dealt briefly with individualism and imperialism, though he did not relate them to one another. Discussing what he called "pure individualism", he pronounced it an unacceptable doctrine, running against the "instincts of humanity" by attempting to separate "individual and social rights". Governments simply had to intervene in the affairs of society in order to ensure justice.[25] On the subject of imperialism, he was even less a "value-free" social scientist. The crisis of Empire had been reached once more, he pointed out, just as in the eighteenth century. But this time the road toward imperial unity, in which the dominions would be given a share in developing and administering imperial policies, was obviously the one that had to be followed. "If independence is no longer to be the future ideal of the colonies, and since geographical reasons forbid a complete amalgamation, it looks as if the manifest destiny of the colonial system must now be sought in imperial federation," he concluded.[26]

Before anyone even suspected that Leacock would develop into a leading humorist, he had achieved fame as a serious entertainer in the cause of imperial unity. In 1906 he called upon the members of the Toronto Canadian Club "to have done with the cry of Canada first".

23. *Nonsense Novels* (1911; reprinted in the N.C.L., Toronto, 1963), pp. 38-53.
24. Bernard Semmel, *Imperialism and Social Reform* (London, 1960), p. 25. Of course American progressives were not immune to imperialism. See W. E. Leuchtenburg, "Progressivism and Imperialism: The Progressive Movement and American Foreign Policy, 1898-1916", *Mississippi Valley Historical Review*, XXXIX, December 1952.
25. *Elements of Political Science* (Boston, 1906), p. 369.
26. *Ibid.*, pp. 283-85.

The future of Canada as a united country depended, he insisted, upon the strengthening of the imperial tie.[27]

Far from being "carried from his moorings", as Harold Innis suggested, Leacock, when he spoke of imperialism, was expressing the essence of his social and political ideas. At one level, he was concerned about the future of imperial organization and made it a subject of both academic study and public advocacy – the two rarely being distinct.[28] But at a much more significant level, imperialism was far more than an arid question of institutional political science, or another counter in the chequerboard of world power politics, though Leacock was concerned to save Canada from the seductions of the Monroe Doctrine.[29] For Leacock, imperialism was a panacea for the ills that beset the country and these ills were primarily spiritual. They were the ills of a society where men, in Leacock's opinion, were almost totally concerned with their petty, selfish, material interests – interests defined by the values of a pecuniary culture. Without a new spirit, a new idealism, Canada as a community would perish. That new spirit, in Leacock's judgment, would be provided by a commitment to the cause of imperial unity. That was the message of his widely distributed pamphlet *Greater Canada: An Appeal: Let Us No Longer Be A Colony*, first published in the *University Magazine* in 1907.

At the outset of his manifesto Leacock made it plain that his concern was for the national future of Canada. "To many people in Canada," he wrote,

> this imperialism is a tainted word. It is too much associated with a truckling subservience to English people and English ideas and the silly swagger of the hop-'o-my thumb junior officer. But there is, and must be for the future of our country, a higher and more real imperialism than this – the imperialism of the plain man at the plough and the clerk in the counting house, the imperialism of any decent citizen that demands for his

27. "The Imperial Crisis", *Proceedings of the Canadian Club of Toronto, for the Year 1905-06* (Toronto, 1906), p. 118.
28. "Responsible Government in the British Colonial System", *American Political Science Review*, I, May 1907, 355-92; "The Political Achievement of Robert Baldwin", *Addresses delivered before the Canadian Club of Ottawa, 1903-09* (Ottawa, 1910), pp. 160-65.
29. "Canada and the Monroe Doctrine", *The University Magazine*, VIII, 3, October 1919, 352-74.

country its proper place in the councils of the Empire
and the destiny of the world.[30]

But what was the point of this new imperialism? It meant the involvement of Canadians in the affairs of the wider world, the real
world. It meant leaving the parochialism of Canadian politics, and
the materialism and corruption of Canadian society. It would, in
short, give Canadians a spirit, a nationalism, to match the potential
greatness of the country.

> Would that the soul of its people were commensurate
> with its greatness. For here as yet we fail. Our politics,
> our public life and thought, rise not to the level of our
> opportunity. The mud-bespattered politicians of the
> trade, the party men and party managers give in place
> of patriotic statecraft the sordid traffic of the tolerated
> jobbery. For bread, a stone. Harsh is the cackle of the
> turkey-cocks of Ottawa, fighting the while as they
> feather their mean nest of sticks and mud, high on their
> river bluff. Loud sings the Little Man of the Province,
> crying his petty Gospel of Provincial Rights, grudging
> the gift of power, till the cry spreads and town hates
> town, and every hamlet of the countryside shouts for
> its share of plunder and of pelf. This is the tenor of our
> politics, carrying as its undertone the voice of the black-
> robed sectary, with narrow face and shifting eyes, snarl-
> ing still with the bigotry of a by-gone day.[31]

The evil and corruption of Canadian life and politics was obviously deep-seated; almost, one would have thought irradicable. Leacock
knew that no mere institutional tinkering, no minor political reform
could change that condition. Something more profound, akin almost
to a religious experience, was called for. "This is the spirit that we
must purge," he wrote. "This is the demon we must exorcise; this is
the disease, the cankerous worm of corruption, bred in the indolent
security of peace, that must be burned from us in the pure fire of
an Imperial patriotism that is not theory but a passion. This is our
need, our supreme need of the Empire – not for its ships and guns,
but for the greatness of it, the soul of it, aye for the very danger
of it."[32]

30. *Greater Canada*, p. 2.
31. *Ibid.*, p. 5.
32. *Ibid.*, p. 6.

Here then was Leacock's prescription for the ills of a society dominated by the moguls of the Mausoleum Club and the turkey-cocks of Ottawa. Whether Canadians lived on Plutoria Avenue or in Mariposa, their vision was blurred by parochialism and materialism. To overcome this corrupt condition, Leacock appealed to the purgative power of patriotism. He was thus one of a long and distinguished line of Canadian intellectuals, reaching back to the Canada First Movement and forward to *Canadian Dimension*, who have sought to solve Canada's problems by a strong injection of nationalism. For Leacock, nationalism and imperialism were one. Here, of course, Leacock parted company with Veblen who expressed nothing but cynicism about the uses of patriotism – at least until the Great War broke out. But perhaps the difference was not so radical: Veblen's "socialism" and Leacock's "imperialism" were both designed as cures for plutocratic social darwinism.[33]

The doctrine of social darwinism, in Leacock's judgment, was both morally reprehensible and politically dangerous. His writings contain several attacks on the doctrine, but nowhere did he express himself more forcefully than in a rather pessimistic essay entitled "The Devil and the Deep Sea", published in the *University Magazine* in December 1910. The belief which holds that "whatever is, is right" is a belief leading to the deification of power, a sanctification of the law of the jungle. Its social results, Leacock maintained, could be seen everywhere. "The nation cuddles its millionaires, cinematographs itself silly with the pictures of its prize fighters, and even casts an eye of slantwise admiration through the bars of its penitentiaries."[34] This pecuniary culture resulted from the triumph of social darwinism.

In his non-fictional writings Leacock devoted little space to the role of the businessman in Canadian society, though his fictional work applies considerable imagination to this problem, particularly in the *Arcadian Adventures*. Here we find the businessman as university president, the church as counting house, and the leisure class as cultural illiterates. Nor did Leacock disguise his scepticism about the praise heaped upon the businessman for his acumen. The tale of

33. Daniel Aaron, *Men of Good Hope* (New York, 1951), p. 226, and David Riesman, *Thorstein Veblen* (New York, 1960), pp. xii-xiv and chapter V.
34. "The Devil and the Deep Sea", *Essays and Literary Studies* (New York, 1916), p. 59.

Tomlinson, the wizard of finance, was nothing less than a thorough debunking of the Horatio Alger myth.[35]

The triumph of commercialism distressed Leacock most in the field of higher education. Probably no character in Leacock's writings is treated less sympathetically than President Boomer, whose Plutoria University "taught everything and did everything".[36] Leacock's ideal university was, of course, Oxford.[37] But his views are best summed up in a sad and witty essay entitled "An Apology of a Professor", first published in 1910. There he denounced the decline of true learning and the rise of professional education. In the new educational mill, busily grinding out its products, the truly dedicated professor was lost. And in the larger society his plight was even more desperate. "But in these days when money is everything, when pecuniary success is the only goal to be achieved, when the voice of the plutocrat is the voice of God, the aspect of the professor, side-tracked in the real race of life, riding his mule to Padua in competition with an automobile, may at least help to soothe the others who have failed in the struggle," Professor Leacock remarked gloomily.[38] Leacock wanted the university to remain a spiritual oasis in a materialistic desert, but instead he was witnessing the triumph of what Veblen was later to christen the "captains of erudition".[39]

Another puppet of the plutocrats, in Leacock's view, was the politician, and he devoted a great deal of space to expounding this viewpoint. This was the theme, of course, of "The Great Fight for Clean

35. *The Arcadian Adventures of the Idle Rich* (1914; reprinted in the N.C.L., Toronto, 1959), pp. 22-36.
36. *Ibid.*, p. 39.
37. *My Discovery of England* (1922, reprinted in the N.C.L., Toronto, 1961), pp. 72-97.
38. "An Apology of a Professor", *Essays and Literary Studies*, p. 35. In his response to the commercialization and bureaucratization of the university Leacock, like Veblen, is a good example of Richard Hofstadter's remark that "the central theme of progressivism was revolt against the industrial discipline; the progressive movement was the revolt of the unorganized against the consequences of organization" (*The Age of Reform* [New York, 1955], p. 214). "My Financial Career" expresses this spirit to perfection. See *Literary Lapses*, pp. 1-4.
39. Leacock's description of Plutoria President Boomer, published in 1914, anticipated Veblen's "captain of erudition" in an uncanny way. See *Arcadian Adventures*, p. 40, and Thorstein Veblen, *The Higher Learning in America*, (New York, 1918), pp. 250-51. See also Stephen Leacock, "The University and Business", *The University Magazine*, XIII, 4, December 1914, 540-49.

Government".[40] Commenting on the Liberal victory in the general election of 1908, Leacock informed an English audience that neither of the Canadian political parties had any clear principles or philosophy. He proceeded to explain why.

> In Canada, indeed, to those who have is given. Office brings with it control of expending Departments whose pecuniary favours, even apart from corruption, fall upon the constituencies in a fructifying shower. In a new country such as ours, public works, railways and canals, become words to conjure with. A wharf is built here, a railway branch there, a river dredged, a new post office building is erected, all on a lavish and handsome scale calculated to stir the gratitude of local contractors with a lively sense of favours still to come. And if to this is added the machination of the dark lantern politician, the timber-limit man, the town site speculator, and the room-for-all land agent, then the Canadian government is able to entrench itself in a fortress wellnigh impregnable.[41]

But Leacock did not believe that the politicians were entirely to blame; the people were corrupted because they were corruptible. Here Veblen's ethic of "pecuniary emulation" was at the heart of the explanation: "We are still a nation in the groping stage, groping for money; when we have got it and enough of it, we may hope to turn honest men." Moreover, he wrote in a later essay, there was the god of bigness that seemed to blind Canadians to questions of quality. Undiscriminating immigration into the Canadian West, he feared, would result in a gulf between Eastern and Western Canada that would be most serious. "The Canadian toad swells and distends in vain emulation of the bulk of the American ox," he declared in a resounding plea for selective immigration.[42]

With these views of the dynamic of Canadian politics, "The Great Election in Missinaba County" takes on a rather less humorous colouration. For all its wit, bathed in the warm sunshine of Mariposa,

40. *Arcadian Adventures*, pp. 139-57.
41. "Sir Wilfrid Laurier's Victory", *The National Review*, 52, 311, January 1909, 831-832.
42. "Canada and the Immigration Problem", *The National Review*, 57, 338, April 1911, 337.

that chapter might well be viewed as one of Leacock's most bitter satires, perhaps exceeding anything in the *Arcadian Adventures*. The point may be simply stated: the election of 1911, concerned as it was with the issue of reciprocity, touched Leacock deeply, since he believed that the future of the Empire depended upon its outcome. He personally campaigned for the Conservative cause. Yet in Mariposa the winning candidate, the Conservative, Josh Smith, obviously had no interest in, or understanding of, what Leacock believed to be the central issue. The values of Josh Smith, small-town hotelkeeper, were obviously no different than those of the Clean Government Association. Mariposa and the Mausoleum Club were one.

Personally Leacock was delighted with the Conservative victory in 1911. He viewed it as a "plebescite of eight million people on this half of the continent in expression of their earnest wish for an enduring union with the Empire".[43] Subsequently he fought hard for the adoption of an imperial defence policy that would ensure a common imperial front. "Let the government try to hold the people of Canada from a British war," he predicted, "and the streets would run with blood of civil conflict, and the Confederation of Canada break instantly asunder."[44] When " a group of eighty-seven elderly gentlemen" in the Canadian Senate "smashed their walking sticks through the windows of the constitution"[45] by rejecting Borden's Naval Aid Bill, Leacock doubtless hoped that the Conservatives would take the imperial question to the country. But they did not, for they too were mere politicians.

Since Leacock had long preached that patriotism was the necessary purgative for materialism, the Great War brought the testing time. In 1909 he had feared that Canadians were in danger of forgetting "the lean, eager patriotism and sacrifice of a people bred for war", and would merely "ply in peace the little craft of gain and greed".[46] The coming of war brought a great outpouring of patriotism. But it did not bring an end to profit. Once more Leacock rose to denounce the "smug hypocrisy" of those who placed profit ahead of patriotism,

43. *The Great Victory in Canada*, reprinted from *The National Review*, 58, 340, November 1911, 12.
44. "What Shall We Do About the Navy?" *The University Magazine*, X, 4, December 1911, 546.
45. "The Canadian Senate and the Naval Bill", *The National Review*, 61, 365, July 1913, 986.
46. *Greater Canada*, p. 2.

and to call for a selfless national win-the-war campaign.[47] He hoped the war would usher in a new era sharply in contrast with a past where "our whole conception of individual merit and of national progress has been expressed in dollars and cents".[48]

The Great War in no way dampened Leacock's personal enthusiasm for the cause of imperial unity but by the war's end he had concluded that the cause, however just, had little future. One of the few significant alterations which he made in his "new and enlarged" 1921 edition of *Elements of Political Science* was in the section on imperial organization. Where he had presented imperial federation as a practical proposal in the earlier editions, he was now forced to write that "the events of the war have entirely changed the outlook. All proposals for a formal federation and for a supreme parliament and for pan-imperial taxes are drifting into the background of academic discussion."[49]

But the declining significance of the imperial cause did not weaken Leacock's desire to humanize the plutocracy he still saw around him. "The real governing forces in North America," he wrote in 1919, "are such things as Big Business, the Manufacturers, the Labour Unions and, in various forms, National Hysteria."[50] National hysteria meant public opinion, particularly the public opinion which had brought about the evil of prohibition. In fact, the decline in his hope for imperial union coincided with the publication of Leacock's one systematic attempt to express his views on social reform and the limits of individualism.

That attempt, *The Unsolved Riddle of Social Justice*, which Leacock published in 1920, was hardly a clarion call for the radical restructuring of Canadian society. Yet when measured against the views of other middle-class reformers of the time – W. C. Good's *Production and Taxation in Canada*, Salem Bland's *The New Christianity*, or W. L. M. King's *Industry and Humanity* – its strong reformist tone is undoubted. And it is in this book, more than anywhere else, that Leacock examines the social consequences of industrial plutocracy. "Few persons can attain adult life," he wrote, "without being pro-

47. "Our Organization for the War", in Miller, *The New Era in Canada*, pp. 409-21.
48. "Democracy and Social Progress", *ibid.*, p. 32.
49. *Elements of Political Science* (Boston, 1921), p. 280.
50. "The Warning of Prohibition in America", *The National Review*, 73, 437, July 1919, 682.

foundly impressed by the appalling inequities of our human lot. Riches and poverty jostle one another upon our streets. The tattered outcast dozes on his bench while the chariot of the wealthy is drawn by. The palace is the neighbor of the slum."[51]

Poverty in the midst of plenty, Leacock argued, was the natural consequence of the "age of machinery"[52] when the individual was allowed an unrestricted right to increase his wealth and power, to society's detriment. But the war had shown the way out of this condition. First, it had brought the end of superfluous production, thus showing that production could be primarily for use and not for profit.[53] But the war also illustrated that the state could, and should, shoulder a large responsibility for the well-being of the citizen. "If every citizen owes it to society that he must fight for it in case of need," Leacock maintained, "then society owes to every citizen the opportunity of a livelihood.[54]

In future, then, unrestrained individualism would have to give way to a broad state responsibility for social reform. This reform, of course, fell substantially short of socialism, a doctrine which, after a rather superficial examination, Leacock dismissed as fit only for "a community of saints".[55] Nevertheless, Leacock goes very far towards outlining a concept of the welfare state that went well beyond what Canadians were to enjoy for some decades. "Put in the plainest terms," he wrote, "we are saying that the government of every country ought to supply work and pay for the unemployed, maintenance for the infirm and aged, and education and opportunity for the children".[56]

Leacock's ideal was the middle-class liberal one of equality of oppor-

51. *The Unsolved Riddle of Social Justice* (Toronto, 1920), p. 14.
52. *Ibid.*, p. 23.
53. *Ibid*, pp. 30-31.
54. *Ibid.*, pp. 127-28. If Leacock had been following Veblen's writings in these years he might have been less hopeful about reform in the postwar years. Writing in *The Dial* in 1919, Veblen predicted an immediate return to plutocratic "normalcy". See Aaron, *Men of Good Hope*, p. 208.
55. *The Unsolved Riddle*, p. 94. In attacking socialism Leacock chose an easy, and dated, target: Edward Bellamy. Perhaps this was because his book was designed for a popular audience. But the same approach is used in the *Elements of Political Science* despite the fact that in the 1921 edition he included in his bibliography the first-rate critical account of modern socialism published by his fellow political economist at Queen's University, O. D. Skelton. See *Socialism: A Critical Analysis* (Boston and New York, 1911).
56. *The Unsolved Riddle*, p. 140.

tunity. He had no doubt that that condition could not be attained unless the state assumed responsibilities that would take it far beyond anything dreamed of in traditional *laissez-faire* theory.

III

The Unsolved Riddle of Social Justice marked Leacock's full acceptance of the character of the new Canada that had emerged from the Laurier and Borden years. What he now advocated was that public policy should be brought into line with the conditions of an industrial and urban society. He was attempting to provide some guidance in overcoming a problem which J. S. Woodsworth had perceived even before the outbreak of the Great War. "The fact is that in Canada," Woodsworth had written, "industrialism has been suddenly thrust into what was essentially an agricultural society. . . . Improvement comes slowly and is resisted, because the Canadians who largely dominate the situation do not understand the new social order. Country-bred men, essentially individualistic in thought and ethics, have attained positions of responsibility in highly organized industrial concerns."[57] These were the wealthy plutocrats, dozing in their plush chairs in the Mausoleum Club, "practically every one of [whom] came from Mariposa once upon a time."[58]

It was the character of a country in the process of transition from Mariposa to the Mausoleum Club that had always been Leacock's essential concern. He may occasionally have yearned for the simple life of an agrarian past, but he knew all too well that rural life in Canada was far from idyllic.[59] He may even have sympathized with his good friend Andrew Macphail, who never ceased to praise the virtues of the rural life and denounce the evils of industrial society.[60] Perhaps he was partly describing himself when he wrote of Macphail:

> I am certain he never quite knew what he believed and
> what he didn't; but underneath it all was a deep-seated
> feeling that the real virtue of a nation is bred in the

57. J. S. Woodsworth, "Some Aspects of Immigration", *The University Magazine*, XIII, 2, April 1914, 190.
58. *Sunshine Sketches*, p. 149.
59. *The Boy I Left Behind Me* (Toronto, 1947).
60. Andrew Macphail, "The Conservative", *The University Magazine*, XVIII, 4, 419-43.

> country and that the city is an unnatural product. To-
> wards plutocrats, bankers, manufacturers and such, he
> felt a little bit as a rough country dog feels towards a
> city cat. He didn't quite accept them. Andrew would
> have made a fine radical, if he hadn't hated radicalism.[61]

Whether because of his training as a political economist, or for
some more personal reason, Leacock resisted the temptation to turn
his back on the urban-industrial world he saw emerging. Instead, he
tried to come to terms with it, even while he criticized it, satirized
it, laughed at it. Yet for all the serious problems which came as part
of industrial society, Leacock believed that it contained potential for a
better life than any time in the past. "Only a false mediaevalism can
paint the past in colors superior to the present," he wrote. "The haze
of distance that dims mountains with purple, shifts also the crude
colors of the past into the soft glory of retrospect. Misled by these,
the sentimentalist may often sigh for an age that in nearer view
would be seen filled with cruelty and suffering."[62] Here is no yearn-
ing for a lost Arcadia. Nor does one find it in his fiction. *Sunshine
Sketches of a Little Town* and *The Arcadian Adventures of the Idle
Rich* both document the emergence of the new Canada, just as their
contemporary, *Maria Chapdelaine*, might be seen as heralding the
death of the old.

The contradictory elements in Leacock's social and political views
are much less apparent when they are woven together into a whole,
the imperialism and the critique of plutocratic individualism going
hand-in-hand. But some of the contradictions, or vaguenesses, still
remain, for Leacock was both analysing and reflecting a period of
profound transition. It is impossible, therefore, to categorize his
views with an easy "ism". He was surely not a "Tory of the
eighteenth century",[63] nor can he be transformed into nothing more
than an American progressive. He drew from both of these traditions,
the latter probably more than the former if only because it had more
relevance to the society in which he was living. Yet here, too, he
drew upon social-imperialist thinking in Great Britain. But above all,

---

61. "Andrew Macphail", *Queen's Quarterly*, Winter 1938, pp. 451-52.
62. *The Unsolved Riddle*, p. 24.
63. Desmond Pacey, *Creative Writing in Canada* (Toronto, 1961), p. 117.

Leacock was concerned with Canadian problems, and was part of a Canadian intellectual tradition.[64]

That Canadian tradition has been characterized by repeated efforts to raise questions about the quality of Canadian life when the gross national product seemed the major concern. It has also been characterized by an attempt to give Canada a self-consciousness and an identity. Leacock belonged to and enriched that tradition. But to categorize him further would be to do violence to the eclecticism that has given that tradition so much of its strength. A writer of Leacock's quality should perhaps be allowed the not very serious last word, even when describing his own political views. "Liberal Conservative," he wrote, "or, if you will, a Conservative Liberal with a strong dash of sympathy with the socialist idea, a friend of Labour, and a believer in Progressive Radicalism. I do not desire office but would take a seat in the Canadian Senate at five minutes' notice."[65]

It can only be regretted that senatorial status was never achieved. It would certainly have brought laughter, and perhaps even reform.

---

64. Carl Berger, in *The Sense of Power*, examines this tradition for the first time in an analytical and convincing fashion.
65. *The Hohenzollerns in America* (Toronto, 1919), p. 218.

The American Revolution and Indian History

S. F. WISE

"He has excited domestic insurrections among us, and
has endeavoured to bring on the inhabitants of our
frontiers, the merciless Indian Savages, whose known
rule of warfare, is an undistinguished destruction of all
ages, sexes, and conditions."

Declaration of Independence.

The picture of the cruel, arrogant, treacherous and essentially un-
American Tory so long a part of traditional American historiography
on the American Revolution has been undergoing revision in recent
years, as scholars like R. R. Palmer, W. H. Nelson, Leslie Upton and
others have focused attention upon the ideological, social and economic divisions within the Thirteen Colonies that made for Loyalism.
Although the stock image of the Tory is probably too inherent a part
of the American historical consciousness to disappear altogether, a
much more informed appreciation of the character of those "domestic
insurrections" referred to in the Declaration of Independence is
certainly emerging.

Nothing like this has happened, or is likely to happen, to the

Indian dimension of the Revolution. Although there have been a few isolated attempts to look at the Revolution as a phase in Indian history, chiefly by historians whose interests are anthropological, the weight of historical opinion, whether American, British or Canadian has reflected, in more temperate language, the outrage of the Declaration of Independence, the wartime propaganda of Franklin and Adams, the denunciations of the Whig opposition in Parliament, and the horror stories of nineteeth-century American patriotic history. Theodore Roosevelt, in *The Winning of the West*, condemned the British government for using the Indians. "The sin consisted in having let them loose on the borders; once they were let loose it was impossible to control them. . . . the fact must ever rest a dark stain on their national history." G. M. Wrong dismissed the Indians as "dangerous and useless allies"; C. P. Lucas found them "unstable as friends, ferocious as foes" and "not fit helpmates for Englishmen in fighting Englishmen". Piers Mackesy, though much more balanced, reflects the same stream when he says, with reference to Burgoyne's inability to recruit Indians in the numbers he had hoped for, that this was "no great loss, for except as scouts they proved worse than useless, and their savagery made effective propaganda to rally the enemy's militia".[1]

Now it is beyond question that Indians operating as the auxiliaries of regular forces were seldom effective, and it is also undeniable that the Indian way of war was not governed by the same restraints that have from time to time modified the manner in which Europeans have fought. But the root assumptions of the traditional historiography go deeper than this. They are that the Indians were instruments to be "loosed", that had Britain forbore from using them, the Americans would have preserved a neutrality towards them, and that it is possible to speak of "Indians" without distinctions when making statements about their role in the Revolution. These notions are at best half-truths.

To write of "Indians" as if they were one people is historically as absurd as the now discarded stereotype of "Tories". On the eve of the Revolution the northern superintendency of Sir William Johnson contained several distinct Indian groupings, each with its tribal

1. Theodore Roosevelt, *The Winning of the West*, 2 vols., New York, 1894, II, 4; G. M. Wrong, *Canada and the American Revolution*, Toronto, 1935, p. 324; C. P. Lucas, *A History of Canada, 1763-1812*, Oxford, 1909, p. 158; Piers Mackesy, *The War for America, 1775-1783*, London, 1964, p. 130.

divisions. The behaviour of Indian tribes within each grouping varied considerably, in accordance with the past history of the tribe, its degree of exposure to white culture, its past associations with French or English, its geographical position, its relationship with other tribes and its own patterns of conduct. The Micmac and Malecite of Nova Scotia had had a long relationship with the French in opposition to the British and the New Englanders. The same was true of the artificial confederation called the Canada Indians or Seven Nations of Canada, made up of such shattered eastern Algonkian tribes as the Abenaki, migrant Iroquois, a few transplanted western Indians and the remnants of the Huron confederacy. The Six Nations, the most important northern grouping, had historically aligned themselves with the English and the American colonists against the French, for reasons familiar to every student of Canadian history. The Seven Years' War had ended the quasi-independence of this confederacy by removing the opportunity for balancing English against French, a policy they had skilfully pursued for generations. Along the Ohio River, and directly exposed to frontier encroachment, were the Delaware and the Shawnee, both Algonkian in origin and both historically affiliated with the Six Nations in the Indian equivalent of a vassal relationship. Less immediately affected by settlement but historically tied to the French fur trade were the tribes of the Ottawa confederacy, the Ottawa, Chipewa and Potawatomi, dispersed about the shores of Lakes Huron, Michigan and Superior. Between the Ottawa confederacy and the little known tribes of the Plains Sioux were tribal groupings under pressure from both, and more apt to be involved in Indian than in white politics. Along the western shores of Lake Michigan were to be found such tribes as the Menominee, Folsavoin, Winnebago, Sac and Fox; farther to the south were tribes of the Miami or Wabash confederacy, including the Miami, Kickapoo, Mascouten and Piankashaw. No single explanation can account for the behaviour of all these groupings during the Revolution, or even from year to year as the war went on.

II

Most of the misconceptions about the Indian part in the Revolution originate in the American national myth, but they can be found as well in the arguments used by the parliamentary opposition to

Lord North's government and to the war policies of Lord George Germain, the Secretary of State for the American Department. The only full-dress debate in Parliament upon the British use of Indians took place in late 1777 and early 1778, following upon the disaster that overtook Burgoyne's expedition. At the beginning of his campaign, Burgoyne had issued a bombastic manifesto to the colonists, inviting them to rally to the royal standard and accompanying his invitation with a threat of Indian reprisal:

> I have but to give stretch to the Indian Forces under my direction, and they amount to Thousands, to overtake the harden'd Enemies of Great Britain and America . . . wherever they may lurk. If . . . the phrenzy of hostility should remain, I trust I shall stand acquitted in the Eyes of God & Man in denouncing and executing the vengeance of the state against the wilful outcasts. The messengers of justice & of wrath await them in the Field, and devastation, famine, and every concomitant horror that a reluctant but indispensable prosecution of Military duty must occasion, will bar the way to their return.[2]

As it happened, Burgoyne had not thousands, but at most seven or eight hundred Canada Indians under two inexperienced British officers, and a handful of Ottawa under the redoubtable Canadian officer, St. Luc de la Corne.[3] His manifesto had enormous propaganda repercussions in New England, particularly after some of his Indians murdered Jane McRea, a young woman engaged to a British officer. During the summer and fall of 1777 the militia of New York and New England began to gather against Burgoyne, inspired in part by a flood of propaganda of which the following is a relatively light-hearted sample:

> *I will let loose the dogs of hell,*
> *Ten thousand Indians who shall yell,*
> *And foam and tear, and grin and roar,*
> *And drench their moccasins in gore.*

2. J. M. Hadden, *A Journal kept in Canada and upon Burgoyne's campaign in 1776 and 1777*, Albany, 1884, pp. 59-62.
3. P.A.C., Series Q 13, Carleton to Germain, 26 June 1777, 188-89; Hadden, 78, 474.

They'll scalp your heads, and kick your shins,
And rip your guts, and flay your skins,
And of your ears be nimble croppers
And make your thumbs be tobacco-stoppers.[4]

Although, except for the murder of Jane McRea, nothing resembling the atrocities promised by Burgoyne had taken place, the Indian part in the campaign had been so inflated by American pamphleteers that Lord Suffolk was unwisely prompted to defend their use by declaring that "it was perfectly justifiable to use all the means that God and nature put into our hands" to suppress rebellion. The Earl of Chatham, "shocked" at the enunciation of principles "equally unconstitutional, inhuman and unchristian", violently attacked the ministry for loosing upon "your Protestant brethren" savages whose known method of warfare was murderous barbarity.

> What! to attribute the sacred sanction of God and nature to the massacres of the Indian scalping knife – to the cannibal savage, torturing, murdering, roasting and eating – literally, my lords, eating the mangled victims of his barbarous battles! Such horrible notions shock every precept of religion, divine or natural, and every generous feeling of humanity. . . . I call upon the spirit and humanity of my country to vindicate the national character: I invoke the genius of the constitution.[5]

Chatham's oratory set the tone of subsequent debate, both in Lords and Commons. His rhetoric made a deep impression, in spite of its obvious hypocrisy. The fact was, as General Amherst reluctantly pointed out, that he, under orders from the administration Chatham had led during the Seven Years' War, had himself used Indians against the French, a circumstance that led Lord Denbigh to term Chatham "the great oracle with the short memory". The real heart of the opposition's attack, aside from the general political advantage they sought, was that Indians were being used not against the French (after all, they had been so employed for more than a century in North America), but against their own flesh and blood. Frenchmen

---

4. Lynn Montross, *The Reluctant Rebels: The Story of the Continental Congress, 1774-1789,* New York, 1950, p. 212.
5. T. C. Hansard, *The Parliamentary History of England from the Earliest Times to 1803,* XIX, London, 1814, 18 November 1777, 368-70.

were one thing, but as Chatham said, it was execrable that Britons should "loose these savage hell-hounds against our brethren and countrymen in America, of the same language, laws, liberties and religion, endeared to us by every tye that should sanctify humanity".[6]

By far the ablest, and certainly the longest, speech on the employment of Indians was made in the Commons by Edmund Burke. His prime contention was that the Indians were unique among peoples in the ferocity with which they made war. They had "but two principal objects" in fighting; one was "the indulgence of their native cruelty", the other was "the glory of acquiring the greatest number of scalps" and "the gratifications arising from torturing, mangling, roasting alive by slow fires and frequently even devouring their captives". Past use of this cruel people in wars with the French was of no weight, for the imperial rivalry which had caused the two powers to become entangled with the Indians no longer existed. The ministerial argument that if Britain did not employ the Indians, the Americans would, was baseless. Congressional policy from the outset had been to establish Indian neutrality. Like other opposition speakers, he cited the resolution of the committee for Indian affairs of the Congress of 30 June 1775, which called for "proper talks to the several tribes of Indians, for engaging the continuance of their friendship to us, and neutrality in our present unhappy dispute with Great Britain". The government contention that great care had been taken to prevent the customary cruelty of the Indians he thought a joke, for if that were the case, there would be no point in using them, for as troops they were worthless. At huge expense the government had bribed into the field savages whose only accomplishment was to debase the character of Great Britain in the eyes of the world, and to destroy any lingering hope that the Americans would unite with the British government in securing a lasting and cordial peace.[7]

The case put forward by the North government for the use of Indians consisted of two simple propositions, beyond which no government speaker would go. The first was, as North himself, in replying to a question, had put it to the House as early as 20 November 1775, that "there was never any idea of employing the Indians, until the Americans themselves had first applied to them", an argument reiterated during the 1777 debate. The second was that given the nature of the Indian attitude towards warfare referred to by Burke,

6. *Ibid.*, 5 December 1777, 509, 511; 18 November 1777, 370.
7. *Ibid.*, 6 February 1778, 694-99.

they "would not have remained idle spectators". Germain put both arguments in a nutshell:

> Now taking the disposition of the Indians with the applications which had been made to them by the colonies, it amounted to a clear, undisputed proposition, that either they would have served against us, or that we must have employed them. This being the alternative, he contended for the necessity of employing them, and was ready to submit his conduct on that ground, to the judgment of the House.[8]

How accurate was the ministerial argument that the government had not considered using Indians until the Americans actually did so? What can be said for it is that it contains a certain small measure of truth, in that it reflects the indecision and temporizing of the ministry during the period preceding actual hostilities. In one respect, the argument was quite true. The superintendent of the Northern Indian Department, Sir William Johnson, had bent his efforts to secure the neutrality of the Six Nations confederacy. When fighting broke out in 1774 between settlers on the Ohio lands of the Vandalia Company and the Shawnee and other Indian tribes of the region, Johnson managed to restrain the Six Nations from joining in the struggle at a conference held at Johnstown in June, 1774. Colonel Guy Johnson, Sir William's nephew and successor, (Sir William died during the conference) continued to follow this line for the rest of 1774 and well into 1775, after the Shawnee war had been overtaken by the deepening quarrel between the Crown and the American colonies. As late as mid-1775, when events in Boston clearly forecast the nature of the conflict to come, Johnson appears still to have urged neutrality upon the Six Nations at a conference held at Oswego.[9]

8. *Ibid.*, XVIII, London, 1813, 20 November 1775, 994; XIX, 6 February 1778, 700-1.
9. E. B. O'Callaghan, (ed.), *Documents Relative to the Colonial History of the State of New York*, 15 vols, Albany, 1853-1887, VIII, Proceedings at a Congress with all the Chiefs and Warriors of the Six Nations, June-July 1774, 474-78; Proceedings of Col. Guy Johnson with the Six Nations, 3 December 1774, 521; Proceedings of the Commissioners of the Twelve United Colonies with the Six Nations, 15 August – 2 September 1775, 630-31. Johnson later changed his story, probably as the result of the switch in British policy, and claimed that he persuaded the Six Nations at Oswego to participate actively in the war. *Ibid.*, Journal of Col. Guy Johnson from May to November 1775, 660.

But the superintendent of the Indian Department was subordinate to the commander-in-chief of British forces in America, General Thomas Gage. During the same period that Guy Johnson was working for the neutrality of the most important Indian group in his area of responsibility, the Six Nations, the military authorities were setting in motion quite a different policy. As early as 4 September 1774, Gage inquired of Carleton whether a body of Canadians and Indians could be recruited "for the Service in this Country, should matters come to Extremities". In addition to his well-known pledge of a Canadian regiment, Carleton in reply indicated that the Seven Nations Indians could probably be recruited, although "you know what sort of People they are". When pressed for a more positive response, Carleton pointed out that the responsibility for control of the Indians, including the "Domiciliés" (Canada Indians) of Quebec, rested with Guy Johnson, but assured Gage that not only they "but all the neighbouring Indians are very much at your Disposal, whenever you are pleased to call upon them, and what you recommend shall be complied with".[10] Carleton's obvious reluctance to take the initiative, and the restraints imposed upon Gage by the Earl of Dartmouth, Secretary of State for the American Department, during the period when the ministry still hoped for a peaceful settlement, prevented the commander-in-chief from following up this first overture. Then, on 12 June 1775, just five days before Bunker Hill, Gage sent Dartmouth the news of Ticonderoga, which would justify Carleton attacking the insurgents on his frontier, and, he added, "we need not be tender of calling upon the Savages, as the Rebels have shewn us the Example by bringing as many Indians down against us (at Boston) as they could collect". At the same time Gage appears to have written to Guy Johnson ordering him to switch from the neutrality policy to one of encouraging active association of the Six Nations and other tribes with British arms. Dartmouth acted immediately upon receiving Gage's despatch; and on 24 July Johnson was instructed by him to "lose no time" in inducing the Six Nations "to take up the hatchet against His Majesty's rebellious subjects in America". This was the crucial policy decision, taken by Dartmouth on the receipt of a single despatch giving no details whatever of the

10. Adam Shortt and A. G. Doughty, (eds.) *Documents Relating to the Constitutional History of Canada, 1759-1791*, 2 vols, Ottawa, 1918, II, Gage to Carleton, 4 September 1774, 583-84; Carleton to Gage, 20 September 1774, 584; Carleton to Gage, 4 February 1775, 662.

facts alleged. Dartmouth's successor, Germain, who took office in November, was much more vigorous in pushing the use of Indians than Dartmouth had been. One of the reasons he gave for replacing Carleton with Burgoyne as head of the planned expedition from Canada was that Carleton's "hesitation in using Indians" told against him.[11]

The fact was that Gage's despatch gave the ministry the kind of pretext it was looking for; had there been real doubts about the policy a much more deliberate approach would have been taken before adopting it. Since 1763 the Crown had maintained, through the Indian superintendencies, an elaborate alliance system not only with the Six Nations, their traditional allies, but also with those Indian nations once associated with the French. As the imperial legatee of the French fur trade, Great Britain inherited as well the Laurentian strategy upon which the trade had been built. The appearance of a few Stockbridge (Mohican) Indians at Lexington and the siege of Boston was the only excuse needed to put into operation the costly mechanism of the Indian Department.

As it happened, Gage was right about the American use of Indians, though the step the ministry later attributed to the Continental Congress had in fact been taken in March 1775 by the Massachusetts Congress, when it enlisted a number of Stockbridge Indians as minutemen. On 1 April, this body went further by requesting the Rev. Samuel Kirkland, a Massachusetts missionary to the Oneida, to persuade the Six Nations to "whet their hatchet" or "at least engage them to stand neuter". Missions were sent at the same time to the Indians of Nova Scotia, the Abenaki of St. Francis, and the Iroquois of Caughnawaga. The remarkable Ethan Allen had also attempted to enlist the support of the Caughnawaga Indians; his letter to them was intercepted by Carleton. The Continental Congress, however, ignored such unauthorized activities in resolving to secure

---

11. P.A.C., CO 5, 92, Gage to Dartmouth, 12 June 1775, 102; N.Y. Docs., VIII, Dartmouth to Johnson, 24 July 1775, 596; Germain to Burgoyne, August 1776, quoted in Mackesy, p. 106. In his Journal, Guy Johnson refers several times to a letter written him by Gage early in June, ordering him to enlist the Six Nations. See N.Y. Docs., VIII, Journal of Col. Guy Johnson from May to November 1775, 660. Although no copy of the letter has been found, it was probably written on or about 7 June 1775. On that date General Gage wrote Governor Legge of Nova Scotia ordering him to "secure the Indians to our Side". P.A.C., Series A, 94, Gage to Legge, 7 June 1775, 133.

Indian neutrality on 30 June, although another resolution on the following day called for "an alliance with such Indian nations as will enter the same" whenever it should be proven that the British were using Indians. At a conference at German Flats on the Mohawk in August, Congress' commissioners secured a promise of neutrality from a part of the Six Nations that included almost the whole of the Oneida and Tuscarora, and a similar conference at Pittsburgh in September with the Shawnee, Delaware, Ottawa and Mingo had the same outcome.[12]

Even before it had become apparent that the British intended to make full use of Indians, however, Benjamin Franklin had proposed "a perpetual alliance, offensive and defensive" with the Six Nations; in December, Congress resolved to call upon the St. Francis, Penobscot and St. John River Indians, and voted presents for them; and by 25 May 1776 it had swung so far from the idea of Indian neutrality that it resolved "that it is highly expedient to engage the Indians in the service of the United Colonies". On 3 June General Washington received its authority to employ "not more than 2000 Indians" in the campaign against Canada. Only four days after the outburst of the Declaration of Independence against the British use of "the merciless Indian savage", Washington was authorized to employ immediately the Indians of Maine and Nova Scotia.[13]

It is fair to conclude that both ministerial and opposition arguments in England were correct, up to a point. Americans had tried to employ Indians as allies, though not by authority of the Philadelphia Congress; Congress, on the other hand, had indubitably encouraged Indian neutrality at the outset. The British, for their part, though pursuing a pacific course through the Indian Department,

12. Justin Winsor, *Narrative and Critical History of America*, 8 vols., Boston, 1884-1889, VI, 613, 615; Peter Force, *American Archives*, 4th series, 6 vols., Washington, 1837-1853, I, 1347-49; II, 942, 1444, 1501; P.A.C., Q 11, Carleton to Dartmouth, 15 May 1775, 161; J. H. Smith, *Our Struggle for the Fourteenth Colony*, 2 vols., New York, 1907, I, 283; P.A.C., Q 11, Ethan Allen to the Councillers at Kocanawago, 24 May 1775, 193-94; N.Y. Docs., VIII, Proceedings of the Commissioners of the Twelve United Colonies with the Six Nations, 15 August to 2 September 1775, 618; W. H. Mohr, *Federal Indian Relations, 1774-1788*, Philadelphia, 1933, p. 34; L. P. Kellogg, *The British Regime in Wisconsin and the Northwest*, Madison, 1935, p. 134.
13. Continental Congress, *Journal*, II, 21 July 1775, 198; *ibid.*, III, December 1775, 401; Winsor, VI, 616-17; N. V. Russell, "The Indian Policy of Henry Hamilton, a Revaluation", *Canadian Historical Review*, XII, 1930, 23.

had few real misgivings about securing Indian help. The scruples of neither side were deeply entrenched, as the rapid move from the policy of neutrality to one of active solicitation of Indian assistance demonstrated.

III

The motivations of the white belligerents in the Revolution are sufficiently clear with respect to the Indians. What of the Indians themselves? Indian history becomes "history", unfortunately, only when it impinges upon white affairs, and a grasp of Indian motivation is gained only from evidence that has passed through the filter of white interpreters. For the most part, an assessment of Indian behaviour during the Revolution comes from such inadequate sources, and from an analysis of their actions. If, as Burke thought, the sole object of Indian warfare was the gratification of their lust for killing and scalp-hunting, then fighting on either side would satisfy them. But to deny the Indians some conception of their own interests would be to deny them humanity. It is surely suggestive that, among the northern tribes, Congress was able to win the support only of the Stockbridge Indians, part of the Oneida and Tuscarora, a small number of the Abenaki and Caughnawaga among the Seven Nations, and for a brief period a handful of Malecite Indians of the St. John River.

Of course, the odds in the contest to win Indian help were heavily weighted in favour of the British. Much more easily and cheaply than the Americans, the British could produce the trade goods upon which the Indians had become so dependent. Throughout the Revolution, they controlled the western posts, the chief outlet for trade goods. For years before the Revolution, the Indian Department had been in the hands of men whose paternalistic protection of the Indians had itself been a protest against the formlessness and indiscipline they considered the chief quality of frontier society, and whose chief endeavour had been to impress the Indians with the essential difference between the benevolence of the Crown and the incorrigible greed of the colonists. Only one Indian Department employee, George Croghan, took the American side, and he had left the department in 1772.[14] American historians have striven to show

14. A. T. Volwiler, *George Croghan and the Westward Movement*, Cleveland, 1926, pp. 230-31, 324-25.

that such factors as these account for Indian support of the British, when in fact they are merely the considerations which would bring about a friendly neutrality.[15]

But on top of British goods, arms and friendship was added the abiding Indian fear of encroachment upon their tribal lands. To tribes under demographic pressure, the Revolution was an opportunity. Pontiac's rising had shown that even a large confederacy of hitherto un-allied nations could not defeat the whites. The Shawnee war had been the blind hopeless retaliation of a tribe goaded beyond its endurance. The Revolution, however, restored a familiar division, with the British assuming the role of the French as the protectors and leaders of the Indians. There was no basis in fact for the contention of Germain and North that Great Britain employed the Indians to prevent their use by the Americans; with few exceptions there was no prospect of such an eventuality. For those tribes menaced by colonial expansionism, the chance was too good to let slip. Within two years of the commencement of hostilities in 1775, the only tribes of the Northern Department which had not gone to war against the United States were those of Nova Scotia and the distant west.

In explaining the behaviour of Indian groups during the Revolution, the tribes of the maritime region have a special place. The relative unattractiveness to settlement of their tribal lands had saved them from the extermination or dispersal that had been the lot of their seaboard brethren to the south at an early stage of English colonial history. Both the Micmac and the Malecite had joined the French against the New Englanders in the seventeenth and eighteenth centuries, and against the English in Nova Scotia after 1713. Nothing had occurred since 1763 to change the Indian outlook, although the establishment of the tiny New England settlement of Maugerville on the St. John River may have been of some significance in changing the attitude of the neighbouring Malecite. Lacking any strong interest in a war between enemies, the maritime tribes were simply "available" to whichever side chose to solicit their services. Procrastination by Legge's government in Nova Scotia meant that the Americans of Massachusetts got in the first bid. On 19 July 1776, for a cash payment, the representatives of Massachusetts concluded a treaty with the Malecite and Micmac in which the Indians agreed to furnish "600

15. See, for example, Ray Billington, *Westward Expansion*, New York, 1949, p. 174.

strong men" to join the American army at New York for a period of three years. Nothing whatever came of this treaty except a temporary rise in maritime Indian prosperity. When Jonathan Eddy launched his assault on Fort Cumberland, he managed to recruit sixteen Malecite at Maugerville; as the British commander observed, even this could have been prevented "had the smallest attention been paid to their Chiefs in the neighbourhood of St. Johns, which by some strange mistake has been entirely omitted". The situation was rectified in May 1777 at a conference on the St. John between Colonel Arthur Goold and the Malecite, and future amity ensured when the sloop *Vulture* captured two American vessels from Machias loaded with presents for the Indians.[16]

The entry of France into the war necessitated a further treaty with the tribes; the value they placed upon extinguishing their traditional ties with the French was 577 pounds, 2 shillings and ninepence. One further flareup, the result of French tampering, occurred among the Micmac of the Miramichi from May to July of 1779. "In the King of France's name" they terrorized the small English fishing settlement and robbed the inhabitants of tools and clothing. A trader from Canada, William Ross, managed to escape from them by posing as a Frenchman; they "placed such confidence in him, that they complied to all his proposals; but a little after he was gone they were informed he was only a Scotchman". Ross got in touch with Captain Hervey, R.N., of H.M.S. *Viper*, who arrived off Miramichi under French colours and welcomed aboard several Micmac "dressed in the best Cloaths belonging to the Inhabitants", and bearing the French Admiral D'Estaing's proclamation to the Canadians and Indians. The masquerade over, Hervey concluded a treaty with the Indians, buttressed by a threat from Haldimand to bring the wrath of the Six Nations down upon them.[17]

16. P.A.C., Series A, 99, Treaty of alliance and friendship entered into and concluded by and between the governors of the State of Massachusetts Bay and the delegates of the St. Johns and Mickmack Tribes of Indians, 19 July 1776, 10-19; *ibid.*, 96, Sir George Collier to Germain, 21 November 1776, 322; ibid., 97, Arthur Goold, Speech to the Indians of St. John, 11 May 1777, 189-92; *ibid.*, Goold to Arbuthnot, 28 May 1777, 208-10; D. C. Harvey, "Machias and the Invasion of Nova Scotia", C. H. A. *Report*, 1932, pp. 20-21.
17. Series A 98, Hughes to Germain, 12 October 1778, 181-82; *ibid.*, 99, Hughes to Germain, 16 January 1779, 3-4; P.A.C., Series B, 119, Memorial of the Turbulent Proceedings of the Indians in the River Miramichi between the 15th May and the 20th July 1779, 66-71; Captain Augustus Hervey, Pro-

For the remainder of the war the maritime tribes turned a deaf ear to blandishments from the nest of American rebels at Machias, Maine, and from the French. In this theatre British and Americans had begun upon an equal footing: they were both cordially disliked by the Indians. Since neither tribe had anything to fear from either Nova Scotian or New England expansionism, the outbreak of the Revolution meant nothing to them. British money and British goods – and British sea power – were enough eventually to secure the friendly neutrality of these tribes; "half Boston, half English".[18]

Among the Canada Indians, the Abenaki of St. Francis had been in generations past the spearhead of French partisan warfare against the New England frontiers. This tribe had been shattered by war, the final blow being Robert Rogers' punitive raid during the Seven Years' War. The Abenaki were in no danger of losing their lands or their lives in the Revolution; their territory was rugged and uninviting, and their villages were relatively safe from incursion. To a large extent they appear to have shared the Canadian habitant's apathy towards the war; in order to gain their help Carleton had to promise to grant them more land. They do not seem to have participated actively after the disastrous Burgoyne campaign; a few individuals, notably Joseph Louis, engaged as couriers or guides for American emissaries to the Canadians, but they were the exception. If the Abenaki had no great love for the British, they had less for the Bostonians.[19]

Quite different again was the response of other Seven Nations villages to the Revolution, notably the Iroquois centres of St. Regis and Caughnawaga. A fairly significant number of Indians from these villages maintained connections with the Americans, but what the British authorities called perfidy was as much the outcome of their past history and present situation as the "loyalty" of the Six Nations was of theirs. During the Seven Years' War the Indians of St. Regis and Caughnawaga had displayed a quite dispassionate attitude to-

ceedings with the Indians of Miramichi, July 1779, 59-66; Treaty of Peace and Friendship concluded by Augustus Hervey . . . with John Julien Chief of the Miramichi Tribe of Indians, 28 July 1779, 72-74; Message sent to the Mickmacks living at Miramichi . . . by the Governor of Canada, 23 August 1779, 82.

18. P.A.C. Series A, James Hawker to Sir George Collier, 4 July 1777, 228.
19. J. A. Maurault, *Histoire des Abenakis*, Sorel, 1866, pp. 582-83; P.A.C. Series B, 111, Campbell to Haldimand, 11 February 1779, 54-55; *ibid.*, 113, Mathews to Campbell, 13 October 1780, 110-11.

wards the disputes of the whites; from 1763 to 1775, while the Ohio
tribes were attempting to fend off white encroachment, the Caughnawaga were engaged in litigious bickerings with the Jesuits and the
civil authorities; and when the Revolution broke out, these Indians
and those of Lac des Deux Montagnes almost succeeded in their aim
of being enemies to none and friends to all. The strong infusion of
New England blood in all the tribes of the St. Lawrence lowlands, and
the nearly complete security of their lands from encroachment by
settlers, combined to sharpen their capacity for shrewd bargaining.
The ideological appeals of either side meant nothing to them; and
during the American invasion of Canada their weathervane behaviour frustrated both Montgomery and Carleton. The outcome of the
Burgoyne campaign seems to have convinced many of the Canadian
Iroquois (who formed the majority of the Indian auxiliaries) that
Britain was not going to win the war, but hemmed about as they
were in the northern cockpit of British power, they could not give
full rein to their politic decision to side with the probable victors.
Therefore they gave laggard assistance to the British for the rest of
the war, while maintaining the fullest connection possible with the
Americans. A small number of St. Regis and Caughnawaga Indians,
in the summer of 1780, left their villages and made their way to
Oneida territory in New York. From this vantage point they distributed propaganda originating in American headquarters in Albany
throughout the Canadian villages and to the Six Nations as well.
Many of the rumours that caused ferment in Canada, such as the
perennial story about a French fleet coming to blockade the St. Lawrence, originated with them; while their conduct served to work upon
Six Nations' feelings of isolation and betrayal. When an officer of the
Indian Department tried to enlist their services to help the Six Nations against the Sullivan expedition in 1779, he found that they
"seem more disposed for goeing to hunt Beaver & Deer".[20] Although
the Seven Nations of Canada gained no military renown during the
Revolution, they suffered no crippling losses, nor were their villages
and fields first ravaged and then taken from them. They were neither
Burke's bloodthirsty savages nor Indian patriots of the Brant type.
Instead, they seem to have appreciated fully the futility of bitter-end
resistance to the white, and lacking any cause of their own, rode out
the Revolution by playing one side off against the other.

20. *Ibid.*, 113, Haldimand to Campbell, 8 April 1779, 13; *ibid.*, 111, Campbell
    to Mathews, 27 September 1779, 129.

Another pattern of Indian behaviour again was that of the far western tribes of the Illinois country. To counter the effects of George Rogers Clark's occupation of virtually the whole of the Illinois country in July 1778, Henry Hamilton, the lieutenant-governor at Detroit, launched a counter-offensive relying almost entirely upon Indian help. "As the effects of pushing a force supported by the zeal of the Indians . . . have not yet been tryed", he wrote enthusiastically to Haldimand, "I hope to be excused if perhaps too sanguine". Hamilton was putting his faith in tribes remote from the settlement frontier. Such tribes as the Kickapoo, Potawatomi, Mascouten, Piankashaw, Miami and Ouiatenon joined Hamilton eagerly enough, but they melted away once Fort Vincennes had been taken. What Hamilton discovered was that these Indians had no great interest in the war, aside from the presents and loot they could obtain; when these prospects were exhausted, they returned to the hunt or to their homes. When Clark suddenly appeared before Vincennes in February 1779, all that was left of Hamilton's force were a few regulars from Detroit and some scouting parties of Ottawa, and Hamilton was compelled to surrender. Despite this result, it was decided in 1780 to base another campaign upon the same undependable peoples. Partly this was because enormous sums had been spent by the Indian Department in maintaining the trade and friendship of these groups. Haldimand was appalled to discover that it was costing more to maintain the friendship of the tribes west of Michilimackinac and Detroit than it was to maintain the Six Nations in the field. As Haldimand observed, their "wavering Dispositions" had been held by presents alone; nevertheless, some use should be made of them to justify the huge expense of their friendship. The attempt proved as unhappy as the Hamilton fiasco. What was supposed to happen was that some one thousand Indians and traders were to seize St. Louis and Cahokia on the Mississippi in order to cut the American supply line from New Orleans, while another body of Indians was to move into the Illinois country. If all went well, perhaps even New Orleans might be taken from the north. The Mississippi force included two hundred Sioux, and several hundred warriors from the Menominee, Sac, Fox, Iowa and Winnebago tribes. This curious force disintegrated on making its first acquaintance with the artillery of the St. Louis garrison. The other wing of the great offensive collapsed when a French trader told the Potawatomi that the Illinois was garrisoned by four thousand French troops. The Detroit commandant, De Peyster, complained that "it is cruel that a single lying Rascal . . . should stop three hundred Indians", and sent them out again, only to have them become embroiled in a renewal of the ancestral feud with the Piankashaw, of much more interest to them than the war against the Americans.[21]

In contrast to the behaviour of all other northern Indian groupings stands the conduct of the bulk of the Six Nations and the Ohio Indians, that is, the Delaware, Shawnee, Mingo or Ohio Seneca, Wyandot and to a slightly lesser extent the Ottawa confederacy. Among all these tribes only a part of the Oneida and Tuscarora, a small group of Moravian Delaware (the "Praying Indians"), and a band of Delaware living uncomfortably close to Fort Pitt remained neutral or gave some limited assistance to the Americans. All these tribes, in varying degrees, were confronted with the moving frontier of American settlement; and all of them, with the exceptions noted, chose to oppose and attempt to throw back this movement. Had there been no revolution, an Indian explosion would still have occurred. It was the misfortune of the American settler that Indian resistance to him coincided with the needs of the British. The Revolution provided the war-bands with both food and weapons and the help of the Loyalist Rangers and the officers of the Indian Department. Only in this sense were the Indians "loosed".

For these Indians, the first act of the Revolution was not Lexington or Bunker Hill, but Lord Dunmore's War. It was only with the utmost difficulty that Johnson had persuaded the Six Nations from going to the assistance of the Shawnee and Delaware. The experience of the Six Nations in fighting as part of the St. Leger force at Oriskany in 1777 had been quite as unfortunate as that of the Canada Indians with Burgoyne. Unlike the Canada Indians, however, most of the New York Iroquois felt they had no choice but to fight on for their lands. Joseph Brant, the most eloquent of all Six Nations spokesmen, voiced both the hope and the despair of his people, when in speaking of the invasion of their lands by General Sullivan in 1779

21. Ibid., 122, Hamilton to Carleton, 8 August 1778, 115-16; Hamilton to Haldimand, 22 September 1778, 167-68; Hamilton to Haldimand, 24 January 1779, 266-72; ibid., 97-2, Brehm to Haldimand, 17 April 1780, 307-18; ibid., 54, Haldimand to Germain, 25 October 1780, 342-47; ibid., 100, De Peyster to Bolton, 10 March 1780; ibid., 97-1, Sinclair to Haldimand, 15 February 1780, 285; ibid., 97-2, Sinclair to Haldimand, 29 May 1780, 349-52; Sinclair to Haldimand, 8 July 1780, 389-92; ibid., 100, De Peyster to Bolton, 16 May 1780, 373; ibid., 122, De Peyster to Haldimand, 31 August 1780, 538.

he said, "if we beat the Rebel Army, they will never invade our Country again", but at the same time reflected that "of course their intention is to exterminate the people of the Long House". It is significant that the first major raid undertaken by the Six Nations was that on the rich Wyoming valley, their traditional hunting ground and the first area to be flooded by white settlement after the Seven Years' War.[22]

The position of the Ohio tribes was the same. Nothing could be more explicit than the following statement made by them to George Morgan, Congress' commissioner for Indian affairs at Fort Pitt:

> You have feloniously taken possession of part of our country on the branches of the Ohio, as well as the Susquehanna, to the latter we have some time since sent you word to quit our Lands as we now do to you, as we don't know we ever gave you liberty, nor can we be easy in our minds while there is an arm'd Force at our very doors, nor do we think you, or anybody else would. Therefore to sue you with more lenity than you have a right to expect, we now tell you in a peaceful manner to quit our lands wherever you have possessed yourselves of them immediately, or blame yourselves for whatever may happen.[23]

This is not the place to recount the history of the war on the borders of New York, Pennsylvania, Virgina and Kentucky between 1777 and 1782. It was a war of sudden descents upon little frontier farming communities, of ruthless attacks upon the isolated dwellings of pioneer husbandmen, a war of ambush, burning, slaughter and widespread material destruction. It was a war in which the Indian object was not to occupy ground but to kill, ravage and destroy, to depopulate and restore to primitive virginity land which had felt the plough. It was a war of countless pin-prick raids at widely scattered points along the vulnerable frontier, made by silent and swiftly moving bands normally numbering less than one hundred warriors. The thread that ran through it was the unrelenting resolve of the Six

22. *Ibid.*, 100, Brant to Bolton, 19 August 1779, 231; Brant to Daniel Claus, 19 August 1779, quoted in H. Swiggett, *War Out of Niagara*, New York, 1933, p. 196; James Sullivan, (ed.), *The Papers of Sir William Johnson*, 10 vols., Albany, 1921-, IV, Johnson to Amherst, 30 March 1763, 70-71.

23. J. A. James, *The Life of George Rogers Clark*, Chicago, 1928, citing Morgan's letter book for 2 February 1777, p. 41.

Nations and Ohio Indians to hurl back white interlopers from their territory. They were neither beasts howling for blood for its own sake, nor merely paid pawns of the whites. For them, the Revolution was another bitter episode in a struggle as old as European settlement in North America. For the historian, it was another phase in the losing struggle of primitive peoples against the irresistible expansion of European technological civilization. This is why unknown numbers of Americans died in the Revolution without seeing a battlefield, why gutted and blackened buildings stood desolate in a great swath of ruin curving for a thousand miles across the northwest, and why the Revolution was not one war but two, waged simultaneously but for entirely different reasons and for entirely different ends.

Sir Robert Borden, the Great War and Anglo-Canadian Relations

ROBERT CRAIG BROWN

Historians of modern Canada are agreed that the Dominion's participation in the Great War resulted in a fundamental change in the Anglo-Canadian relationship. And though they may argue over the precise nature of the change they credit Sir Robert Borden with responsibility for the transition which took place. Borden was at once the instrument and the embodiment of the transition. Before the First World War, with the exception of Canada's direct relations with the United States, at no time was Canadian advice crucial, or even influential, in the determination of imperial foreign policy. But in the winter of 1918-19 Borden, representing Canada, sat in the highest councils of the Empire-Commonwealth, contributing to decisions on imperial foreign policy. That was indeed a far cry from the state of affairs when Sir Robert had first gone to London to speak for his country in discussions about naval policy just six years earlier. Then, in the summer of 1912, all he secured in return for a promise of a contribution to the imperial navy was the privilege of wistful participation in an advisory committee with a grandiose title but increasingly less influence over foreign policy. Significantly, Asquith and Harcourt pointed out to Borden this negative interpretation of Canada's participation in the Committee of Imperial Defence both at the time and in retrospect.[1] Strangely, Borden seemed to ignore the cautionary advice of the British prime minister and the colonial secretary. He chose to interpret the concession more positively: "No important step in foreign policy would be undertaken without consultation with such a representative of Canada," he told the House of Commons on his return.[2] He regarded it as an important initiative towards Canadian responsibility in foreign policy, temporarily sufficient though not the ultimate goal. Of course, many "important steps" were taken without consultation with Canada, or, for that matter, with the C.I.D. In Canada, between the 1912 visit and the beginning of the war, the Senate quashed the Canadian part of the bargain by rejecting Borden's naval bill. Attitudes to policy had been expressed in the inconclusive naval debate, but no opportunity presented itself for their transformation and practice.

In mid December 1913 Loring Christie, recently recruited by Borden as legal advisor to the Department of External Affairs and governmental factotum, pointed out the inconclusiveness of Canadian foreign policy in a memorandum for the prime minister. "The Canadian people must sooner or later assume a control over foreign policy (i.e. over the issues of peace and war) no less effective than that now exercised by the people of Britain or by the U.S.A." Reflecting on the crystallization of attitudes that had come out of the naval debate, and over-simplifying them, Christie saw only two routes for Canada:

1. Participation in the C.I.D. discussions was based on the 1911 Imperial Conference resolution which included the phrase, "when questions of naval and military defence affecting the Oversea Dominions are under consideration". Harcourt's despatch of December 10, 1912 noted that "We [Asquith and Harcourt] pointed out to him [Borden] that the Committee of Imperial Defence is a purely advisory body and is not and cannot under any circumstances become a body deciding on policy. . . ." See Department of External Affairs, *Documents on Canadian External Relations*, I, 1909-1918 (Ottawa, 1967), no. 390, p. 276 and no. 401, pp. 276-77. (Hereafter referred to as DCER).

I would like to thank Mr. Robert Bothwell, who was my research assistant in the summers of 1968 and 1969, for his assistance and suggestions in the preparation of this paper. Mr. Bothwell is preparing a study of Loring Christie for his doctoral thesis at Harvard University.
2. See his speech of December 5, 1912, on Naval defence. Canada, House of Commons Debates, 1912-13, cols. 692-693.

(A) By separating their own foreign policy from that of the Empire and by controlling it through their own Dominion Government.

(B) or by insisting that the foreign policy of the Empire be separated from the domestic affairs of Britain and entrusted to a government responsible no less to Canadian than to British voters. . . . it follows that in assuming control of foreign affairs, Canadians will either commit their country to final separation from the Empire or to becoming an organic part of it . . . .

He added that most Canadians, however, "do not grasp the reality of these two alternatives, neither of which is palatable, nor do they understand that it is impossible to evade one or the other."[3]

It is the purpose of this paper to suggest that Canada's participation in World War I and the consequent strains it produced in the Anglo-Canadian relationship provided the opportunity to clarify the objectives of Canadian foreign policy and to achieve responsibility in foreign affairs without having to accept either of the "unpalatable alternatives" presupposed by Loring Christie.

The first step in the process was to articulate Canadian justification for participating in the war at Great Britain's side. Once done, the Canadian statement became both the background and the framework for the Canadian case in subsequent disputes with the British government and, with constant reiteration, a statement of Canadian war aims. Significantly, Canada's enunciation of explicit war aims was unique among the autonomous Dominions. No other Dominion government spent as much time and effort elaborating what were defined as national war aims as did the Canadian. As early as August 6, 1914, Borden instructed Christie to draw up the initial statement. Sir Robert believed it was imperative to "justify the action of Great Britain"[4] and, more important, establish why Canada should follow the British lead. Canada did not participate in the war simply because when Britain was at war Canada was at war. Rather, Canada was involved in "a struggle in which we have taken part of our own free will and because we realize the world-compelling consideration which its issues involve". Those considerations were larger than the Anglo-

3. Public Archives of Canada, Borden Papers, Memo from L.C., December 10, 1913, no. 67875.
4. P.A.C., Christie Papers, II, file 6, Borden to Christie, August 6, 1914.

Canadian relationship, larger than the welfare of the Empire. What the Kaiser had called into question was "the future destiny of civilization and humanity" and "the cause of freedom".[5]

For Borden this was more than pious rhetoric. Like a good prosecuting attorney, he wanted to establish his texts and marshall the facts necessary to his brief. He referred Christie to Oppenheim's volume on international law, specifically to his concept of the "community of interests" of "civilized states". He asked Christie to

> lay particular stress upon the refusal of the . . . Emperor to accept the mediation which was so earnestly sought by . . . Grey and which doubtless would have prevented the war. Emphasize also the weakness of the excuses which the Emperor offers and . . . the violation of the treaty . . . guaranteeing the neutrality of Belgium.

Borden's use of the word "justify" was deliberate. The Emperor had violated the norms of conduct of "civilized states" and it was necessary to apportion blame. Germany and, at least at this stage of the war, more particularly the Kaiser, was being arraigned. Justification was to be established or discredited by a process not dissimilar to that of a trial, and then enforced by the united action of Canada in fulfillment of its "duty to the world".

Canadian war aims, couched in the terminology of legal moralism, were constantly stressed by Borden. The war was a struggle to punish the German "military aristocracy" for disturbing the peace of the world and to prevent it from doing so again. The war was just; being just it had to be pursued – and here lies an important distinction from the later attitudes of Smuts and Sir Henry Wilson – until the objective was unequivocally attained. "Probably no part of the Britannic Commonwealth was more disinterested in reaching a decision as to its duty," Borden wrote in 1918. "We are ready to fight to the last for the cause as we understand it, for every reasonable safeguard against German aggression and for the peace of the world."[6]

At the heart of Borden's concept of Canadian war aims was the assumption that the law must be used as an instrument of war, as

5. "Canada at War", A Speech . . . by . . . Borden", November 18, 1916, pp. 7-9.
6. Department of External Affairs, Borden Papers, Peace Conference, file 18, Borden to L. S. Amery, August 22, 1918.

the basic rationale for Canadian participation in the war. The law was the bedrock of civilization – "the chief insignia of a civilized nation are orderly government and respect for the law."[7] The law must be protected if civilization was to endure; it must be the active agent in the prosecution of a just war. In the past it had been the most suitable instrument used by civilized men to eliminate inequality and bondage. Now that inequality and bondage under the Kaiser threatened the civilized states, the purposefulness of the law must be reasserted. Borden told the Lawyers Club in New York City that "the purpose of the law must be found in some help which law brings towards reaching a social end."[8] During the war that social end was the punishment of the Kaiser's Germany, the salvation of the "civilized states" and the eventual establishment of a higher international order.

Total involvement in the war, of course, meant the acceptance of great sacrifices for Canada and its people. But because the call to duty was based upon the righteousness of the cause there would be attendant benefits to the participants. At the front the humdrum life of the average young man would be enlivened by a sense of commitment, an exercise of mind, spirit and morality which was tested in physical endeavour and sacrifice. It all could be, the English scholar Gilbert Murray observed, "one form at least of very high happiness".[9] Borden believed that the beneficial social effects of making war extended to all Canadians.

> They have learned that self sacrifice in a just cause is at once a duty and a blessing, and this lesson has both inspired and ennobled the men and women of Canada. It was indeed worth a great sacrifice to know that beneath eagerness for wealth and apparent absorption in material development there still burned the flame of that spirit upon which alone a nation's permanence be founded. One must move among our people to realize their overmastering conviction that the justness and greatness of our cause overpower all other considerations and to comprehend the intensity of the spirit

7. Speech to New England Society, New York, December 22, 1915. Borden Papers, no. 175538.
8. "Canada at War", *op. cit.*, p. 5.
9. Cited, Arthur Marwick, *The Deluge* (London, 1967), p. 48.

which permeates and quickens every Canadian community.[10]

He was convinced that out of Canada's commitment to what
Arthur Marwick has called "a deeply felt sense of moral purpose"
would come a better Canada and a better world. "The character of a
nation is not only tested but formed in stress and trial, through
sacrifice and consecration to duty," he told a London Opera House
audience in August, 1915.[11] A month later the Canadian Club in
Ottawa heard the prime minister suggest that the war would "prove
to be the death of much that marred and hindered the progress and
development of civilization and democracy. Shall we not hope and
indeed believe, that this war may prove the birth pang attending the
nativity of a nobler and truer civilization."[12]

Loring Christie, reflecting his, as distinct from Borden's, close
connections with the Round Tablers, was more specific in his hopes
for Canadian war aims. In a burst of imperial enthusiasm he told
Charles Magrath that the war offered "the greatest opportunity ever
held out to a young nation", "a chance at least to save our soul of
Canada". The path to salvation was through recognition by Canadians of "this crying need of coming together", of the necessity of
the "members of the British Commonwealth" to "deliberately join
their destinies".[13] But Borden refused to follow his advisor's lead.
Mention of imperial consolidation is seldom found in his speeches
and, when present, is clearly stated as co-operation rather than consolidation. Indeed, on occasion, the prime minister even deleted
"British Dominions" from a Christie draft and inserted "Canada" in
the final address.[14] Again and again he placed more stress on Canada's
duty to civilization at large than did Christie. Christie hoped for
the "coming together" of the British Empire; time and again in his
speeches Borden looked to a "noble and truer civilization", the "re-
generation of civilization".

Canada's war aims were nationally defined, general, moral and un-
selfish. They provided the high-minded purposefulness which Sir

10. "Canada at War", *op. cit.*, p. 8.
11. Borden Papers, no. 175500-07.
12. *Ibid.*, no. 175510.
13. Christie Papers, II, file 3, Christie to Magrath, n.d.
14. Compare, for example, the draft of "Canada at War" in Christie Papers,
    II, no. 1385-92, with the copy of the text in Borden Papers, no. 175560-6
    and the printed pamphlet cited above.

Robert believed was the necessary answer to critics of Canada's war effort. They convinced him of the purity of his and his country's motives in pursuing the war. They convinced him, further, of the superiority of the morality and earnestness of Canada's contribution. This point was brought into sharp relief by the inevitably increased intimacy of the Anglo-Canadian relationship during the war and the resultant conflicts over priorities among the contending partners, both in everyday operations and in ultimate objectives. "So far as Canada is concerned," Borden loftily proclaimed to his fellow members of the Imperial War Cabinet, "she did not go into the war in order to add territory to the British Empire."[15] Behind all of Borden's stormy complaints about the British war effort and Canada's part in it rested the "first principles" of Canada's own war aims.

One matter of continual concern to Borden and his colleagues in Ottawa was the apparent incompetence of the British High Command. Hughes reported in the late spring of 1915 that "complacency is observed on every hand". Though mobilization in Canada was certainly a triumph of luck rather than the consequence of rational planning, Borden did not hesitate to complain to Perley about the "apparent lack of system in the War Office touching the measures being taken here".[16] Perhaps the evidence from the mercurial Minister of Defence, by itself, could be dismissed or heavily discounted. But it did fit with the general impression of discord and disillusionment in 1915 that accompanied the long-delayed realization that the war was a conflict of uncertain duration and scope. On June 16 Borden received a letter from Colonel J. A. Currie "complaining of lack of foresight and incompetence of British. 'They send us on every for-lorn hope.' " The following week Sir Richard McBride returned from England and reported that he was "not optimistic as to result of war. He thinks England did not take it seriously enough at first. He doubts competency of some English generals." The total neglect of the Dominion by the Asquith government meant that there was no opportunity to get evidence to the contrary and only reinforced Canadian doubts. And what Borden saw and heard during his visit to London in the summer of 1915 confirmed his worst fears. "The efforts which Great Britain is making to provide the necessary war

15. DCER, II, no. 14, pp. 13-14.
16. Borden Papers, "Memo on the War Situation" by Hughes, no. 31706-21; Hughes to Borden, May 28, 1915, no. 31777-9; Borden to Perley, June 4, 1915, no. 31698-9.

material, such as guns, machine guns, ammunitions, etc." was hardly, he told his cousin, Sir Frederick Borden, "characterized by reasonable efficiency." Almost desperately, he sought reliable information on the military situation. To his dismay he discovered on the eve of his departure for Canada that Kitchener "had forgotten the preparation of the memo he had undertaken".[17]

Nor was there any improvement as the war dragged on. One observer attributed the disastrous defeat on the western front in the spring of 1918 to the "blundering stupidity of the whiskey and soda British Headquarters Staff", and Borden replied that there was "some ground for that impression".[18] At the War Cabinet meeting of June 11, called to consider the implications of the spring's events, Lloyd George "gave no explanation of how Germans can drive our forces back and inflict greater losses than they incur". But the same day Sir Clifford Sifton, "who is greatly disturbed", did have an answer: "says many British divisions useless and men disorganized." The next day General Currie arrived and "gave an awful picture of the war situation among the British. Says incompetent officers not removed, officers too casual, too cocksure. No foresight."[19]

At another meeting of the War Cabinet on the 13th Borden was scheduled to make a statement on the war activities of the Dominion. After a summary of Canadian war statistics he angrily turned to the subject of the British defeat in France. "There must be a cause for our failure," he observed, adding that "it seems apparent, having regard to the material of which the British Army is composed, that the unfortunate results which have obtained during the past year, and especially during the past three months, are due to lack of foresight, lack of preparation, and to defects of system and organization." He cited Currie's comments comparing Canadian and British troops and leadership, with examples pointedly taken from Passchendaele. There and elsewhere routine and stupidity had frustrated sound planning. British intelligence was invariably worthless. British preparations were inadequate. A British officer had "told [Currie] that in his corps they had nothing comparable [to the Canadian barbed wire] and that in his particular battalion the men were engaged in

17. Borden Papers, Private, Diary, June 16 and 25, August 23, 1915, Borden to Sir Frederick Borden, September 9, 1915. R.L.B. Series, folder 929.
18. Borden Papers, Memoir Notes, no. 2382.
19. Diary, June 11 and 12, 1918.

preparing lawn tennis courts last autumn while the Canadians were erecting barbed wire entanglements."[20]

"Curzon, Lloyd George, my colleagues, the other overseas Ministers, Long etc. gave me very warm congratulations," Borden noted afterward in his diary.[21] And later in the day Lloyd George confessed that so far as the Flanders offensive of the previous summer was concerned, "the Government felt considerable misgivings . . . but were not prepared to overrule their military advisers in regard to the strategy of the war."[22] The explanation was hardly sufficient. Borden believed that "if the British Army Corps had made the same preparation to meet the German offensive as did General Currie and the officers and men of the Canadian Forces, the German offensive could not possibly have succeeded as it did". "One could almost weep," he concluded, "over the inability of the War Office and even of the Admiralty to utilize the brains of a nation at a time when brains are most needed."[23] Until the very end the contrast between the efficiency and success of the Canadian Corps and the incompetence and relative lack of success of British armies remained constantly in Borden's mind. To him it was both evidence and proof of the higher quality and character of the Canadian war effort.

The incompetence of the British High Command, Borden believed, was but a particular manifestation of a more general problem, the persistence of inefficiency and procrastination in the whole British war effort.[24] Another special problem related to this, Borden found on his 1915 visit, was the munitions crisis of that summer. On the first anniversary of the war Borden pointedly told a London audience that "in Canada we began to organize our industries for the production of munitions of war as far back as the end of August, 1914."[25] A few days later at a conference with Bonar Law, Churchill and F. E.

20. Borden Papers, no. 2484-96, Imperial War Cabinet 16, Shorthand notes.
21. Diary, June 13, 1918.
22. DCER, I, no. 340, p. 201.
23. *Ibid.*, no. 341, pp. 201-03.
24. Lord Beaverbrook, who was one of Borden's few sources of information, later described Asquith's "own way of looking at a world at war" in words Borden would have heartily seconded: "His complete detachment from the spirit of the struggle; his refusal to make up his mind on grave and urgent issues of policy; his balancing of one advisor against another till the net result was nil; his fundamental desire to have a peaceful tenure of office in the midst of war . . ." *Politicians and the War, 1914-1916* (London, 1960), p. 226.
25. Borden Papers, no. 175500-07.

Smith, the "grave" munitions crisis was discussed with discouraging results. Borden asked when there would be an ample supply of munitions. Bonar Law said within five months but Churchill "says middle of next year". "Told them I must have definite information."[26] More discouraging was the opinion Borden received at a luncheon with Bonar Law and Lloyd George.

> I had told Law that unless I received definite informa-
> tion as to munitions etc. we should stay our hand.
> L. George delivered statement as to munitions, guns,
> etc. Damning indictment of Department negligence.
> Said Great Britain would not be ready to exert full force
> for year or 18 months.[27]

Borden's feelings were best expressed in a letter to Perley some months later. "Procrastination, indecision, inertia, doubt, hesitation and many other undesirable qualities have made themselves entirely too conspicuous in this war." He recalled his August luncheon with Lloyd George who "in speaking of the officers of another Department said that he did not call them traitors but he asserted that they could not have acted differently if they had been traitors. They are still doing duty and five months have elapsed."[28]

Many of the production problems were solved as time went on. Rationalization of the supply of Canadian munitions for the British war effort, for example, was achieved in November of 1915 with the disbandment of the Shell Committee and the establishment of the Imperial Munitions Board. But the "undesirable qualities" seemed to persist, even to increase their manifestations. So far as Borden could see, the most important result of the 1918 German spring offensive was Sir Henry Wilson's reaction to it; to turn tail and run. Assessing the results of the offensive, Wilson gloomily reported to the War Cabinet on July 31 that "It must be realized that all enthusiasm for the war is dead," and that, though he had no positive recommenda-tion to make, the Allies must, somehow, resolve "to strike in 1919 or stop the war".[29] Wilson was not alone. As early as April of 1917

26. Diary, August 21, 1915.
27. Diary, August 24, 1915.
28. DCER, I, no. 184, p. 104, Borden to Perley, January 4, 1916.
29. Borden Papers, no. 66395-426. Years later Borden contemptuously wrote of Wilson, "Indeed he was the man most faint-hearted, more than any other." Borden Memoirs, II, 815.

Smuts reported to the War Office that a military victory was neither desirable nor necessarily expected. Now, on August 14, he told the War Cabinet that he was "very much against fighting [the war] to the absolute end, because I think that, although the end will be fatal to the enemy, it may possibly be fatal to us too". "Complete military victory may be attainable," he added, "but the risks that we are running are too great and we have to take a more moderate line."[30]

Smuts' speech, Borden thought, "left [him] open to serious attack".[31] Both Wilson's report and Smuts' comments were, at best, wrong-headed. This was no time to counsel compromise or admit of defeat. He had given Canada's answer a month before.

> Canada will fight it out to the end. . . . Let the past bury its dead, but for God's sake let us get down to earnest endeavour and hold this line until the Americans can come in and help us to sustain it till the end.[32]

Looking back, Borden's criticism of the British war effort can easily be matched with uncomplimentary references to much of Canada's own effort. The record, both on the home front and in the Canadian command structure, especially in England, contained more than a little of inefficiency, personal bickering and jealousy, and corruption.[33] And these too played their part in the disruption of Anglo-Canadian relations during the war. But two points can be made in reply. First, the record of the Borden governments in attempting to solve these problems as they came to light was generally creditable, especially so after the formation of the Union Government. More important, such an attack on the Canadian war effort misses Borden's fundamental point. His critique was more of attitudes than of any one or any combination of specific actions. The British, in his terms, were measured for earnestness and commitment to duty and found wanting. Of Borden's own commitment, of his earnestness, and, he believed, of his country's, there could be no doubt. If anything, the opposite was more true. Borden was, perhaps, too "earnest", too committed to winning the war to see, as Smuts did, the long-term consequences of the total defeat of Germany.

30. Borden Papers, no. 2660-72, Imperial War Cabinet 31, Shorthand notes.
31. Diary, August 14, 1918.
32. Borden Papers, no. 2484-96, Imperial War Cabinet 16, Shorthand notes.
33. A portion of this story is very well told in John Swettenham, *To Seize The Victory, The Canadian Corps in World War I*, (Toronto, 1965).

British "traitors" on the home front, incompetence in the field, and wavering in the High Command all served to aggravate even more the third general problem in Anglo-Canadian relations, the political treatment accorded to the Dominion's contribution to the war effort. Until 1917 the British government appeared to treat Canada more like a Crown Colony than the full-fledged nation it deemed itself to be. The Canadian reaction was entirely predictable. It found expression in Borden's famous "toy automata" letter to Perley on January 4, 1916. Two paragraphs bear repeating:

> During the past four months since my return from Great Britain, the Canadian Government (except for an occasional telegram from you or Sir Max Aitken) have had just what information could be gleaned from the daily Press and no more. As to consultation, plans of campaign have been made and unmade, measures adopted and apparently abandoned and generally speaking steps of the most important and even vital character have been taken, postponed or rejected without the slightest consultation with the authorities of this Dominion.
>
> It can hardly be expected that we shall put 400,000 or 500,000 men in the field and willingly accept the position of having no more voice and receiving no more consideration than if we were toy automata. Any person cherishing such an expectation harbours an unfortunate and even dangerous delusion. Is this war being waged by the United Kingdom alone, or is it a war waged by the whole Empire? If I am correct in supposing that the second hypothesis must be accepted then why do the statesmen of the British Isles arrogate to themselves solely the methods by which it shall be carried on in the various spheres of warlike activity and the steps which shall be taken to assure victory and a lasting peace?[34]

34. DCER, I, no. 184, p. 104. Eight days after it was written, Borden instructed Perley not to pass the letter on to the British government. Perhaps Perley at some stage conveyed its general sense to Bonar Law and others but they would hardly have needed to be reminded of Borden's opinions on the subject. I use it here because I think it is an accurate summation of his consistent attitude towards the problems of consultation.

This letter was in response to an exchange of correspondence in late October and early November which opened with a complaint from Borden. He granted the "necessity of central control of Empire armies", he told Perley, "but Governments of overseas Dominions have large responsibilities to their people for conduct of War and we deem ourselves entitled to fuller information and to consultation respecting general policy in War operations." Perley had taken the complaint to Bonar Law but found the colonial secretary's response discouraging. He feigned acceptance of the rightness of Borden's demand but then shifted the responsibility for doing something about it back on the Canadian prime minister – "it is our desire to give him the fullest information and if there is any way which occurs to him . . . in which this can be done I shall be delighted to carry it out." As to consultation on war policy, Bonar Law continued,

> here again I fully recognise the right of the Canadian Government to have some share of the control in a war in which Canada is playing so big a part. I am, however, not able to see any way in which this could be practically done. I wish, therefore, that you [Perley] would communicate my view to Sir Robert Borden, telling him how gladly we would do it if it is practicable and at the same time I should like you to repeat to him what I have said to you – that if no scheme is practicable then it is very undesirable that the question should be raised.[35]

Here, indeed, was the true meaning of the British government's attitude to consultation in high policy. It had been implicit in the words of caution that Asquith and Harcourt had given Borden in 1912. Now, when the matter was being put to the test, when the lives of thousands of young Canadian men were being determined behind closed doors in London, and when the Canadian government had to answer for their destinies to the Canadian people, Sir Robert and his colleagues had to rely upon the tidbits of information gleaned by Perley and Aitken supplemented by press reports. More than this was not possible, at least it could not "be practically done". The onus for correcting this unsatisfactory state of affairs appeared, moreover, to be on the Dominions. But even here it was clear that the colonial

35. *Ibid.*, no. 165, pp. 93-94, no. 172, p. 96.

secretary was in no mood to encourage a Canadian initiative; Bonar
Law had made that quite plain by his suggestion that "it is very
undesirable that the question should be raised".

The "toy automata" letter was neither a momentary outburst of
temper by the prime minister, nor was it solely concerned with high
policy, as important as that might be. Rather it crystallized the
accumulated grievances of Borden and his government over the whole
range of inadequate consultation and co-operation since August 1914.
For Borden, as we have seen, Canadian participation in the Great
War was a domestic as much as it was an external affair; it was a
matter of contracts for munitions and supplies as much as it was a
matter of maintaining the Canadian Corps at strength. The Canadian
involvement was, or at least should be, total. But the procurement
and fulfillment of war contracts was as dependent upon consultation
and co-operation with the British government as was the deployment
of Canadian troops at the front. And in this sphere the British
government had been singularly negligent.

The trouble began early in the war with a complaint over the
letting of contracts for wagons for the British and French armies in
the United States. Borden cabled Perley that "our manufacturers ask
consideration only in cases where they can supply articles of equal
quality at the same cost . . . [but] can obtain no answer from either
government except refusal unaccompanied by any reason." "Not
only the people of Canada as a whole but individuals are making
sacrifices hitherto undreamed of to support Empire in this war. A
very painful and even bitter feeling is being aroused throughout the
Dominion," he continued. "Men are going without bread in Canada
while those across the line are receiving good wages for work that
could be done as efficiently and as cheaply in this country."[36] When
orders did come, when work was finally to be done in Canada, as
with the building of submarines in Montreal, the Canadian government only found out about it when Vickers, the company concerned,
put aside work on a previously ordered Canadian government ice-
breaker. The polite language of the governor general's dispatch
covering the matter did not hide the dismay of the Canadian government over the way in which it had been arranged. Connaught
observed that his government would "be grateful if a somewhat
earlier intimation could be given to them as to the intention of His

36. *Ibid.*, I, no. 93, p. 59.

Majesty's Government in such matters as it seemed inappropriate that an arrangement . . . which involved interference with work undertaken by the company for my Government should in the first instance be communicated to my advisors by the company itself."[37]

Orders for war material eventually came in abundance. In April 1915, the Canadian Pacific Railway was appointed the British government's purchasing agent in Canada. The following month Borden appointed a War Purchasing Commission to co-ordinate and control Canadian and British war contracts (the Shell Committee was specifically exempted from the Commission's purview). And in November, as noted, the Imperial Munitions Board, responsible to the British government, acting in Canada under the chairmanship of Sir Joseph Flavelle in close co-operation with the Borden government, was established. But getting the contracts was only half the problem. Being able to fill them was another matter. Here Canadian shipping was crucial to Canadian war production. At the same time, Canadian shipping was subject to the requisitioning authority of the Admiralty. And the Admiralty exercised their powers with callous disregard of Canadian interests.

After a long series of requests for and then complaints about the lack of consultation with Canada, Borden told Perley that "it is entirely within the mark to say that no such principle has been accepted" by the Admiralty. Most recently they had requisitioned a DOSCO coaster, impairing the supply of Canadian steel for Canadian munitions plants and forcing the latter to buy their raw materials in the United States. The Admiralty "without any consultation with us have felt themselves competent and have taken it on themselves at such a distance to judge of the conflicting needs and interests involved". "It should be clearly recognized, whatever the registry of the ships concerned, if they are regularly engaged by charter or otherwise in what may be distinguished as the local or coasting trade of Canada no action disturbing them should ever be initiated by the Admiralty without consulting us or carried out without our consent." Upon what principle, Borden asked, "is it claimed that the Canadian Government should not be recognized in considering Canadian needs and conditions?"[38] Clearly, upon none whatsoever. As

37. *Ibid.*, no. 106, p. 64. This affair, a classic illustration of the point, is carefully related in Gaddis Smith, *Britain's Clandestine Submarines, 1914-1915* (New Haven, 1964).
38. *Ibid.*, no. 251, pp. 144-47.

Doherty noted in a January 1917 order-in-council, the Admiralty doubtless had the legal power to requisition the ships, but each exercise of that power violated Canada's constitutional rights. "It is the Parliament of Canada alone which constitutionally can determine and prescribe the burdens to be borne by this Dominion or by any of its citizens for the purpose of this or any other war . . . this prerogative must be exercised upon the advice of Your Excellency's Ministers and not upon the advice of the Government of the United Kingdom."[39]

The problem of consultation was, of course, largely resolved with the formation of the Imperial War Cabinet. Reacting to the increasingly harsh complaints from Canada and the other Dominions, and of the even greater burdens they were going to be asked to bear, the initiative came from Lloyd George and his advisors.[40] Lloyd George's motives were decidedly mixed. The first he revealed to Walter Long in December 1916. Because "we must have even more substantial support from them before we can hope to pull through," he wrote, "it is important that they should feel that they have a share in our councils as well as our burdens."[41] But the British prime minister also wished to use the War Cabinet, an *ad hoc* committee under his control, as an instrument against his foes amongst his colleagues, especially the High Command. In July 1918 he told Borden "that for eight months he had been boiling with impotent rage against higher command, they had affiliations and roots everywhere". "It was for the purpose of strengthening his hand in dealing with the situation that he had summoned the Dominion Ministers and the Imperial War Cabinet."[42]

Once the War Cabinet assembled, consultation on all matters of high policy, of war aims and, eventually, of peace terms and conditions took place. Perhaps even Bonar Law would have admitted that it was practical. Hankey later observed to Lloyd George that "the Governments of the Dominions were associated with the work of laying the foundations of the Peace Treaty, which was really begun

---

39. *Ibid.*, no. 277, pp. 158-59. See documents no. 278, p. 163 and no. 285, p. 167 for the resolution of this particular problem.
40. See Thomas Jones, *Whitehall Diary, Volume I, 1916-1925* (London, 1969), p. 12.
41. Lloyd George, *War Memoirs*, IV, (London, 1934), 1733.
42. Diary, July 14, 1918, and Borden, *Memoirs*, II, 827.

at the Imperial War Cabinet of 1917."[43] It was in the War Cabinet that Borden's angry attack on the High Command took place in 1918. As a result, Lloyd George established a Prime Ministers' Committee to report back to the War Cabinet on the whole scope of military policy. After careful deliberation the Committee reasserted the necessity for greater control over military policy by the civilian government. "The Government," the Committee concluded, "is in the position of a Board of Directors who have to insist that before committing the resources of the Company in some great enterprise, they shall be fully appraised of its prospects, cost, and consequences."[44]

In addition, Resolution IX of the Imperial War Conference of 1917 emanated from the meetings of the Imperial War Cabinet. Professor Hancock has written that it was "a resolution of the greatest historical importance which Smuts drafted, and carried through the Imperial War Conference."[45] Hancock's point, Smuts' singular role, is overstated. Writing to R. M. Dawson in 1935, Borden noted that "Smuts and Borden did the drafting; Austin Chamberlain suggested the reference to India. The Resolution was submitted to Long and then to Lloyd George who gave it unqualified approval before it was moved."[46] Sir Robert's diary generally accords with his later letter to Dawson. On March 19 Borden met Smuts for the first time – "He impresses one as a strong and straight forward man." On the 21st the two were joined by Massey on a committee to prepare an agenda for the Imperial War Conference. The next day the three met to discuss the agenda and a resolution regarding constitutional relations. Here an important difference of opinion between Borden and Smuts arose over a critical point in the eventual resolution. Borden's diary entries tell the remainder of the story.

> 22 March, 1917: . . . I insisted on a clause declaring
> our right to an adequate voice in foreign policy.

43. Beaverbrook Library, Lloyd George Papers, Hankey to Lloyd George, July 11, 1938, G/8/18/39.
44. Borden Papers, Memoir Notes, Report of the Prime Ministers Committee, ff. no. 2484, p. 9.
45. Hancock, *Smuts*, I, 429. Hancock's reference reads: "Amery (*My Political Life*, II, 109) says that Smuts was 'the main author' of this historic resolution" (p. 586). We might conclude that there are no Smuts papers relating to the resolution and that Professor Hancock either ignored or discounted the account of the incident in Borden's *Memoirs*, II, 667-77.
46. Borden Papers, no. 149889, Borden to Dawson, January 12, 1935.

Smuts fears this may involve responsibility for financial aid in defence etc. . . .

27 March, 1917: . . . important interview with Long . . . showed him resol^{ns} as to const^1 relations & he thought my draft most suitable. In the evening discussed them with Smuts Massey and Morris & they all agreed.

28 March, 1917: . . . Then War Confer. Gave notice of my res^n on Const^1 relations, having first seen Ward who raised no question. . . .

16 April, 1917: . . . went to Impl. War Confce at 11 and moved res^n respecting con relations. Spoke 15 minutes. Referred to King's position etc. Massey Smuts followed . . . Sinha [here the account differs with the letter to Dawson] proposed amend^t including India in a qualified manner. I accepted. Ward made a long rambling speech 50 minutes no logical idea running through it.[47]

Apparently, then, there were at least two drafts of the resolution, one by Smuts and one by Borden. They were probably much the same regarding the general matter of consultation. In its final form the resolution stated that the Dominions and India should have "effective arrangements for continuous consultation in all important matters of common Imperial concern, and for such necessary concerted action, founded upon consultation, as the several Governments may determine". But it is equally apparent that this statement did not go far enough for Borden. The experience of the preceding war years had convinced him that consultation upon "matters of common Imperial concern," was too ambiguous. It might be left up to the British government to determine what were and what were not "matters of common Imperial concern". They might or might not include "the right . . . to an adequate voice in foreign policy and in foreign relations",[48] and it was this clause which differentiated his

47. Diary, March 19, 21, 22, 27 and 28 April 16, 1917. The account in Borden's *Memoirs* also credits Austin Chamberlain with the suggestion for the reference to India. *Memoirs*, II, 668. However, the record of the Imperial War Conference proceedings matches Borden's diary references. The resolution, as originally moved by Borden, contained no reference to India. After a seconding speech by Massey and remarks by Smuts and Morris, Sir Satyendra Sinha suggested the inclusion of India in the resolution and Borden accepted it. See M. Ollivier (ed.), *The Colonial and Imperial Conferences from 1887 to 1937*, II, Part I, (Ottawa, 1954), 203-4.
48. Borden, *Memoirs*, II, 668.

draft from Smuts'. The simple fact was that the British Foreign Office had the power to commit Canada, legally, to war or to peace. And there was no greater matter of "common Imperial concern" than that. At the same time, as the order-in-council of the previous January had stated, the Parliament of Canada "alone . . . constitutionally can determine and prescribe the burdens to be borne by this Dominion or by any of its citizens for the purpose of this or any other war". It was therefore necessary to include the clause to which Smuts objected at the March 22nd meeting.

"Foreign policy and foreign relations," Borden said in his speech moving the resolution,

> with which is intimately connected the question of the common defence of the Empire, have been under the immediate control of the Government of the United Kingdom, responsible to the Parliament of the United Kingdom . . . this condition . . . has proceeded on a theory of trusteeship which, whatever may be said of it in the past, is certain to prove not only entirely inadequate to the needs of the Empire but incompatible with the aspirations of the people of the Dominions in the future.[49]

Later in the discussion Borden reminded his colleagues of the distinction between the legal powers of the British Parliament and the constitutional rights of Canada. The British Parliament had the legal power to impose a foreign policy upon Canada just as it had the legal power to repeal the British North America Act. "But there is no constitutional right to do so without our assent, and therefore, while there is the theory of predominance, there is not the constitutional right of predominance in practice, even at present." Perhaps thinking back to the quarrel over ship-requisitioning, he added that

> Questions, however do arise with regard to it from time to time. We have had, even since the War began, a question as to the exercise of the prerogative, and a question as to advice upon which the prerogative under certain conditions shall be exercised – upon the advice of the Government of the United Kingdom, or upon the advice of the Government of Canada? Doubtless,

49. Ollivier, *Colonial and Imperial Conferences*, II, Part I, 194.

[upon] the basis which is established by this Resolution they are less likely to arise in the future.[50]

Borden returned from the first series of Imperial War Cabinet
meetings full of enthusiasm for the arrangement. Canada, he had
said in London, "has raised herself to the full rank and dignity of
nationhood".[51] Canada's place at the cabinet table signalled the fact
while side-stepping the danger of centralization. It reconciled the
apparently contradictory aspiration for autonomy of which Canada
was "rightly jealous" and the "necessity of consulation and co-
operation". More important, the Imperial War Cabinet "arose out of
the necessity imposed by events, and I am thoroughly convinced that
it was not premeditated or designed".[52] Borden had told Lloyd George
in a letter of April 26 that it was desirable that "the policy under
which the Imperial War Cabinet has been assembled shall be continued until after the conclusion of the war".[53] In another letter he
went further, expressing confidence that "the usage thus initiated
will gradually but surely develop into a recognized convention".[54]
Elaborating on this point in his report to the House of Commons, he
expressed the hope "that annually at least, and, if necessity should
arise, oftener, there should assemble in London an Imperial Cabinet
to deal with matters of common concern to the Empire".[55]

The enthusiasm was premature. In the interval between the 1917
and 1918 meetings of the Imperial War Cabinet it became clear that
Borden's voice in the determination of imperial policy was predicated
on his continuous presence in London, not in Ottawa. That was both
practically and politically impossible. But while the Dominion prime
ministers were at home, the assistant secretary of the War Cabinet,
L. S. Amery, explained, their governments had "to revert to the old
system of communication through the Colonial Office". Meanwhile,
the 1917 decisions regarding war policy were totally undercut by
events. Nivelle's offensive failed; so did the Russian offensive. The
British War Cabinet sanctioned the Flanders offensive without consultation and with disastrous results. And the German drive in the
spring of 1918 was all too successful. One side of the problem was that

50. Ibid., p. 214.
51. Christie Papers, II, file 3. Speech of May 2, 1917.
52. Borden Papers, no. 175653-87. Speech to House of Commons, May 18, 1917.
53. Ibid., no. 88280.
54. Ibid., no. 175664.
55. Ibid., no. 175660.

the British government "had to shoulder that responsibility for decision-making alone"; the other was that continuous consultation was short-circuited by reliance upon the cumbersome formalized channels of communication between the Colonial Office and the Dominions. They may have been entirely adequate for relations with a nineteenth-century colony in peacetime. But Canada was a twentieth-century nation at war and, as Amery defined the use of those channels, "This is absurd."[56]

Various schemes of improvement were mooted at the 1918 Cabinet and Conference. In the latter Hughes carried through a general resolution calling for administrative changes to facilitate communications. In the cabinet he urged continuous and direct links between the prime ministers and was supported by Borden. Sir Robert added the threat that if Canada did not have "that voice in the foreign relations of the Empire as a whole, she would before long have an independent voice in her own foreign relations outside the Empire".[57]

Amery circulated a long memorandum on the "Future of the Imperial Cabinet-System", advocating an elaborate institutionalization of the War Cabinet scheme and the appointment of "certain Imperial Ministers of State" including imperial Ministries of Defence and Finance.[58] Lloyd George accepted the idea of direct communication between the prime ministers and suggested the appointment of Dominion ministers resident in London to sit in the cabinet when the prime ministers were in their home countries. Further, he wondered if the members of the cabinet might not immediately discuss the constitutional changes which Resolution IX called for after the war. "As regards the wider question of the permanent machinery of Imperial organization, he agreed with Mr. Churchill that it would be easier to set up some machinery during the war than after", and suggested a cabinet committee "investigate the machinery for carrying on the business of the Empire after the war". The Dominion representatives, however, "were not prepared to agree in the desirability of setting up even an informal Committee".[59]

Even that, let alone Amery's scheme, smacked of enough centrali-

56. DCER, no. 497, p. 338. Memo by L. S. Amery, "The Future of the Imperial Cabinet System", June 29, 1918.
57. Borden Papers, No. 2582, Imperial War Cabinet 26.
58. DCER, no. 497, pp. 332-44.
59. Borden Papers, no. 2595, Imperial War Cabinet 27, no. 2603, Imperial War Cabinet 28.

zation to frighten them off. With direct continuous consultation agreed to, it was better to let well enough alone and allow the future to provide for itself. Borden clearly recognized that the Imperial War Cabinet was an *ad hoc* body specially designed to meet the demands upon the imperial government in wartime and, even more, the particular political necessities of the Lloyd George government. Neither was it the appropriate place nor the appropriate time to tinker with the constitution. The important business at hand was winning the war. For that purpose, he told Lloyd George, "I see no better method of attaining co-operation between the nations of the Empire or of giving adequate voice to the Overseas Governments."[60]

Direct communication with Lloyd George proved satisfactory after Sir Robert returned to Ottawa. Borden vacillated over the appointment of a resident Dominion minister in London, probably because of lack of confidence that either Sir George Perley or Sir Edward Kemp, who were both there, could adequately represent his views in the War Cabinet. And, as in 1917, events overtook planning. The strategy mapped out by the Prime Ministers Committee was rendered obsolete by the collapse of the enemy war effort. Within weeks Borden was back in London attending meetings of the War Cabinet to discuss peace and peace terms. Hughes fought for separate representation at the forthcoming Peace Conference with Borden's support.[61] When the War Cabinet moved to Paris in January 1919, under the new name of the British Empire Delegation, the continuity of consultation in foreign relations was maintained.

When war was declared in August 1914, Canada's foreign policy and Canada's role in the determination of imperial foreign policy were conspicuous only in their ambiguity. Only one point was clear. That was that the Borden government was as convinced as was John Dafoe in Winnipeg that it was going to be "Canada's war".[62] Even that was more a posture enunciated in innumerable speeches on war aims than a policy. But the inevitably more intimate Anglo-Canadian relationship during the war contributed directly to the transformation of "Canada's war" from an attitude to policy decisions and demands. The lack of either information from or consultation with

60. DCER, no. 496, p. 331. Borden to Lloyd George, June 28, 1918.
61. See L. F. Fitzhardinge, "Hughes, Borden, and Dominion Representation at the Paris Peace Conference", *Canadian Historical Review*, XLIX, no. 2, June, 1968, 160-69.
62. See Ramsay Cook, *The Politics of John W. Dafoe and the Free Press*, (Toronto, 1963), p. 66.

the British government, the arbitrary interference by the Admiralty in the Canadian war effort on the home front and the apparently futile and endless slaughter of Canada's brave youth because of a mindless and inefficient British High Command induced a very real sense of bitterness about the relationship with Britain on the part of Borden and many of his Ottawa colleagues. All of these factors forced them to think more about *their* war effort, to restate and re-emphasize *Canadian* war aims and to reflect on the British obstacles placed in the path of their fulfillment.

Rightly or wrongly, objectively or otherwise, the Canadians convinced themselves that their part in the whole, whether at home or at the front, was always a little purer than that of the others. Canada, Borden said, did not come back to the Old World to aggrandize the fortunes of the British Empire. Her civilian soldiers were more efficient, their planning was better and more successful. On the home front, after 1917, the money-changers had been driven out, the councils of government had been cleansed and Borden spoke with a fresh and united mandate – English-speaking section – to carry on to victory. There would be no procastination. Canada's voice was that of the "bitter-enders". Unlike Smuts, or General Wilson, Borden regarded a partial peace as incomprehensible and unacceptable. It accorded neither with his nation's professed war aims nor with his nation's response to his appeal in 1917.

The creation of the Imperial War Cabinet averted a serious breach in the Anglo-Canadian relationship during the Great War. Properly, Borden thought, the initiative came from the senior partner in the alliance; not because Britain was senior – *primus inter pares* – but because it was her system, or lack of it, that was deficient and needed to be reformed. Gradually the War Cabinet became an adequate instrument for information and consultation. Through it and its 1918 Prime Ministers Committee Borden and his Dominion colleagues exerted influence on the highest policy decisions for waging war and making peace.

Resolution IX symbolized the change in the relationship. For Borden it was not a statement of Canada's aspirations but of her deeds accomplished; full nationhood and the responsibilities that went therewith were not going to be achieved in 1921 or 1923 or later, they already had been. "Full recognition of the Dominions as autonomous nations" took place in 1917. A postwar imperial conference to consider "the readjustment of the constitutional relations of the

component parts of the Empire" would be just that – a conference
to tidy up the constitution of the Empire-Commonwealth. There
was no time to do that during the war. Beyond that, Borden was
always suspicious of grand schemes like Amery's or of the visionary
planners in the Round Table groups. The experience of the war, the
constant necessity to accommodate to events made him the more
suspicious. He went out of his way to remind the House of Commons
that the Imperial War Cabinet was "not premeditated or designed."
As he had told a Winnipeg audience in 1914, constitutional changes
"have been usually gradual and always practical; and they have been
taken rather by instinct than upon any carefully considered theory."[63]
Flexibility and adjustment to circumstances would be necessary at
Paris and in the post-Peace Conference world. Elaborate constitutional
designs were as likely to impede Canada's evolving nationhood and
its attendant responsibilities as to enhance them.

Sir Robert Borden's role in the Anglo-Canadian relationship during
the Great War has often been characterized as a dramatic shift from
"imperialism" to "nationalism".[64] Probably no one would have been
more surprised by that characterization than Borden. It presumes
an ideological dichotomy between "imperialism" and "nationalism"
and assumes that Canada's national interests were "opposed to the
imperial" interests of both Canada and Britain. For Borden no such
dichotomy existed. Moreover, the "national" interests of Canada and
the "imperial" interests of Canada during the Great War were
demonstrably the same. The point at issue was at once more subtle
and more simple: what kind of relationship did exist and what kind
of relationship should exist between two nation states within the
Empire. World War I provided an opportunity and a catalyst for
clarification of the ambiguities in the international relationship between two states whose "chief tie", Borden told the King in April
1917, was "the Crown". Certainly Borden would have agreed that
the process of clarification was not complete in December of 1918.
Nor, indeed, would it be after the Peace Conference. After all, he had
always argued that it was and should be an ever-evolving process. Still,
when the Imperial War Cabinet meetings came to an end and he
packed his bags for the trip to Paris, Sir Robert was satisfied that his
colleagues recognized that the Great War had been Canada's war.

63. See Borden, The War and The Future, (Toronto, 1917), pp. 126-28.
64. See especially Harold A. Wilson, The Imperial Policy of Sir Robert Borden,
     (Gainesville, 1966), pp. 30, 33.

A Point of View

PETER WAITE

The Anglo-Saxon mind has always been reductionist in character. Explanation, in philosophy and in history, has usually been sought, not through special metaphysical conceptions, but rather by bringing these down to the earth. Thus the complex is reduced to the simple, the mysterious to the obvious, and the grand to the humdrum. Ockham's razor was one of the first, and perhaps is still the purest example of this process. Even material objects were reduced, through Locke, Berkeley, and Hume (that trinity of empiricism) to nothing but sensation. The State, capitalized on the continent, became in this tradition the state, merely an aggregation of people.

Anglo-American history may be thought of as the great heartland of this empirical tradition. Richard Pares' review of Toynbee's ten volumes for the *English Historical Review* in 1956 is entirely characteristic. "All historians," wrote Pares, with his stern eye on Toynbee, "are imposing all the time a pattern of their own discovery upon their material. But they must do this modestly, soberly, and honestly, or else their work will become a monument of uncontrolled ingenuity." That famous preface of H. A. L. Fisher's, which saw in history only one safe rule, to recognize the play of the contingent and the unforeseen, has a diabolical fascination, both for what it says and the tradition it represents.

But I am not going to write about what Frederick the Great called (with good cause) "sa sacré majesté, le hazard". My interest in this brief essay is the kind of remark found, not infrequently, in *Canadian Historical Review* book reviews. "An interesting book, but it has no point of view." The question asked now, too often, is "What is his interpretation?" The new slim and slippery snippets of readings suggest the reflection that where there is no interpretation, or no contrasting interpretations, there is no real history. This is of course demonstrably false. Selection is always a form of interpretation, and we must all select. And on the whole I would prefer to avoid Miss Wedgwood's distinction between "why" history and "how" history; I do not see how any historian can fairly avoid writing both. Let me put the problem another way. In a recent issue of CHR is found the following: "Eschewing commitment to a single, predominant interpretation of Woodrow Wilson's development which has marked some writings, Bragdon has let the sources guide him." Now I know the word "sources" begs nearly as many questions as it answers. I know the Bible can be quoted to serve a variety of ends, and more than one young person has had his equilibrium upset by injudicious indulgence in what must be a too superficial view of the Song of Solomon. By sources I mean what we all mean by sources: the raw material of history.

As we know, E. H. Carr has insisted that none of us can escape our contemporary biases. His argument, broadly speaking, is that before we read *A History of Soviet Russia* we should be well advised to read *A History of E. H. Carr*. And his conclusion seems to imply that there is not much point in trying to escape our biases, for we are defeated before we start. Therefore, he seems to say, let interpretation fairly have its head; let us ride bravely across those careful antiquarian gardens, those gardens which are tended by assiduous but picayune scholars, whose dedication is unfortunately unmatched by any capacity to think. It's an exhilarating experience – who can deny it? Who has not been, for a time at least, swept off his feet by Henri Pirenne's *Mohammed and Charlemagne*? Professor Trevor-Roper, for all his talk, seems never to have quite recovered from the experience. E. H. Carr says, "great history is written precisely when the historian's vision of the past is illuminated by insights into the problems of the present." There is a sense in which this is legitimate enough, but to write the history of Canada in the 1840s in the perspective of the 1920s can produce warped history; can, and has. E. H. Carr would reply that this only means that every generation of historians will criticize its predecessors and that each must write its own version of the 1840s, from its own perspective, for itself; in other words that history is not just a study of the facts, but it is an interaction between the historian himself and his facts. E. H. Carr is a very good and careful historian, one superbly equipped technically; but the juxtaposition of his *History of Soviet Russia* with Isaac Deutscher's *Trotsky* on the question of opposition to the Bolsheviks makes the point. Isaiah Berlin considered the *History of Soviet Russia* "the most monumental challenge of our time to that idea of impartiality and objective truth and even-handed justice in the writing of history which is most deeply embedded in the European liberal tradition".

The truth is, I suppose, that historians like E. H. Carr become uneasy in the absence of any obvious interpretation. They feel that they are drifting without a chart, and furthermore, that the historian they are reading lacks a chart too. Their view of the past compels them to take a point of view; the absence of a point of view is unnerving. It is thus easy for them to say that history of that kind is meaningless, mere recitation of names and places, mere biography, a travesty in fact of what history ought to be. E. H. Carr puts it more graphically, "When you read a work of history always listen out for the buzzing of bees in bonnets. If you can detect none, either you are tone deaf or your historian is a dull dog." *What is History?* is a remarkable book, not less so for being witty and lucid. It is also a dangerous book; my main quarrel with it is that it is defeatist. Carr admits that the historian ought to try to "rise above the limited vision of his own situation, in his own society and in history", and he adds that this fact is partly dependent on the historian's recognition of the impossibility of total objectivity. So far so good; no one would quarrel with that. But he cannot bring himself to go that one stage further and admit that awful prospect that the historian might just possibly concern himself with the pursuit of truth. This is the gloss, I think, that Sir Lewis Namier would have made on E. H. Carr.

It is a truism, of course, that we cannot get at the whole truth. But isn't the aiming at it everything? Must the fact that we cannot realize the whole truth prevent us from trying? Are we to confess defeat before we start? What I am suggesting is an approach to the stuff of history along the lines that Thomas Huxley explained a hundred years ago to that undistinguished Regius Professor of History at Oxford, Charles Kingsley. Huxley wrote,

> Science warns me to be careful how I adopt a view that
> jumps with my preconceptions. My business is to teach
> my aspirations to conform themselves to facts, not to
> try and make facts harmonize with my aspirations.

In 1869 Kingsley died and was succeeded as Regius professor by a
man whose preconceptions were stronger, Sir John Seeley. There is a
delicious story of the Master of Trinity walking home with a colleague after Seeley's inaugural address. "Well, well," said the Master
of Trinity, "I did not think we could so soon have had an occasion
to regret poor Kingsley."

There is a theory in aesthetics that in going to a play we suspend
disbelief and instinctively commit ourselves to the fairy tale on the
stage. I suggest for history the reverse. Let us adopt as a principle
for history the willing suspension of belief. Of course beliefs, theories,
are useful; but they ought to be put aside like other superstitions,
when they do not square with what we find. They probably will be
put aside in any case if they cease to flatter our vanity. Because we
are writing history from a variety of personal viewpoints in Canada
in 1970 we do not have *carte blanche* to indulge our preconceptions.
Our duty, or so it seems to me, is to disencumber ourselves of preconceptions. We can't, of course; but we can try. There are two ways
of looking at this. The first is: I am a creature of my time and place
and the history I write cannot escape these limitations; so I am going
to write the history of Canada between 1900 and 1930 frankly and
openly in the light of my interest in the problems of Canadian society in 1970. The second way of looking at this, and the way I am
urging is: I concede the fact that I am to a great degree a product of
my environment, but my duty as historian is to disengage so far as
I can my historical mind from the evanescent preoccupations of my
time and place, however difficult this may be to do.

I cannot escape the feeling that contemporary relevance is historical irrelevance. This argument can be deemed, not unreasonably,
as a squirrel's view of history, making of the past an antiquarian
jungle; or worse, making it just a great, buzzing, sentimental confusion. The fact that it *is* a great buzzing confusion, sentimental or
not, is, in the view of some critics, no justification for failing to sort
out the confusion. I agree with that. My feeling is that this sorting
out is too readily done in terms of contemporary relevance. Contemporary relevance is just a trick. All generations, Ranke said once, are

equidistant from eternity. Rome in 44 B.C. is as relevant for 1970 as is England in 1844, perhaps more so, it being the year of the assassination of Julius Caesar. It is also fashionable now to make fun of Ranke's naïveté in declaring that he wanted to write history as it really was. What he was insisting on, over-enthusiastically no doubt, was that we be ruled by the documents.

We all know what is wrong with the documents; how much they don't say and how wrong-headedly they say what they do. Few of us in this hunger, as I hope it is, for documentary evidence, neglect the lessons of *Rashomon*, or as it is put more humbly in the Indian tale of the blind men and the elephant. There are few more ruthless denunciations of first-hand evidence than in David Hume's criticism of miracles. And we do not need to go that far; we have the newspapers of Canada before us, past and present. Do they reflect public opinion, do they make public opinion, or do they reflect nothing but party warfare? T. C. Patteson, the editor of the Toronto *Mail*, was supposed to have said, "Oh, well, we have to stab some Grit under the fifth rib every morning!" At this Edward Blake exploded into a metaphor a paragraph long:

> No matter how often the Black Mail has changed owners and captains, crew and pilot – no matter by what merchants she was chartered, what freight she was paid, with what goods she was laden, in what company she sailed, to whom she was consigned – no matter what canvass [sic] she carried, what weather she met, what winds filled, what seas she cross[ed], what tacks she made, what courses she steered, how her compass varied, on what lee shores or shifting sands or sunken rocks she ran – no matter how her rig & hull and armament were changed or how her guns were pointed, what ransom she levied, what fraudulent manifests she carried, what double logs she kept, what false papers she procured, what false lights she showed – no matter what colours she was painted, or what other flags she flied; yet the old craft might be always recognized by the black signal run up when first she reached open water and kept flying ever since, with its pirate's devices of a death's head and cross bones, and the gory form of an unhappy Grit, fresh stabbed under the fifth rib each lawful day.

Patteson actually replied to this diatribe. He hadn't used the expression, but a junior reporter had; in any case it made not much difference. The Toronto *Globe* and the Toronto *Mail* differed little from each other,

> now or at any time in the thirty years I have read
> them, either in the colours they fly or in the maneuvres
> which you so graphically describe. The average news-
> paper is but an echo of the average politician: and a
> stream never rises higher than its source. Some day
> public opinion will be stronger and both will improve.

But would it improve? Newspapers were to a surprising degree also the creatures of their own subscribers. On February 20, 1890, W. H. Montague fought the third of a series of savage by-elections in Haldimand, that had gone on since 1887. Sir John A. Macdonald needed the Catholic vote, and the Catholic Bishop of Hamilton told him frankly if he wanted the Catholic vote, he had better get the Hamilton *Spectator* to be less abusive to Roman Catholics. So Macdonald talked to the editor. Macdonald's report back to the Bishop of Hamilton is full of interest:

> I spoke to him [writes Macdonald] seriously of the
> evil consequences of his harsh language respecting
> Catholicism and Catholics.
>   He admitted frankly that his language had fre-
> quently been strong, that his articles were dashed off
> at night in haste and without being revised, and that
> frequently he has had cause to regret the severity of
> their tone when he and they had time to cool.
>   He promised to be more careful in the future, but,
> said he, "my paper is read principally by Protestants,
> and I am a Protestant". In other words [said Mac-
> donald] the paper must be written to suit the tastes of
> the subscribers.

The editor of the *Globe* admitted that the moderate position the paper had taken on the Riel affair lost it many Protestant subscribers. There is a kind of Gresham's Law at work here: bad newspapers drive out good ones. Pity the poor historian, said the *Nation* once, who attempts to write the biography of Oliver Mowat from the Toronto *Globe* and the Toronto *Mail*. He will end up with two Mowats.

Newspapers are treacherous; they thrive on controversy and excitement. And when desperation, that is dearth of news, sets in they
will manufacture excitement. Television is simply this process in
caricature.

The newspapers are not alone. How much do we ourselves remember of the periods of our own lives that were unruffled and un-
eventful? Our own diaries and journals, if we have them, record
striking events, romantic memories, tragic happenings, amusing
stories that have jarred our consciousness and have so been remembered. History is a record of the unusual rather than the usual. What
passes for history is often real life, but tarted up and tricked out by
the human imagination and by the way human beings remember
things. The even tenor of their way has hardly been a subject of
history at all. There is an ancient Chinese curse, "May you have an
interesting history." Tolstoy put the same idea another way, at the
beginning of *Anna Karenina*. "The life of all happy families is the
same, that of unhappy families all different." The truth is, I suppose,
as Thoreau says somewhere in *Walden* that "the mass of men lead
lives of quiet desperation". That was one reason he went to the
woods, which event he found remarkable enough to write a book
about.

We all know this weakness of primary sources, and I shan't labour
the point further. Because, however, we know the past so imperfectly
is no reason to despair. Nor is it a reason to wrench the past into the
Procrustean torture of a theory. Neither am I urging the historicist
argument, "Tout comprendre c'est tout excuser." I do say, understand first, and judge and interpret later. For this purpose of understanding, all must be grist to our mill; literature, philosophy, sociology, economics. But there are no impersonal forces, only human
beings; men make history. They may act differently in groups than
they do alone, or they may not, but they are still men. History and
sociology have to live together. By a curious irony I find Sociology
100 at Dalhousie using Max Weber's *Protestant Ethic*, while in History 100 we prefer Tawney. I find the dogmatism of some sociologists
distasteful; they find historians mindless and puerile. Both subjects
would be better for informing the other. Goethe says in his essay on
Winkleman in 1805, "Man can achieve much by using his individual
faculties appropriately, but supreme achievements only come when
all his faculties are united." So too history. One should, so to speak,
become soaked in a period until its ways of thinking and doing be-

come meaningful. Some of Professor Creighton's most illuminating pages in *Macdonald* come from this sense of context, as if he had absorbed the half-spoken, but very real ways of a society by a process of osmosis. This is a difficult process at best, especially since mature men, Macdonald for example, do not even act in the terms of the age in which they are living; they tend to operate in terms of a generation earlier. Men do not look to the future; they look to the past. Here the pages of Professor Creighton catch the juxtaposition of generations:

> There are more than a few times when he [Macdonald] seemed to belong most appropriately to the reigns of George III and George IV, to the age which had closed in 1832 with the passage of the Reform Bill. He had its grace, its urbanity, its intelligence and reasonableness, its freedom from sanctimoniousness and cant. Macdonald had never taken himself or his affairs too seriously. In a more solemn age [1878] he still kept something of his jaunty eighteenth-century assumption that politics were the affair not of ponderously instructed professionals but of gifted amateurs. Here in contrast with the manly downrightness and simplicity which the Victorians believed they admired, his methods seemed often devious and subtle. To these mid-Victorian critics it seemed almost incredible that a man who enjoyed life so obviously, who was so frequently lacking in respectable earnestness, who seemed so ready to give up sober work and quiet repose for mere empty enjoyment should have a really solid claim to be considered as a great national statesman.

I am not quite sure that the mid-Victorian Canada was quite as sober as all that, but how little has this to do with 1955, the year when *Macdonald*, Volume II was published!

In other words the writing of history means not the transfer of contemporary values to the past, but the transcending of them. This takes time; research alone requires that the making of history be a slow business. The acquisition of the feel of a period, the mastery of its ways of working and thinking, makes it even slower. I recall Winthrop Bell working on *The Foreign Protestants of Nova Scotia;* for twenty years he did almost nothing else. Just one question on the way ship tonnage was calculated in the eighteenth century took months to unravel. I am not saying this kind of history can easily be emulated; Winthrop Bell had given up teaching at Harvard, and lived in Chester on a private income. But I do think it is history to be admired; not for nothing did he earn a Ph.D. from Göttingen in 1914. Instant history is easy to do, easy to publish, easy to sell, and quick to die. That solid, compact, huge tome, *The Foreign Protestants of Nova Scotia*, is as near to being imperishable as any work of history published in Canada in recent years.

What I am suggesting is not without its dangers. There is always the risk of drowning in the period: of falling into antiquarianism, a preoccupation with the miniscule. At a first stage this can be useful; at a second, harmless; at a third, cloying; but finally it defeats the purpose of history. As John Morley put it in 1914, "vast and countless accumulations of insignificant facts, sterile knowledge and frivolous antiquarianism". There is, in other words, a serious problem of selection. A second danger is still more serious. This is of becoming a member of the school of history described as "one damn thing after another". That is a loaded expression, of course. Life itself is one damn thing after another. We can in retrospect impose a pattern upon what has happened in our own lives, and try to give it shape, or direction. There may be a shape and a direction to it; but usually such impositions ignore the many choices that have been open to us. Of course we have made choices, but upon what basis? A consciousness of where we were going, doubtless, some of the time; in others, however, fortuitous events have made the choice for us; how often has accident changed the course of our lives!

Thus the chronicle, whether it be of one's own life, or of the multifarious events in the world around it, is the raw material of history, that is shaped by ourselves, or by historians, sometimes into a clear pattern, sometimes not. But the avoidance of the danger posed by that awful phrase, "one damn thing after another", is often held to justify the imposition on the past of theories of change, of cause and effect, that represent distortions far worse than the "je ne sais pas" of the chronicle, or, for that matter, of Michel de Montaigne.

Nevertheless, it is to be remembered that the past does not describe, not as a rule anyway, how it itself changes, any more than we describe how we change. But we do, and it does. We must make speculations about change, though we do so, inevitably, at the peril of honest history. It has been argued, and by good historians, that the value of any work of history lies fundamentally in the adequacy of its theory of change. To argue that human nature does not change is really, for such historians, an abdication of the historian's responsibility for divining the structure that underlies cause and effect. On this question historians divide, I suppose, into two kinds, rather resembling Isaiah Berlin's famous classification of hedgehogs and foxes: the hedgehogs, whose architectonic minds see history as a pattern, or as the exposé of an argument; and the foxes whose minds run empirically, and who tend to see history as a tale, sometimes a sorry one, of human nature. In these terms Harold Innis is a hedgehog. I sense myself already classified, by the argument of this essay, as a fox. Professor Creighton is perhaps, as Berlin described Tolstoy, a fox who would like to be a hedgehog. This classification is of course too neat; in any case it is, as Ved Mehta says in the *Fly and the Fly-Bottle*, an argument without end.

My theme can be summed up by an ironic sign that many have doubtless seen: "My mind's made up: don't confuse me with facts." Perhaps these words we can remember when we walk through the doors of archives with that visceral excitement of things to come, and with, let us also hope, a sense of dedication to what the documents have to tell us, besides what we have to tell the documents.

Donald Grant Creighton:

A BIBLIOGRAPHY OF HIS ACADEMIC WRITING

1931

"The Struggle for Financial Control in Lower Canada, 1818-1831", *Canadian Historical Review*, vol. 12 (2), June 1931, 120-44.

1933

"The Commercial Class in Canadian Politics, 1792-1840", *Papers and Proceedings of the Canadian Political Science Association*, vol. 5, May 1933, 43-58.

1937

The Commercial Empire of the St. Lawrence, 1760-1850. Toronto, The Ryerson Press. Reprinted by The Macmillan Company of Canada Limited under the title *The Empire of the St. Lawrence*, 1956.

"The Economic Background of the Rebellions of Eighteen Thirty-Seven", *Canadian Journal of Economics and Political Science*, vol. 3 (3), August 1937, 322-34. Reprinted in Easterbrook and Watkins (eds.), *Approaches to Canadian Economic History*. Toronto: McClelland and Stewart, The Carleton Library, 1967, pp. 222-36.

1938

"The Victorians and the Empire", *Canadian Historical Review*, vol. 19 (2), June 1938, 138-53. Reprinted in R. L. Schuyler and H. Ausubel (eds.), *The Making of English History*. New York: The Dryden Press, 1952.

1939

British North America at Confederation: A Study prepared for the Royal Commission on Dominion-Provincial Relations: Appendix 2. Ottawa, King's Printer.

"Conservatism and National Unity", in Ralph Flenley (ed.), *Essays in Canadian History*. Toronto: The Macmillan Company of Canada Limited, pp. 154-77.

1941

"Federal Relations in Canada Since 1914", in C. B. Martin (ed.), *Canada in Peace and War: Eight Studies in National Trends Since 1914*. London: Oxford University Press, pp. 29-57.

1942

"The Course of Canadian Democracy", *University of Toronto Quarterly*, vol. 11, April 1942, 255-68.

"Economic Nationalism and Confederation", Canadian Historical Association *Report*, pp. 44-51. Reprinted in *Confederation*. Toronto: University of Toronto Press, 1967.

1943

"George Brown, Sir John Macdonald and the 'workingman'," *Canadian Historical Review*, vol. 24 (4), December 1943, 362-76.

1944

"Canadian History in Retrospect and Prospect" (with G. W. Brown), *Canadian Historical Review*, vol. 25, December 1944, 357-75.

"Ontario" (with Helen Marsh), *Canadian Affairs*, vol. 1, no. 16, September 1944.

Dominion of the North: A History of Canada. Boston, Houghton Mifflin.

1945

The Writing of History in Canada. University of New Brunswick Founders' Day Address, Fredericton, New Brunswick.

"Canada in the English-Speaking World", *Canadian Historical Review*, vol. 26 (2), June 1945, 119-27.

1948

"An Episode in the History of the University of Toronto", *University of Toronto Quarterly*, vol. 17 (3), April 1948, 245-56.

"Sir John Macdonald and Canadian Historians", *Canadian Historical Review*, vol. 29 (1), March 1948, 1-12.

1950

"Sir John Macdonald and Kingston", Canadian Historical Association *Report*, pp. 72-80.

"The Dominion: Genesis and Integration", in G. W. Brown (ed.), *Canada*. Toronto: University of Toronto Press, pp. 99-123.

1952

John A. Macdonald: Vol. I: The Young Politician. Toronto, The Macmillan Company of Canada Limited.

1955

John A. Macdonald: Vol. II: The Old Chieftain. Toronto, The Macmillan Company of Canada Limited.

"Education for Government", *Queen's Quarterly*, vol. 61, Winter 1955, 425-33.

1956

"Old Tomorrow", *The Beaver*, vol. 287, Winter 1956, 6-10.

"Towards the Discovery of Canada", *University of Toronto Quarterly*, vol. 25, April 1956, 269-82.

"The Past Half-Century, 1906-56". Address on the occasion of a dinner celebrating the fiftieth anniversary of United Grain Growers Limited, Calgary, United Grain Growers.

1957

"Macdonald and Manitoba", *The Beaver*, vol. 287, Spring 1957, 12-17.

"Presidential Address", Canadian Historical Association *Report*, pp. 1-12.

"Sir John A. Macdonald", in C. T. Bissell (ed.) *Our Living Tradition*, first series. Toronto: University of Toronto Press, pp. 48-62.

Harold Adams Innis: Portrait of a Scholar. Toronto, University of Toronto Press.

1958

The Story of Canada. London, Faber and Faber.

"Canada", in H. Moseley (ed.), *The Romance of North America*. Boston: Houghton Mifflin, pp. 41-83.

"The United States and Canadian Confederation", *Canadian Historical Review*, vol. 39 (3), September 1958, 209-22.

Dominion of the North (revised and enlarged edition). Toronto, The Macmillan Company of Canada Limited.

1959

A Long View of Canadian History (with Paul Fox). The text of talks originally given on the CBC on June 16 and June 30, 1959. Toronto, CBC Publications.

1964

The Road to Confederation: The Emergence of Canada, 1837-1867. Toronto, The Macmillan Company of Canada Limited.

The Confederation Conference. Charlottetown, Prince Edward Island Centennial Committee.

1966

"Introduction", in J. B. Brebner, *North Atlantic Triangle*. Paperback edition: Toronto, McClelland and Stewart Ltd., The Carleton Library, 1966.

1967

"The 1860s", in J. M. S. Careless and R. Craig Brown (eds.), *The Canadians*. Toronto, The Macmillan Company of Canada Limited.

"John A. Macdonald, Confederation and the West". Address given on the anniversary of the birthdate of Sir John A. Macdonald. Winnipeg, Manitoba Historical Society.

1970

Canada's First Century. Toronto, The Macmillan Company of Canada Limited.

List of Contributors

R. CRAIG BROWN, *Associate Professor of History, University of Toronto*

J. M. S. CARELESS, *Professor of History, University of Toronto*

LOVELL C. CLARK, *Associate Professor of History, University of Manitoba*

RAMSAY COOK, *Professor of History, York University*

GEORGE P. DET. GLAZEBROOK, *formerly Professor of History, University of Toronto*

ROGER GRAHAM, *Douglas Professor of Canadian History, Queen's University*

KENNETH W. MCNAUGHT, *Professor of History, University of Toronto*

JOHN S. MOIR, *Professor of History, Scarborough College, University of Toronto*

W. L. MORTON, *Vanier Professor of Canadian History, Trent University*

CHARLES P. STACEY, *Professor of History, University of Toronto*

PETER B. WAITE, *Professor of History, Dalhousie University*

PATRICK C. T. WHITE, *Associate Professor of History, University of Toronto*

ALAN WILSON, *Professor of History, Trent University*

S. F. WISE, *Director, Canadian Armed Forces Directorate of History*